MW01253679

Hinduism and the 1960s

ALSO AVAILABLE FROM BLOOMSBURY

Bloomsbury Companion to Hindu Studies, Jessica Frazier
Hinduism Today, Stephen Jacobs

Hinduism and the 1960s

The rise of a counter-culture

PAUL OLIVER

B L O O M S B U R Y

LONDON · NEW DELHI · NEW YORK · SYDNEY

Bloomsbury Academic

An imprint of Bloomsbury Publishing Plc

50 Bedford Square	1385 Broadway
London	New York
WC1B 3DP	NY 10018
UK	USA

www.bloomsbury.com

Bloomsbury is a registered trade mark of Bloomsbury Publishing Plc

First published 2014

British Library Cataloguing-in-Publication Data
A catalogue record for this book is available from the British Library.

ISBN: HB: 978-1-47253-303-6
PB: 978-1-47253-155-1
ePDF: 978-1-47252-765-3
ePub: 978-1-47253-078-3

Library of Congress Cataloging-in-Publication Data
Oliver, Paul, author.
Hinduism and the 1960s : the rise of a counter-culture / Paul Oliver.
pages cm
ISBN 978-1-4725-3303-6 (hardback) – ISBN 978-1-4725-3155-1 (paperback) –
ISBN 978-1-4725-2765-3 (ePDF) – ISBN 978-1-4725-3078-3 (epub)
1. Hinduism–Social aspects. 2. Counterculture. 3. Nineteen sixties. I. Title.
BL1215.S64O55 2015
294.509'046–dc23
2014012908

Typeset by Newgen Knowledge Works (P) Ltd., Chennai, India
Printed and bound in India

To Lyn

Contents

PART ONE The rise of a counter-culture 1

1 The intellectual roots of the 1960s counter-culture 3

Introduction 3
The nature of a counter-culture 5
Factors leading to the creation of the 1960s counter-culture 7
The beat generation and Eastern religions 10

2 Social and political movements of the counter-culture 17

The hippie movement 17
The environmental movement 18
Civil rights 21
The peace movement 22
Equality in relation to gender and sexual orientation 24

3 Spirituality in the counter-culture 31

Introduction 31
The nature of a guru 32
Hindu spirituality 33

PART TWO Hinduism and the
counter-culture 43

4 The philosophy of Hinduism and its attractions
for the counter-culture 45

Introduction 45
The Hindu religion 46
The Upanishads 47
The Bhagavad Gita 49
Hindu philosophy and practice 52

5 Transcendental Meditation and the Beatles 57

The Maharishi 57
The Beatles 62

6 Drugs, enlightenment and Hinduism 69

The Vedic ritual 69
Experiments with hallucinatory drugs in the West 71
A psychedelic culture 74
Links with Hindu culture 75

7 Ahimsa, Gandhi and the peace movement 81

Attitudes to peace in the 1960s 81
The history of non-violence in Indian culture and religion 86
Gandhi and ahimsa 87
The Vietnam War 90

8 Sexual liberation, tantra and the Kama Sutra 93

Life before the 1960s 93
The changes of the 1960s 94
The contribution of Hindu culture 98
The equality of women 101
Gay equality 102

9 Ashrams, communes and the hippy lifestyle 105

Introduction 105
The ashram 106
The Hindu teacher 108
Communal living 111

10 Ayurvedic medicine and naturalistic well-being 117

Introduction 117
Thoreau, 'Walden' and Hindu philosophy 118
Sustainability 119
Ayurveda 120

11 Yoga, mysticism and spiritual consciousness 129

The eclecticism of the 1960s 129
The internal life 132
Universalism in the Hindu religion 133

PART THREE The legacy in contemporary lifestyle 141

12 Overland to India – a modern pilgrimage 143

Introduction – the route 143
Interacting with the local people 146
The British in India as a formative influence 148

13 Meditation and a secular religion 157

Introduction 157
The spread of yoga in the West 161
Meditation in the West 162
Meditation as a therapy 165

14 The seeker and an alternative to the consumer society 169

Introduction 169
Counter-cultural ethics 170
Statements of principle 172
Symbols of change 174
Hinduism and individuality 176

References 179
Glossary 185
Index 187

PART ONE

The rise of a counter-culture

1

The intellectual roots of the 1960s counter-culture

Summary

This chapter analyses the ideas and philosophies which combined to help create the 1960s counter-culture. There is first an exploration of the concept 'counter-culture', and of how the latter term may be applied to social movements in the 1960s. This chapter continues with a discussion of the economic expansion of the period after the Second World War, and of the social opportunities created for young people. There is finally an evaluation of the beat generation writers such as Kerouac and Ginsberg, and the interest which they demonstrated in Eastern religions.

Introduction

In the autumn of 1960 it was the height of fashion for secondary school children to be seen carrying a well-known work of English literature. The novel concerned had a bright orange cover, and had been first published in an unexpurgated form by Penguin Books in August of that year. The book was Lady Chatterley's Lover by D. H. Lawrence. Many considered the work too explicit in terms of sexual content, and the publishers found themselves the subject of a prosecution under the 1959 Obscene Publications Act. The trial, which received a great deal of publicity at the time, ended on 2nd November, with Penguin Books being found not guilty. With hindsight, the trial has been seen as making possible a much more liberal approach in the media and in publishing in particular. Many have taken it as a key moment at the start of a decade which would later epitomize a range of personal freedoms previously unknown.

Six days after the end of the Penguin Books trial, a young democratic senator from Massachusetts was elected as the new president of the United States. John F. Kennedy was inaugurated in January 1961 and initiated a domestic and social policy which among other things sought to eliminate racial discrimination and segregation, and to improve rights for women. Although he was not successful in his short administration in totally transforming society, his personal commitment to these issues did a great deal to set the tone for the coming decade. Many young people, however, would not be happy with the pace of change in terms of personal freedom, and throughout the decade, would engage in protest and opposition to the established political order.

Although Kennedy set out in his presidency to reform some aspects of American society, he also came to power at a time of major ideological differences between the West and the Soviet Union. There was enormous anxiety about the potential spread of communism, and the Castro administration in Cuba was seen as a particular threat to the United States. In April 1961 there was a failed attempt by the United States to destabilize the Castro regime, with the 'Bay of Pigs' invasion. Just over a year later the Soviet Union attempted to establish missile bases on Cuba, and although the confrontation was resolved in October 1962, it brought the world uncomfortably close to a nuclear conflict (Dobbs, 2009). There was also an increasing level of tension in Vietnam, and during 1961 American support for South Vietnam was gradually extended, leading ultimately to a full-scale American involvement in the Vietnam War. The risks to world peace seemed so significant at this time, that an extensive peace movement developed throughout the 1960s, particularly through the intervention of young people and students. Young people wanted autonomy and self-determination. They did not want to live in a world involved in major armed conflict.

Medical advances were also resulting in important social developments. In 1960 the oral contraceptive pill became available in the United States, and the following year in Great Britain. For the first time this provided women with an easily administered and relatively certain form of contraception, and gave them control over when they would have children. In terms of career planning, it enabled women to delay starting a family, and gave them the freedom to pursue education and training for longer. This in turn gave young women the opportunity to take a more active economic role in the family and in society.

Freedom was also an ambition for people on a national as well as an individual scale. Since the end of the Second World War, colonial countries had increasingly aspired to independence. In February 1960, the then British prime minister, Harold Macmillan gave a speech in South Africa in which he acknowledged the legitimacy of these aspirations. It became known as the 'Wind of Change' speech, indicating the political changes which were sweeping across Africa. A number of former British colonies in Africa subsequently gained their independence over a fairly short period of time, for example, Uganda in 1962 and Kenya a year later.

There was thus at the beginning of the 1960s an increasing demand for freedom, equality and autonomy in many areas of life. Where inequalities were deeply embedded within the existing social structure, as for example, with race and gender inequalities, the coming decade would see a concerted challenge to these existing cultural norms.

The nature of a counter-culture

Although social change began to become evident at the beginning of the 1960s, it was the result of gradual changes which had been happening throughout the 1950s. As in all wars, the Second World War had been a time of extensive interaction between different social groups and classes, nationalities and ethnic groups. In part this interaction resulted in a questioning of the accepted norms and conventions of society. While some people wanted to retain the existing conventions, others began to realize that they need not accept the received social structures and could seek to change society.

The term counter-culture tends to be used where a sub-culture evolves which is significantly different from conventional society in terms of values and patterns of behaviour. Such a counter-culture often exhibits an antipathy towards the established institutions of society. It could be argued that counter-cultures have existed since society has existed, since only through periodic challenges to the prevalent power structures, can society change (Goffman and Joy, 2005). Indeed one might further argue that it is part of the concept of a counter-culture that it seeks to subvert the existing society.

However, just as a society is a complex, multi-faceted organism, so too often is a counter-culture. The latter may not possess a single, dominant ideology. During the 1950s, as the American economy expanded, it resulted in an increasingly materialistic and technology-based society. Many young people of the developing counter-culture rejected this view of society (Roszak, 1995). However, although anti-materialism was a fairly pervasive perspective throughout the 1960s counter-culture, there were many other issues which were equally or even more important to some groups of young people.

Within a Marxist perspective one might assume that a counter-culture would be largely a working-class movement, opposing the perceived hegemony of bourgeois economic power. However, the 1960s was a period of relative economic affluence in the West, coupled with low unemployment. Many of the young members of the counter-culture of that time came from a middle-class background and had a number of different lifestyle choices at their disposal. However, they were often alienated from the values and culture of their parents, and sought to challenge the predominant paradigm of society.

In terms of discussing the counter-culture of the 1960s it is important to clarify not only the geographical extent of the phenomenon but also its temporal limits in terms of having a finite end point. Throughout this book, as we discuss the counter-culture in 'the West', we will define this as broadly signifying the United States and Europe, while at the same time acknowledging that its influence affected other parts of the world, including for example Australia and Canada. In addition, as we move on to discuss the relationship between the counter-culture and India, we will see that there has been a continuous cultural and religious interaction between the West and India since the eighteenth century.

As has been alluded to earlier a counter-culture is often political in nature, in that it seeks to transform society. Indeed it may well be radical and revolutionary in nature, in terms of rejecting gradual change in society and wanting rapid transformation. Such was the case in May 1968 in Paris when students protested on a large scale, wanting *inter alia* much more democratic control over the education system in France, with changes in both the pedagogy and curriculum in French universities. This particular facet of the broader counter-culture of the time had much in common with the movements in the United States and Britain, in that French students were opposed to the pervasive materialism of the West. Interestingly the students were joined in their protests by industrial workers in many parts of France (Ross, 2002). This combination of students protesting on the streets of Paris, and of large-scale strikes, nearly resulted in the fall of the government of President Charles de Gaulle.

Of course a cultural movement does not simply start and finish as a closed entity, unaffected by other factors. A counter-culture evolves from other movements and later evolves into new developments in society. It will almost certainly leave its mark on society, but essentially a counter-culture exists as part of a continuum, representing the continuing evolution of society. For this reason, it is not easy to establish a clear beginning and end for a counter-culture, and this certainly applies to the youth movement of the 1960s. It is useful, however, to establish some notional time limits, and to do this one could consider the beginning and end of a major political event of the period. One of the major targets of youth protest during the 1960s was the perceived lack of morality of the war in Vietnam. There were strong objections not only to the American involvement but also to the unethical methods employed such as the use of defoliants and napalm. The war could be approximately dated from 1960 to 1975. By late 1960, the National Liberation Front of North Vietnam (the Viet Cong) had determined to force American advisors from South Vietnam. Equally by 1961 President Kennedy felt that he had to stop communist expansion in Vietnam in order to affirm American authority in the world. The stage was thus set for the expansion of the conflict. It continued until April 1975, when the then American president Gerald Ford announced that the war was over. As the ending of the Vietnam War was such a major goal of young people, it is reasonable to take 1975 as a notional ending for the counter-culture, although this has to be seen as merely a convention.

There were, however, many other sources of protest for young people involved in the 1960s counter-culture. These included gay rights, gender equality, race equality, the peace movement, the environmental movement and civil rights. The at least partial achievement of some of the goals of the counter-culture in relation to these issues almost certainly influenced its gradual decline during the early 1970s. In addition, this decline was also almost certainly affected by the oil crisis of October 1973. The embargo created by middle-Eastern oil-producing countries had a negative effect on Western economies. This no doubt resulted in young people being more concerned with employment and the other practicalities of life than with the protest movement.

Factors leading to the creation of the 1960s counter-culture

The rise of a counter-culture during the 1960s was the result of a number of factors during the 1950s, economic and political, but also social and cultural. The immediate aftermath of the Second World War saw the beginnings of a major economic boom in the West, partly as a result of the need to rebuild the infrastructure of Western Europe. This economic boom was to last for approximately 30 years and would bring a standard of living for ordinary working people, which previous generations could have considered scarcely possible. The American Marshall Plan was conceived in order to help with the reconstruction of Europe and contributed many millions of dollars to this end. The Plan lasted from 1948 to 1952, and during this period the economies of Western Europe expanded rapidly.

The young people of the counter-culture were born either during the last few years of the Second World War or during the first decade after the end of the war. The latter period was one of considerable increase in the birth rate and became known as the 'baby-boomer' period (Feeney, 2012). The baby boomers, born as they were during a period of economic expansion, enjoyed a standard of living much better than children before the war. This generation benefited a great deal from large amounts of government money invested in education, and in Britain had unprecedented access to free higher education. The expansion of educational opportunities enabled working-class children to aspire to professional careers and well-paid jobs, even if in reality many were held back by other social factors outside their control. The Robbins Report of 1963 recommended that the number of universities should be rapidly increased and that access to a university education should be based upon merit.

Life did not, however, return to normal very quickly after the Second World War. Britain had suffered enormous damage to its infrastructure; there had been many casualties and the general population had suffered large-scale privation in many ways. This privation also continued to some extent after the war. Food rationing, for example, although gradually phased out in the years after the war, did not finally end until July 1954. As members of the armed forces returned from combat duties, there was considerable adjustment necessary when rejoining civilian life. There was not in the 1940s compared with now, the same awareness of, nor sensitivity to, the psychological damage induced by warfare. Two successive generations had now experienced war on a global scale, and there was among younger people an understandable desire to create a different kind of world. This challenge to received values was aided to a considerable degree by technological advances. The 1950s saw for the first time the widespread availability of television. Not only did this bring entertainment programmes, but perhaps more importantly for social change, it brought programmes which disseminated ideas and encouraged political debate. Current affairs programmes such as 'Panorama' in the United Kingdom and 'See it Now' in the United States were first broadcast in the 1950s. Such programmes exposed viewers to a multiplicity of different perspectives on the world and encouraged them to think critically about the society in which they lived. The first long-playing (LP) records became available in 1948. These records with multiple tracks helped the distribution of music of different genres and further aided an increasing cultural diversity in society.

Perhaps the most famous and iconoclastic of those who helped to re-shape the society of the 1950s were the so-called beat generation. The members of this informal group met initially in New York City and consisted of poets, writers and travellers who threw themselves into a style of life which was completely at odds with convention. Notable members included Allen Ginsberg and Jack Kerouac. The 'beats' became notorious for typically using a variety of different drugs and having non-conventional sexual relationships.

Jack Kerouac was born in 1922 in Massachusetts of French–Canadian parents and was able to speak and write in the form of the French language characteristic of Quebec. He was briefly a student at Columbia University in New York and later started writing. After the war he met Neal Cassady, a drop-out and inveterate traveller, and together they travelled extensively in both the United States and Mexico. These journeys became the subject of Kerouac's book 'On the Road' which he wrote in 1951 (Kerouac, 2012). The celebrated manuscript of the novel consists of one long strip of paper nearly 40 metres long. Kerouac made this by taping together separate sheets, so that he could type without a break. It was difficult for Kerouac to find a publisher for 'On the Road' because it was written in such an unconventional style. However, it was eventually published in 1957.

'On the Road' made Kerouac very famous, and he was subsequently represented as the spiritual leader of the beat generation. However, he did not really consider himself as an unconventional character. He remained very serious about his Roman Catholic faith, and if anything thought of himself as a Catholic author. He died in October 1969 aged 47 years, from internal bleeding caused by excessive consumption of alcohol.

In terms of a literary philosophy, Kerouac was characterized by a spontaneity in his writing, which had parallels with the 'stream of consciousness' approach. The commitment to a philosophy of spontaneity led the beat writers to an interest in Zen, an affinity which we explore later in this chapter. In general terms the beats did not do a great deal to change institutional practice or legislation in relation to say drug acceptance or different forms of sexual relations. On the contrary, they lived their lives in an uninhibited style and acted as a model for future social change in the 1960s. By the late 1950s, the beat generation had helped to create the social movement known as the 'beatniks' which had a similar philosophical approach to life. The beatniks did not concern themselves greatly with using the political system to transform society. However, with the evolution of the beatniks into the hippie movement of the 1960s, there was a much stronger interest in the creation of socio-political movements and in an active political consciousness.

Allen Ginsberg (1926–1997) lived long enough to span both the beat generation and the hippie movement. He was born in New Jersey of a Jewish family. He attended Columbia University where he met Jack Kerouac and his friend William Burroughs. Ginsberg had an affinity with communism, and was given the pseudonym 'Carlo Marx' by Kerouac, in 'On the Road'. Ginsberg's poem 'Howl' was published in 1956 (Ginsberg, 2009). In many ways it is a personal account of the beat generation, its main characters and their beliefs. The poem, however, contains allusions to the use of drugs and to explicit sex and was the subject of an obscenity trial in 1957 which mirrored that of Lady Chatterley's Lover three years later. As with the latter case, the publishers were found not guilty of publishing an obscene work. Ginsberg played a key role in the counter-culture of the 1960s. He was, for example, at the forefront of protests against the Vietnam War and was also a leading figure in the liberalization of laws against homosexuality.

William Burroughs (1914–1997) was a writer who worked in a variety of genres, and was a student at Harvard University in the 1930s. When he left university he visited Europe and immersed himself in the gay sub-culture of Austria. When he went back to the United States he was eventually rejected for army duty, and decided to move to New York where he was a member of Jack Kerouac's circle of friends. However, while living in New York Burroughs became a heroin addict.

In 1954, he decided to live in Morocco, attracted by a variety of factors including the climate and the relaxed lifestyle. It was there that he wrote 'Naked Lunch', a novel which was perceived as obscene in some quarters, but which was eventually published in 1959 (Burroughs, 1990). Seven years later the novel was the subject of another obscenity trial in the United States, but a court in Massachusetts decided that it could not be considered obscene. Burroughs obtained a post lecturing in creative writing in 1974, at the City College, in Harlem, New York. He was unhappy in this job, however, and left within a year. From the late 1970s onwards he was regularly taking heroin and died in 1997 as a result of cardiac problems.

The beat generation and Eastern religions

In 1958 Jack Kerouac published 'The Dharma Bums' a semi-autobiographical book which recounts the interaction between Buddhism and his everyday life (Kerouac, 2008). Kerouac was taught about Buddhism by his friend, the poet Gary Snyder, who appeared in The Dharma Bums under the pseudonym 'Japhy Ryder'. During the mid-1950s Kerouac was very serious about his studies of Zen and shared a cabin in California with Snyder, where they spent a great deal of time discussing Zen. Some readers and Buddhist scholars thought that Kerouac's understanding of Buddhism as displayed in the book was rather superficial. However, there are many aspects of Zen which exhibit spontaneity and subjectivity. These are very often demonstrated after a monk has spent many years devoting himself to a rigorous training in meditation and physical work. It is possible that some readers of Kerouac felt that he had not submitted himself to a sufficiently long period of training in order to be able to say something original or profound about Buddhism.

It sometimes appears that there are two threads running simultaneously through Kerouac's life, and which appear in The Dharma Bums. The first is his love of the purity of the American forests, and the wilderness areas which he came across on his travels back and forth across the United States. This love of nature relates very closely to his understanding of Zen, and the tranquillity and peace of being far from urban development. Secondly there is an undoubted attraction which Kerouac possessed for urban culture and the 'literary life'. He loved the stimulus provided by large cities, the conversations with other writers and the impetus which these all provided for his own writing. Throughout his life, there remained a strong spiritual theme in Kerouac's existence. The internal, reflective life was very important to him, whether stimulated by his Catholic roots or by elements in Buddhism.

Allen Ginsberg nourished a strong interest in India, and thought that he might find there a form of spiritually oriented society very different from that of the United States. He had been consistently opposed to the materialistic culture which seemed to be dominant in the United States, and also to a general lack of a spiritual dimension to life. Ginsberg went to India in May 1963, with his partner Peter Orlovsky, in search of a culture where spirituality remained central to existence (Ginsberg, 1996). Allen Ginsberg had always carried his philosophy of anti-materialism to a personal level, by trying to live simply and not amassing too many material goods. In India he continued to live extremely frugally and made a special effort to meet working-class people and to try to understand their concepts of religion and the divine. He and Orlovsky maintained the practice of living in very basic accommodation while in the sub-continent.

While in India, Ginsberg set out to learn as much as he could about the culture, and to gain fresh insights which would be of use to him back in the United States. In preparation for his stay in India, Ginsberg had studied the Bhagavad Gita and other Indian scriptures, and also learned as much basic Hindi as he could. While in India he learned particularly about the philosophy of ahimsa, and the Gandhian non-violent protests against British imperialism. He was much influenced by this approach in terms of how he himself protested against the Vietnam War. Ginsberg and Orlovsky visited many of the cultural and religious sites in northern India, including Sarnath near Varanasi, Allahabad and Kolkata. While in the latter city, Ginsberg went regularly to the burning ghats alongside the river to watch the cremations. He found it difficult to adjust to the way in which the cremation of a body was openly visible to all. He compared this style of treating the body at death with the much more clinical approach in the West. He began to treat these cremations as a learning experience, during which he gained an appreciation of the impermanence of existence, as in the teachings of the Buddha. He also became acquainted with the common practice of chanting mantras. There seemed to him to be a connection here with the reading of poetry, and when he returned to the United States, he continued the practice of chanting Sanskrit mantras, particularly for the feelings of calmness which they induced.

Ginsberg tried to make regular contact with sadhus and other religious mendicants in order to learn about their spirituality and philosophy of life. He was especially interested in the way in which wealthy Indians could be prepared to give up all the wealth which they had accumulated during a lifetime and become a sadhu. He contrasted this with the American attitude of constant accumulation of wealth, and of the conception of wealth as an indicator of the worth of a person. In India, he noted with interest that other values were used as yardsticks to measure the worth of people. These thoughts lead him to an interest in the principle of non-attachment, whether this was in relation to wealth, to possessions or even to the gaining of enlightenment or moksha. One particular feature which Ginsberg noted about Hinduism was its flexibility and capacity to incorporate a range of different divinities and belief systems from other faiths. This tolerance towards other religions, and relativism in terms of belief and faith, inspired him in relation to his own perception of other religions. In addition, while in India, Ginsberg acquired a sense of the extent to which spirituality could permeate the ordinary existence of people, whether wealthy or poor.

Ginsberg took a variety of drugs on a regular basis while in India. One of the main purposes of this seemed to be an attempt to gain spiritual insights, by as rapid a method as possible. He did not appear to want to devote himself to prolonged periods of meditation or other spiritual practice in order to gain enlightenment. When Ginsberg had a meeting with the Dalai Lama, he apparently suggested that the latter try drugs. However, not unexpectedly, the Dalai Lama refused and said that the key means of gaining enlightenment was to control and discipline the mind.

While in Kolkata in 1963 Ginsberg met writers and poets who were members of the literary group, 'The Hungry Generation'. The man often regarded as the leader of this group was the poet Malay Roychoudury. Ginsberg became close friends with Malay and his brother Samir, and stayed with them in the city of Patna in Bihar.

The Hungryalists, as they were often known, were famous or notorious in a number of ways. In their work they often wrote in the vernacular of the streets and slums, in order to give a voice to the poorer, lower-caste people. The poets of the movement were often in trouble with the authorities because of the radical nature of their output. The content of their work often challenged the norms and values of colonial times. One of the best-known poems of the group, which is perhaps representative of their work, is Malay Roychoudury's 'Stark Electric Jesus'.

It could be argued that Ginsberg and the other members of the beat poets who visited India primarily took ideas from the culture of the sub-continent, rather than there being a flow of ideas from the West towards the East. However, the previous exposure of India to Western culture had principally been mediated via the colonial experience, and the beats provided an alternative to this set of values. This perhaps explains why the beat poets and the radical Bengali poets of the Hungry movement found that they shared many ideas.

A different kind of contribution made by Ginsberg was to publicize through the medium of his poetry some of the poverty and suffering in the Indian sub-continent. In a later visit to India in 1971 during the Bangladesh Liberation War, he wrote the poem 'September on Jessore Road' as a result of seeing thousands of refugees trying to escape from the fighting. Jessore road links the town of Jessore in Bangladesh with the Dum Dum area of Kolkata, and was one of the main routes for refugees seeking security in India.

Ginsberg's interest in Indian culture and religion continued throughout his life. In 1965 when he had returned to the United States from India he became a keen supporter of Bhaktivedanta Swami Prabhupada, the founder of the International Society for Krishna Consciousness (ISKCON). Swami Prabhupada had first travelled to the United States in 1965 with the express purpose of spreading the philosophy of Vaishnavite Hinduism. Ginsberg met the Swami and was interested in his teachings, taking up the chanting of the name of Krishna as a mantram. He helped the Swami in settling in to the United States, and in founding the first ISKCON temple in New York City in 1966. During the later 1960s Ginsberg supported the dissemination of the philosophy of Krishna consciousness within the counter-culture, particularly in California.

Ginsberg also maintained a strong interest in Buddhism, and sometimes referred to himself as a Buddhist. In 1974 Chögyam Trungpa, a Buddhist teacher in the Tibetan tradition, founded Naropa University in Colorado. Trungpa invited Allen Ginsberg and others to establish a department at the university which was subsequently named the 'Jack Kerouac School of Disembodied Poetics'. The School specialized in the areas of literature and creative writing, and much of the teaching had a central theme which drew upon both Eastern and Western spiritual and literary traditions.

It is probably a truism that no social trend arises in a complete vacuum, and the same can be said for the interest of the beats in Eastern religion. Like all wars, the Second World War had resulted in an extensive mixing of cultures, and this was particularly true of the conflict in the Far East. Both British and American troups encountered faiths which were new to them, and this no doubt expanded the consciousness of people in their home countries. This was particularly true of the Western seaboard of the United States, such as in California, which faced across the Pacific to countries where, for example, Buddhism was the indigenous religion.

Even prior to the Second World War, however, there had been important contacts between Eastern religions and the West. In India, early contacts with the West were not exclusively concerned with trade. Western scholars were very interested in Sanskrit and began to realize the wealth of literature written in that language. Some Western scholars began a systematic study of the language, and translations of key religious texts started to become available. Charles Wilkins translated the Bhagavad Gita into English in 1785, and in 1804 Abraham Anquetil-Duperron, a French student of Sanskrit, translated the Upanishads into Latin.

One of the most significant contacts between India and the West in the nineteenth century took place when Swami Vivekananda, an Indian spiritual teacher, lectured at the Parliament of World Religions in 1893 at Chicago. Swami Vivekananda came from Calcutta and was a disciple of the teacher Ramakrishna. Vivekananda set out to bring Hindu teachings to the attention of the West. At the Parliament of the World's Religions, Vivekananda gave a number of talks on Hinduism and Buddhism. His central message was to articulate the basic links between all major religions, and of the need for tolerance between different faiths. Vivekananda's talks had a profound influence upon his audiences, and his contribution marked the beginning of a much wider interest in Indian philosophy in Western countries (Vivekananda, 1982a).

In the latter part of the nineteenth century there were other developments designed in part to further an understanding of Eastern religions, including Hinduism. In 1875 Helena Blavatsky established the Theosophical Society in New York. The aims of the society were among others to further the study of different religions, particularly Eastern religions, and to encourage people of different ethnic groups and faiths, to live and work together in harmony.

One of the beliefs of the Theosophical Society was that at various times in the history of the planet, a spiritual teacher would appear who would have a profound effect upon the development of the human race. In 1909, members of the society at their centre at Adyar in India became acquainted with a young man called Jiddu Krishnamurti, who was considered to be a future spiritual leader. He was given an excellent formal education by members of the society, but it appears that he felt he was being to some extent manipulated by members of the society. By the mid-1920s Krishnamurti was beginning to feel disenchanted with the society and finally decided to leave it completely. From that point onwards he devoted his time to giving lectures on religious matters. In later life he did not associate himself with any particular religious or philosophical school but through his writings and talks became a celebrated teacher (Krishnamurti, 2010). Although he did not specifically or exclusively disseminate Hindu ideas, he was nevertheless responsible for an enhanced interest in Hinduism in the West. He died in 1986 at the age of 90 years.

The beat generation thus had much to say about Western society in the 1950s, whether about the perceived preoccupation with consumerism or about the values of autonomy and free expression. Their orientation towards society appears to have laid the groundwork for the more systematic critique of society which took place in the 1960s. In the next chapter we examine the transition from the beats of the 1950s to the hippie movement of the 1960s, and in particular, the wide range of social movements which had their origins in that decade.

Further reading

Burroughs, W. S. (2013) *Rub out the Words: Letters 1959–1974*. London: Penguin.

Charters, A. (ed.) (1992) *The Portable Beat Reader*. London: Penguin.

Kerouac, J. (2012) *Big Sur*. London: Penguin.

Miles, B. (2010) *Ginsberg: Beat Poet*. London: Virgin.

Trungpa, C. (1984) *Shambhala: The Sacred Path of the Warrior*. Boston, MA: Shambhala.

Yinger, J. M. (1982) *Countercultures: The Promise and Peril of a World Turned Upside Down*. New York: Free Press.

2

Social and political movements of the counter-culture

Summary

This chapter examines some of the main areas of social action which took place during the 1960s. It could be argued that the single most important event of the period was the Vietnam War. This gave rise to a movement for peace, which was linked in the minds of many with the Civil Rights movement. Other important areas of activism included the environmental or 'green' movement, and the wide range of organizations which campaigned for equality in terms of gender and sexual orientation. Permeating the entire period was the socio-cultural hippie movement. This chapter explores these movements, and the impact which they started to have on society.

The hippie movement

It can be argued that the beat movement was fundamentally existential in nature rather than espousing a particular philosophy. The beats wished to experience life in all its fullness and complexity, and to live in the manner advocated by many mystics of different persuasions – 'in the moment'. At various times they criticized the materialism of American society and supported the notion of autonomy and individualism. This extended to ideas of personal liberty reflected in a relaxation of sexual relationships and the taking of different types of drugs. Nevertheless they seemed to eschew the idea of propagating a specific social or political philosophy and of attempting to transform society in a particular direction. As the 1950s moved into the

1960s there was however an increasing sense among the counter-culture that society did need changing in a number of ways. The principal link between the beat generation or beatniks of the 1950s and what became the hippie movement of the 1960s was arguably Allen Ginsberg who had consistently demonstrated a concern for social change. As we shall see he was active throughout the 1960s in a range of social movements.

Although we tend to associate the beats with the 1950s, and the hippies with the 1960s, it is very rare in the development of society that we can demarcate social trends precisely. One movement tends to merge with another over time. The origin of the term 'hippie' is uncertain, although it appears to be related to the use of the word 'hip' among jazz afficionados in the 1940s and 1950s in the United States. If someone was 'hip' it broadly designated them as fashionable, trendy, 'with it', 'cool', in vogue and contemporary. It also suggested a very relaxed and insouciant approach to life. There are also implications of a relaxed attitude towards sexual mores and drug use.

As the hippie movement developed its own character during the early 1960s, it generally became associated with San Francisco and in particular with the Haight-Ashbury area of the city. Inexpensive accommodation in the area made it attractive to impecunious young people. In 1967 the song about San Francisco 'Be sure to wear some flowers in your hair', acted as a clarion call for young people to travel to San Francisco, which remained in the popular consciousness as the epicentre of the hippie movement.

The environmental movement

One of the philosophical approaches which permeated the hippie movement was that of naturalism. Although environmentalism could not be clearly delineated as precisely urban or rural, there was a definite trend towards the ideal of living in a rural democratic community, growing one's own food, living on a vegetarian or vegan diet and consuming only what was necessary for a self-sustaining existence. Many rural communes, structured along these lines, developed in the United States during the 1960s, and the philosophy subsequently spread to many parts of the world (Matthews, 2010). In fact this model of living acted as a precursor for the green movement which was to attract increasing popularity during the next half-century.

It is not to argue however that the hippies were the first to advocate a naturalistic, organic lifestyle. During the period following the English Civil War a group of political reformers called the True Levellers sought to establish agricultural communities in which people worked together to grow crops and share these between members. The idea was to take over common land and to use it productively in this way. The name 'True Levellers' came from the group's ideology of democratic equality and of sharing food and other resources. The group was led by Gerrard Winstanley (1609–1676). The main philosophical inspiration for the Levellers came from Protestant Christianity and a form of interpretation which today we would recognize as distinctly socialist. Although the group was not a direct threat to the affluent land-owning classes, the latter still considered them as challenging the established political order. Their practice of cultivating historically shared land for agriculture led them to be popularly known as 'Diggers'. The radical movement represented by the Diggers proved not to be long-lasting in practical terms, but it helped to sustain the concept of socialist agricultural communities.

It is interesting that in 1966–1967 a group which assumed the name 'San Francisco Diggers' established themselves in Haight-Ashbury and followed the broad principles of the original Diggers. They were essentially a food cooperative. Members typically collected surplus food from supermarkets and restaurants, and prepared meals for free distribution to the poor and homeless. They assumed the broad ideological approach of the original Diggers but without the element of Christian Socialism. The over-riding ideal was one of the sharing and redistributing of natural resources rather than wasting them.

Mahatma Gandhi was also well-known as an advocate of communal, rural living. In 1910 during Gandhi's campaigns for civil rights in South Africa, a friend donated a farm for the use of Gandhi and his followers. It was close to Johannesburg and was named Tolstoy Farm after the celebrated Russian writer. The membership of the community fluctuated as people came and went. The community was also multi-cultural and multi-faith. People grew their own food and followed Gandhi's philosophy of vegetarianism and non-violence. There was a school for the children, and the overall philosophy was one of self-reliance. Given the variety of religions represented in the community, a great emphasis was also placed on religious tolerance and understanding. Tolstoy Farm has served as a model for spiritually inspired cooperative living since its inception.

Gandhi lived at Tolstoy Farm for approximately four years and then returned to India in 1915. He was hoping to establish an ashram or religious retreat where he could continue with the same sort of self-sufficient agricultural activities. By 1917 Gandhi had established such an ashram in Gujarat, adjacent to the Sabarmati river, near the town of Ahmedabad. It was here that Gandhi and his followers founded a centre for agriculture and religious practice. It became known as Sabarmati Ashram and is still active today as a museum, library and resource centre for the study of Gandhi's philosophy.

Much of Gandhi's philosophy was concerned with leading a simple life and using only a minimum of natural resources compatible with effectively sustaining life. This approach is also linked in Indian philosophy with a respect for all living creatures and a desire not to do any harm to other living beings. As a child Gandhi was very much influenced by the Jain religion, well-known for its strict philosophy of non-harm towards living things (Long, 2009). Indeed Jain monks will often gently sweep the path ahead of them as they walk in order not to harm any small organisms on the ground. There is also a philosophical link here with Buddhism. One of the key concepts of Buddhism is impermanence, the notion that all living and non-living matter will eventually disintegrate. To put this in the style of speaking of some Buddhists we might say that all aggregate matter eventually and inevitably disaggregates. Once we truly understand this, we do not want to do anything to further the process of disaggregation. Hence we refrain from harming other living beings.

India has a long tradition of adhering to such principles long before the time of Gandhi. One of the most celebrated advocates of living in harmony with other living beings was the Mauryan emperor Ashoka (304–232 BCE). Ashoka ruled over most of the Indian sub-continent. During the early part of his reign he was concerned to acquire new territories, and was regarded as a fierce and relentless military commander. However, disturbed by the slaughter of his campaigns he converted to Buddhism, and set about constructing many of his political policies upon Buddhist philosophical principles. While he did not completely ban the eating of meat, he placed limitations upon the killing of animals for food. He established hospitals, and also centres for the treatment of sick animals. In addition he planted many thousands of trees along the main routes to provide summer shade for travellers.

One of the interesting facets of the reign of Ashoka was that he erected a large number of stone pillars throughout India, upon which he had carved 'edicts' to reflect his philosophical approach to governance, and the way in which he wanted society to develop. These mostly reflected a Buddhist approach to life. One of the most famous pillars is still standing at Sarnath, to the northeast of Varanasi in the state of Uttar Pradesh. The top of the pillar is kept as an exhibit in the museum at Sarnath. It consists of four lions facing outwards at 90 degrees to each other. This sculpture has become the official symbol of India and is used in places such as on stamps. At the base of the Sarnath pillar is a wheel or chakra which symbolizes the teaching of the Buddha. This is used in the centre of the design for the Indian flag.

The 1960s marked the beginning of a rapidly growing awareness of the importance of the environment for the future of the planet. There was a gradual appreciation among the counter-culture that the demands of large corporations may be at conflict with maintaining an ecological balance whether in the indiscriminate disposal of industrial waste, or the widespread use of pesticides, there were likely to be negative consequences for the environment. The counter-culture began to see these trends as opposed to their utopian vision of a naturalistic lifestyle. One of the most influential books on the subject was 'Silent Spring' by Rachel Carson, which was first published in 1962, and argued that the use of pesticides such as DDT was having a serious effect upon wildlife (Carson, 1965). She argued significantly that DDT and similar organic compounds accumulated in the bodies of organisms, and that this exacerbated their effects. The validity of her arguments was never universally accepted, but there is no doubting the impact of her book, which acted as a beacon for the developing environmental movement, particularly among young radical environmentalists.

Civil rights

For such young people it was insufficient to provide merely an example of how life might be lived in a rural idyll. Certainly it was important to provide alternative models of living, but this was not sufficient. As the 1960s progressed it became evident that the growing counter-culture saw the importance of direct, non-violent action and protest as one way of proceeding against attacks on the environment. They also saw however the need for legislation to restrict the activities of large industrial corporations who disposed of their waste materials thoughtlessly, or in a manner designed simply to save money. There was thus a real determination to change the world, rather than to attempt merely to take the moral high ground.

The same philosophical approach was also true of the other issues addressed by the counter-culture including the attempt to improve civil rights, which for many black Americans in the 1950s were extremely limited indeed. Despite the advances made during the American Civil War in abolishing slavery, there was, until the mid-1950s in the southern states of America particularly, a society which operated systematic oppression and discrimination against black people. Arguably the major turning point in this discriminatory system came in December 1955, when Rosa Parks, a 42-year-old housekeeper, was travelling on a bus in Montgomery, Alabama, and was asked to give up her seat to a white person. She refused, and was arrested. At that time the front rows in Montgomery buses were designated for white people and the back rows for black people. However, if the bus was full and additional white people got on, blacks were expected to relinquish their seats for whites. Rosa Parks was tried five days after her arrest, and found guilty. On the one hand, in a groundswell of anger at the unfairness of the segregation system, the black community mounted a boycott of the bus system in Montgomery even though this created considerable hardship for those working, who often had to walk a long way to their employment. On the other hand, the boycott also cost the bus company a great deal in lost revenue. The boycott lasted over a year but was finally successful in acting as a catalyst for the removal of racial segregation on Montgomery buses. The leader of the boycott movement had been a young pastor called Dr Martin Luther King.

An increasingly politicized counter-culture was beginning to adopt a variety of forms of non-violent protest to bring about social change. The 'sit-in' was widely used at the beginning of the decade of the 1960s to protest against discrimination practised against black people in coffee bars and restaurants. In 1960 the US Supreme Court had declared illegal the use of racial segregation on buses travelling between different states. Yet this still took place in the south, and groups of black and white young people took part in what became known as 'freedom rides'. They rode on buses travelling across state boundaries, deliberately inviting the antagonism of local people. Many suffered severe beatings and imprisonment.

One of the most notable events to further the civil rights cause in the early 1960s was the March on Washington for Jobs and Freedom which took place on 28 August 1963. This was the event at which Martin Luther King made his famous speech including the phrase 'I have a dream . . .'. Approximately a quarter of a million people gathered in the space before the Lincoln Memorial in Washington, DC to listen to a number of speeches and songs. The March achieved a great deal of publicity for the Civil Rights Movement and exerted pressure on President J. F. Kennedy to enact legislation in this area. The March was also marked by the appearance of Bob Dylan and Joan Baez singing 'When the Ship comes in'.

When President Kennedy was assassinated on 22 November 1963, Lyndon Johnson as vice president was sworn in as president. He supported and continued the civil rights legislation planned by the Kennedy administration, and in 1964 the Civil Rights Act which declared racial segregation illegal was passed. The following year the Voting Rights Act was passed.

The peace movement

The Civil Rights Movement was particularly active during the mid-1960s at the same time as the American involvement in the Vietnam War was expanding. Many civil rights leaders such as Martin Luther King were also committed opponents of the Vietnam War. This was partly because in the popular consciousness, conscription into the army was seen as resulting in a disproportionate number of black and ethnic minority men being sent to Vietnam. The validity of this statistic was challenged by some, but black people certainly continued to believe it to be true.

There was widespread opposition to the Vietnam War based on a number of factors. The war was perceived as not being particularly relevant to American interests, even given an obsession in some political quarters with the spread of communism. Escalating fatalities made the war seem increasingly futile, and the manner in which it was conducted appeared to reflect the unethical employment of military power by the United States. Events such as the My Lai massacre in March 1968 strengthened protests in the United States (Bilton and Sim, 1993). University and college students were at the forefront of protests. Student protests were not only founded upon a moral and political opposition to the Vietnam War. The risk of being 'drafted' seemed to students to be enhanced by the policy of the Nixon presidency in May 1970 to invade Cambodia, and hence to appear to extend rather than limit the Vietnam War. Protests took place on a number of American campuses. Tragically, at Kent State University in Ohio, the National Guard was called in on 4 May 1970 to disperse a crowd of students, and opened fire on them. Four students were killed.

The deaths at Kent State University had a dramatic effect across the country. Many student campuses were virtually closed by protest marches and students withdrawing from classes. Nearly 500 higher education campuses were closed by these actions. A major march was held in Washington, DC, and a number of military buildings around the country were set on fire. The pressure upon the Nixon regime to end the war increased and increased.

The draft was often perceived as an illogical and badly administered process. The folksinger Arlo Guthrie released a song 'Alice's Restaurant' in 1967, which highlighted some of these inconsistencies. Guthrie had a conviction for dropping litter, and had to declare this as part of the evaluation process for conscription. As a result of this conviction he was exempted from the draft. The song recounts this story, and became a celebrated lyric within the counter-culture and anti-war movement.

Popular music, and particularly folk music, played a major role in articulating the feelings of the counter-culture towards the Vietnam War. The lyrics of Bob Dylan's songs were particularly important in this regard. However, if any song reflected the contemporary mood, it could be said to be Country Joe McDonald's 'I feel like I'm fixin' to die rag', which he played at the Woodstock Festival in August 1969. Its ironic lyrics tended to summarize many of the views of the counter-culture towards the war in Vietnam.

Throughout the mid to late 1960s there was also systematic opposition to the Vietnam War from intellectuals who saw the war as an example of American imperialism. They generally highlighted the consequences of the war for poor Vietnamese villagers who normally earned their living from agriculture. They pointed to the way in which the war was destructive of the natural environment in Vietnam, and hence having an adverse effect on the cultivation of crops.

One of the foremost of these opponents of the war was Professor Noam Chomsky of the Massachusetts Institute of Technology. In an article entitled 'The Responsibility of Intellectuals' (Chomsky, 1967) he posed the question of the extent to which ordinary citizens could separate themselves from the actions of their governments during time of war. Even more so, he pointed out that intellectuals have arguably an even stronger responsibility because of their academic training. They are educated to analyse concepts and ideas and have a responsibility to examine the ethics and logical validity of arguments. This responsibility was particularly important in relation to such events as the Vietnam War where so many lives were at risk.

Another prominent Vietnam protester during the 1960s was Abbie Hoffman. Educated at Brandeis University and the University of California, Berkeley, he was one of the leaders of an anti-war protest march on the Pentagon in October 1967. The following year Hoffman was involved in a major protest during the Democratic National Convention in Chicago. There were violent confrontations between police and demonstrators, and Hoffman was arrested along with other demonstrators who were subsequently described as 'The Chicago Eight'. Hoffman was found guilty but this decision was rescinded on appeal.

Allen Ginsberg, who had been prominent among the beat generation, continued his social protest activities throughout the 1960s. In November 1965 he was one of the organizers of an anti-Vietnam War protest at Berkeley, California. It was anticipated by the protesters that they would face a number of pro-war demonstrations and that there was likely to be violence. Ginsberg suggested that the anti-war protesters hold flowers and handed these to any opponents they encountered. This was probably the first instance of the peaceful strategy which became known as 'flower power'.

Equality in relation to gender and sexual orientation

The 1960s was also a period of concerted effort by many groups to achieve genuine equality for women and for those people of a different sexual orientation to the majority. The exploration of gender issues as a serious question of social politics and philosophy did not start with the 1960s. The philosopher who perhaps had the most significant influence immediately prior to the 1960s was Simone de Beauvoir. Born in Paris in 1908, she was the lifelong friend and intellectual colleague of Jean-Paul Sartre. They were both philosophy students together in Paris in the late 1920s and were associated with the philosophical movement of existentialism.

Simone de Beauvoir's key work in relation to feminism was 'The Second Sex' (De Beauvoir, 1989) originally published in 1949. In this work she argued that girls were not born with all of the psychology or predispositions of women but acquired these through a process of socialization. This view was in harmony with the philosophy of existentialism which asserted that human beings are born and subsequently grow to maturity in a particular role, partly through the effects of socialization and partly through the choices they make in relation to the kind of person they would wish to become. De Beavoir therefore distinguished between the nature of an inherited gender role and the nature of gender as a socialized condition. This distinction opened up the possibility for women that they did not need to subordinate themselves to a gender role defined for them through their up-bringing, education or societal background. They were free to create for themselves the gender role which they perceived as appropriate for them. Their social world was to some extent a blank slate upon which could be written the needs and aspirations of women. This philosophical approach was in harmony with the general spirit of the age in the 1960s as it stressed the relevance of human freedom and autonomy in determining the lives of women. De Beauvoir's book was extremely influential and served as a reference point for much of the later writing on feminism.

As an example of de Beauvoir's determination to live her life in the way she saw fit, in 1971 she joined a number of other French women in signing a statement that she had an illegal abortion during her life. Over 300 other French women, some of them very famous in public life, also signed. The purpose of the statement was to argue that although it was illegal, the decision to have an abortion should rest with the woman. The statement resulted in the issue of abortion becoming something of a feminist cause célèbre in France, and in 1974, as a result of legislation promulgated by Simone Veil, it became legal to have an abortion during the first ten weeks after conception.

During the Second World War there had been a tendency for women to work in more traditionally male occupations because of the large number of men in the armed forces. One might have thought that with the end of hostilities women would remain in these occupations, perhaps to replace those men who had been killed in action. However, it seems that after 1945 women tended to revert to their traditional role of housewife. If they did remain in work, many took up posts with less status than male colleagues. This situation appeared to continue throughout the 1950s. Only a relatively small number of girls and young women were able to continue their education and aspire to a professional career. This applied to a greater or lesser extent in both the United States and Europe. The priority for many young women, as indeed for their parents, was that a daughter should primarily seek to make a successful marriage rather than establish herself in a professional career.

One woman who did succeed in breaking through this stereotype was the American, Betty Friedan, who attended Smith College in Massachusetts. In the late 1950s she collected data from some women who had attended college at the same time as her, and also from some other respondents. Many of them were housewives and she was interested in the extent to which they were happy with their lives. It appeared from the data that many of the interviewees were to varying degrees unhappy and would have preferred to have a career, rather than being a housewife. In 1963 Betty Friedan published the results in her book 'The Feminine Mystique' (Friedan, 2010). The 'feminine mystique' of the title derived from the fact that many of the respondents had extremely comfortable lives from a material point of view, yet that this was insufficient for them to attain happiness. Betty Friedan's argument was that women, just as much as men, needed educational and intellectual stimulus, and the satisfaction that comes from a rewarding career. The book was very influential and did a great deal to remind the young women of the 1960s counter-culture that they could aspire to have whatever role they wanted in society.

In the same year as the publication of Betty Friedan's book President J. F. Kennedy oversaw the enactment of the Equal Pay Act in the United States, which, with some exceptions, assured equal pay between the genders, for work of a similar type. This act had a significant effect in terms of improving women's wages relative to those of men. Issues related to feminism gathered momentum as part of the counter-culture during the 1960s, and in 1966 a group of women in the United States founded the National Organization for Women to act as a pressure group for women's issues.

Several important books on feminist issues were published at the end of the decade of the 1960s. Kate Millett published 'Sexual Politics' for example in 1970. In the ten years which had elapsed since Betty Friedan was conducting her research, it was becoming more and more common for women to establish themselves in an academic career and to contribute to the intellectual debate about gender issues. Kate Millett for example had studied at the universities of Minnesota and Oxford and gained a PhD from Columbia. In 'Sexual Politics' (Millett, 1970) she argued that Western society was permeated by patriarchal views and attitudes which reinforced male dominance in society. These values, she asserted, were reproduced through such means as literary works which continued to portray women as subservient to men. She argued strongly that these patriarchal values had to be challenged in order to enable women to be liberated, and able to lead autonomous, fulfilling lives, free from the yolk of male domination.

A widely read and influential book of the period was 'The Female Eunuch' by the Australian-born academic Dr Germaine Greer. Published first in 1970, it initiated extensive debate on the role of women in society (Greer, 2006). She argued that girls are socialized to view traditional family life as the most appropriate milieu to fulfil themselves. However, she asserted that this environment did not enable women to experience their full sexuality, and that they should explore other contexts for rearing children and having sexual relationships. She also argued strongly against the treatment of the female image as a product to be marketed. The reduction of women to a consumer commodity had a negative effect on their sexuality, and was also disempowering, particularly for those who felt they failed to attain the idealized image of women portrayed in the media.

What is interesting is that as we look backwards from the second decade of the twenty-first century, many of these ideas within feminism and the women's movement seem very familiar. Even though much remains to be done in terms of equality for women, these arguments have attained a considerable degree of acceptance. However, if it were not for the insights and persistence of these and other writers, the changes in subsequent decades would never have been brought about.

The fight for gay rights in England also started to come to fruition in the 1960s, but only after a period of immense struggle which started in the 1950s. During that decade there had been a gradually increasing unease about the number of prosecutions for homosexuality and as a result the government established a committee under the chairmanship of Lord Wolfenden to evaluate legislation concerning what were then offences with regard to homosexuality. The committee's report was published in 1957, and recommended that homosexual acts taking place in private, between consenting adults, should not be considered as criminal behaviour. The next decade was one of considerable debate on the issue, but finally in 1967 the Sexual Offences Act was passed. This Act contained some of the elements of the Wolfenden Committee report. For homosexual acts to be legal, they had to be in private, and between participants of 21 years or older.

The mid-1960s also saw an increasing use of the term 'gay' to describe a homosexual. The term tended not to be associated with some of the more pejorative connotations of 'homosexual', and the gradual transition in terminology did a great deal to facilitate an evolution in the social definition of homosexuality.

Although in England the 1967 Sexual Offences Act did not resolve all issues of concern to the gay community, it at least represented a clear basis in law from which further campaigns for liberalization could take place. In the United States the legal situation was rather more complex, given historical differences between individual states, and between state and federal legislation. The general atmosphere in the United States during the mid-1960s towards gays was relatively negative. Conservative elements in society viewed them as being subversive towards the cohesion of society, and there were occasions of harassment and arrest of gays by the police. Attempts were made throughout the decade to organize systematic opposition to this type of treatment, and also to try to change public attitudes towards gays. However, it remained difficult for gays to find places to gather or socialize, where they would not be subject to intimidation. Some clubs, bars and cafes became known as places where gays would meet, and one such place was the Stonewall Inn, in the Greenwich Village area of New York City. In June 1969 a group of police officers entered the club and started to take details of some of the customers. Altercations ensued and some arrests were made. Others objected to being arrested and the situation quickly became rather disorderly with the police losing control. Gay sympathizers and other onlookers from the neighbouring area started to gather, and the police soon found themselves in a rapidly escalating public order disturbance. This event received a great deal of publicity in the media during the next few days. It focused public attention on the rights of the gay community to meet peacefully and to socialize without the risk of intervention by the police. In retrospect, the events at the Stonewall Inn tended to stimulate a gradual change in public attitudes, and to give the gay community a greater sense of determination in seeking more fairness of treatment (Carter, 2005).

Prior to the riot at the Stonewall Inn, gay activism had generally been limited to persuasion and advocacy of the gay cause. After Stonewall however, there was a change of emphasis with the creation of much more radical gay and lesbian groups. Many gay people had been involved in anti-Vietnam War protests during the decade, and had experience of direct, non-violent street protests. They brought this kind of social consciousness to the gay movement. There was a gradual realization that the issue of gay rights was fundamentally political, and needed to be approached from a political perspective. The Gay Liberation Front was an informal association of different gay groups established in New York in the aftermath of the Stonewall events. Branches were established elsewhere, including in the United Kingdom in 1970. Other lobbying and activist organizations developed subsequently, including 'Stonewall', named after the bar in New York.

The Second World War had created an enormous upsurge in world society, resulting in the mixing of people of different cultural backgrounds and social classes. After the war, there was a tendency for some people to want to return to the perceived stability of pre-war society. However, the young people of the counter-culture were not prepared to do this, and had a different vision of the future. This vision included the kinds of change discussed in this chapter, and a society based on variation rather than conformity. This variation included among other things the different types of spiritual experience which are the subject of the following chapter.

Further reading

De Groot, G. J. (ed.) (1998) *Student Protest: The Sixties and After*. London: Longman.
Goodman, P. (1960) *Growing Up Absurd: Problems of Youth in the Organized Society*. New York: Vintage.
Hall, S. (2006) *Peace and Freedom: The Civil Rights and Anti-War Movements in the 1960s*. Philadelphia, PA: University of Pennsylvania Press.
Marcuse, H. (2002) *One-Dimensional Man: Studies in the Ideology of Advanced Industrial Society*. London: Routledge.
Yates, N. (2010) *Love Now Pay Later: Sex and Religion in the Fifties and Sixties*. London: SPCK.

3

Spirituality in the counter-culture

Summary

This chapter analyses the type of society which existed before the period of the 1960s, and how this affected the aspirations of the counter-culture, particularly in terms of spirituality. It looks at the concept of the guru in Eastern religions, and the influence which this had on young people seeking a personal spirituality. Finally this chapter explores the lives and philosophies of a range of teachers who were influential towards the evolving counter-cultural movement.

Introduction

The parents of the baby-boomer generation were brought up in a pre-Second World War society which was characterized by social conformity, class differences, a relative absence of individual freedoms and a general lack of educational and other opportunities, except for the children of rich families. As the baby boomers grew to maturity towards the 1960s, they tended to reject this sort of society and aspired to a very different way of life. Similar social forces were at work in the world of religion. After the war the prevalent religious world view in Europe and in the United States was Christian. Christianity provided a moral framework for society, and the validity of this paradigm went largely unquestioned. It was typified by a range of religious injunctions such as the Ten Commandments. However, just as the young people of the counter-culture rejected the concept of social conformity, they also refused to accept religious and moral conformity. However, it would be wrong to suggest that young people of the period did not seek some principles by which they could live their lives. They simply did not want to subscribe to oppressive injunctions which left little room for personal expression or autonomy.

In terms of spirituality and an associated moral framework, young people of the 1960s did not want to be constrained within a rigid paradigm; they wanted the freedom to pick and choose from a wide range of religious practice and experience; they wanted to retain their own sense of autonomy and they wanted the self-determination to be able to change their approach to spirituality if and when they wanted. When they practised within a particular tradition they typically wanted to try to find a direct experience of the world, the universe or the divine, rather than simply the knowledge that they had complied with certain religious injunctions. This need for subjective spiritual experience attracted them to mystical approaches such as Kabbalah or Sufism, and to Eastern religions such as Zen Buddhism or Hinduism.

The nature of a guru

It is the norm within such traditions for there to be 'teachers' or gurus, who interpret the religion for their followers. The guru may encompass a number of roles, from passing on a knowledge and understanding of scripture, to explaining religious ritual. In addition, however, a guru in the sense of Eastern religions also tends to explain ways in which the religious tradition is relevant to everyday life. Individual gurus may differ in the way in which they do this and may offer their own particular interpretation to their disciples. During the 1960s there were many cases of teachers coming to the West in order to establish religious communities, and also of young people travelling to Asia in search of a guru. Some teachers had a long period of experience and training within a religious tradition, whereas in the case of some others this was less so. Overall, however, the 1960s was a period in which the diversity of world religions was brought into the public consciousness, and young people began to reflect more on the many opportunities for spiritual experience.

One of the religious writers and teachers of the 1960s who perhaps best espoused a sense of autonomy and a firm determination to explore his own spiritual pathway was Alan Watts. He was born in the south of England in 1915, and in his teens became a member of the Buddhist Society in London. In 1938 Watts moved to New York, where he continued with his studies of Buddhism, concentrating on the Zen tradition. He subsequently entered a Christian seminary and remained involved with the Christian Church until about 1950. Settling in California, he taught Eastern religions in San Francisco at the American Academy of Asian Studies. It was through this institution that Watts made the acquaintance of Gary Snyder, the poet and academic, who himself was linked with the beat poets. Throughout the 1950s and 1960s Alan Watts broadcast a number of radio and television programmes on Eastern religions and gave numerous public talks. He was a prolific writer, and published a number of influential books which continue to be widely read (Watts, 1957, 1988).

Watts was eclectic in his writing and philosophy, integrating ideas from Taoism, Buddhism and Hinduism. He died in California in 1973. He was extremely popular as a writer and lecturer throughout the 1960s, and there are perhaps a number of reasons for this. He did not concentrate on teaching the formal concepts of Buddhism or Vedanta, but tried to relate these ideas to people's everyday lives. He emphasized the practical relevance of the teachings of Eastern religions such as the use of meditation to help people cope with periods of psychological stress. Many of the books of the period tended to discuss the philosophy of different religions and it was not easy for readers to apply this theoretical writing to their own lives. His approach was almost inevitably a personal, subjective interpretation of the teachings of Buddhism and Hinduism, but this appealed to many young people of the counter-culture who wanted to find their own spiritual way. Whether or not Alan Watts sought it, he was in effect cast in the role of a spiritual guru for many thousands of people. His non-traditional approach to the teaching of religion inspired young people who were seeking a sense of meaning in life, but who could not accept the traditional, formal teachings of established faiths. In fact Alan Watts had apparently found it difficult to accept religious traditions which defined a specific belief system as the one for people to accept. He appeared to want the freedom to decide which particular teachings were relevant to him. He was eclectic in his interests which ranged from mystical approaches in Hinduism, to Chinese calligraphy, environmental issues and meditation. During his life he gave lectures at a number of universities, but he was never an academic in the formal sense. His non-traditional approach to spirituality appealed to the demand of the counter-culture to find different ways of looking at religious life, and the popularity of his writings continued long after his death.

Hindu spirituality

One of the most influential spiritual movements of the counter-culture was that of Vedanta. This term in Hinduism refers to the teachings derived from the texts known as the Upanishads. These are philosophical works which comment on and analyse the Vedas. Vedanta is characterized by the assumption that human beings are intrinsically divine. They have within them an element which is derived from God, and the purpose of life is to enable each individual to unite with this divine element and thus to perfect themselves as human beings.

The central purpose of the guru within Hinduism is to guide and assist the spiritual student in attaining this religious union with God. The guru employs a variety of practical strategies to help students, including meditation, the analysis of scriptures, the repetition of mantras and the practice of yoga.

This approach of enabling the individual to attain a form of spiritual fulfilment was very attractive during the counter-culture. It was not an approach which depended upon submitting to a set of religious rules, but rather one which encouraged each individual to find their own unique pathway to God. This appealed to the autonomous, individualistic mood of the 1960s.

Within the Vedanta philosophy, the idea of seeking to perfect the individual and to unite his or her soul with God was the essential element of all religious practice. Indeed, for Vedantists, all religions were seen as broadly following the same aim. They might employ different techniques, and they might have different scriptures, but ultimately for Vedantists the purpose of all religions was seen as achieving a mystical union with God. The manner in which this was to be achieved was not as important as the goal itself. One result of this philosophy was that the various external manifestations of a religion were not perceived as of prime importance in the religious quest. They might assist adherents in achieving their goals, but they were not of central importance.

Historically, one of the best-known advocates of this approach to religion was the nineteenth-century Bengali teacher, Ramakrishna (1836–1886). He explored other religions besides Hinduism and argued that all of the world's principal religions were the same in that they aimed at the achievement of a union with the divine.

Ramakrishna and his teachings were very influential, and several of his disciples established well-known religious organizations. Vivekananda founded the Ramakrishna Mission in 1897, and Swami Abhedananda established the Ramakrishna Vedanta Society in 1923. A leading figure in the development of Vedanta in the West was Swami Prabhavananda. He was born in 1893 in a village near Calcutta. As a young man he met a number of people who had been close to Ramakrishna. He encountered Sarada Devi, the wife of Ramakrishna, and also Brahmananda who, along with Vivekananda, had been a leading disciple of Ramakrishna. Prabhavananda finally became a monk of the Ramakrishna order in 1921. In 1923 he was asked by senior monks to travel to California to become head of the San Francisco Vedanta Society, and under his inspiration the Society expanded considerably during the next few years. He finally established the Vedanta Society of Southern California. Prabhavananda became a leading spiritual teacher of the counter-culture in the California of the 1960s, and knew Alan Watts (1972) along with the writers Christopher Isherwood (1980) and Aldous Huxley (1954). He died in 1976.

The idea of attaching oneself to a guru became very popular in the 1960s. There are a number of possible explanations for this. Young people of the counter-culture were looking for some kind of inspirational leadership, and yet they tended to be alienated first by political leaders who were taking them deeper and deeper into a complex war in the Far East, and secondly by business leaders who were creating a society ever more dependent on materialism and consumerism. Traditional religious experience appeared to offer nothing new, and hence many young people turned to the idea of having a spiritual teacher or guru, usually associated with an Eastern religion.

The concept of a guru has a long tradition in Indian society. Linguists have suggested a number of etymological origins for the term, but one suggestion is that the word derives from the Sanskrit for dark and light. A guru, on this explanation, is a person who helps the devotee move from spiritual darkness into spiritual light. Within many Hindu traditions, the guru is thought to be necessary for the adherent to achieve spiritual fulfilment or enlightenment. In other words the analysis of the holy scriptures, although helpful, is not considered sufficient to enable someone to achieve liberation. The aspirant needs the practical, spiritual advice of a teacher, who can interpret the scriptures and guide the aspirant towards a mystical union with God.

As the role of the guru is so important in the spiritual search, it may place the disciple in a situation of dependency in relation to the guru. It thus becomes essential that the aspirant is very careful in the choice of a guru. During the 1960s some gurus attracted a somewhat negative reputation. This was particularly so in the case of teachers in-charge of some new religious movements, where they were alleged to have had exploitative relationships with younger members of their organizations. Certainly gurus who had travelled to the West appeared to have different attitudes in relation to their role. Some who had been initiated into a specific historical tradition acted according to well-established norms. Others who had established their own religious tradition sometimes acted in a more subjective, idiosyncratic way. There was no clear line of distinction here, but this did point to the need to be circumspect when young people were choosing a guru to follow. A number of possible criteria have been suggested for identifying a potentially suitable guru.

Perhaps the most obvious criterion is that the guru should have a knowledge of the Hindu scriptures and of Sanskrit in order to be able to transmit the traditional teachings of Hinduism. One might also assume a knowledge of practical aspects of the religion such as hatha yoga. However there are examples of gurus who are untutored in an academic sense, but who have acquired a deep sense of spirituality from their own guru. What seems more important is that the guru should be deeply spiritual, and in everyday life should act in an ethical manner. An indication of this is that the guru complies with the basic tenets of his own teaching. For example, if she or he advocates a life of non-attachment to material things, then one would expect the guru to lead a simple life, uncluttered with consumer goods or material possessions. One might also look for indications that the guru tries to serve others rather than be concerned with his own welfare. Some Hindu gurus have acquired a reputation both throughout India and even internationally as religious teachers. However, one would not particularly expect a guru actively to seek disciples, or to acquire a reputation purely in order to enhance or glorify their own position. In fact one would probably expect them to be very modest, and perhaps have a retiring attitude towards society. Certainly one would not expect them to seek wealth or a celebrity status simply for its own sake. They may acquire status and fame as an accidental by-product of their teaching, but this is different from actively seeking an enhanced reputation.

It has to be accepted that different people will apply different criteria when judging a guru, and in the 1960s and early 1970s some members of the counter-culture appear to have placed a high premium upon a guru having a charismatic personality. An example of this would have been Bhagwan Shree Rajneesh (1931–1990), known in his later life as Osho, who was without doubt a highly charismatic teacher. He wrote many books on Hinduism and other Eastern religions (Osho, 1998, 2002). No one can doubt his popularity and influence both during his life and after his death. However, he also came under criticism for the wealth acquired by the Rajneesh organizations, and also for the ostentation of such possessions as the Rolls Royce cars which he acquired.

During the 1960s many young people attached themselves to Indian gurus who had come to the West. Others, however, travelled to India and became disciples of either established Western-oriented teachers or sadhus. The latter are itinerant holy men or women, who lead an ascetic life. They tend to belong to particular denominations or akharas, such as the Juna akhara. Sadhus will normally tend to lead solitary, meditative lives, or perhaps live in small groups. However, at the celebrated Kumbh Mela, held every three years, they gather in very large numbers, converging from all over India for a period of festivities and devotion. Despite the undoubted hardships of the lifestyle, there are documented examples in the 1960s of Westerners joining sadhus to practise their spiritual life (Yorke, 2011).

To those who met and talked to sadhus in the 1960s the impact must have been considerable. Sadhus are very striking in their appearance, often covered in white ash from their holy fires, and with long, matted hair. Much of the purpose of their appearance is to demonstrate a renunciation of the body, and many aspects of the training of a sadhu reflects a determination to abandon all care for the body. Sadhus try to remind themselves continually that one day they will have to shed this physical body, and that the latter will return to the earth and to the air. Philosophically speaking, one of the reasons for smearing ash on themselves is that the ash is a symbol of the earth to which the sadhu must eventually return. Comparisons could be made here with the practices of Ash Wednesday in the Christian tradition. Sadhus consider that their bodies are not their possessions, but that they belong to God. Thus they tend not to be too pre-occupied with the state of their bodies, but live in the present, trying not to have any great concerns for the future.

For a part of the year at least, many sadhus travel northwards to the foothills of the Himalayas and live a reclusive life in caves, meditating and practising yoga. They then return to the north Indian plain, usually at holy places alongside the river Ganges for the remainder of the year. While in the Himalayas life can be very hard, as they often go barefoot, and have very few clothes for protection against the cold. As part of their renunciation of the material world, sadhus will often live close to the cremation grounds along the Ganges. When people bring dead relatives to be cremated, it is a reminder to the sadhus that life is impermanent. One group of sadhus, the Aghoris, take this reflection on impermanence to extremes. They will often carry a human skull around with them and use it as an object of meditation. In addition, they engage in extreme practices, such as eating a small amount of flesh taken from the body of someone being cremated. The purpose of this is not sensationalism for its own sake, but rather to remind the Aghori that just as they consume part of the dead person, they in turn will be consumed by the fire and the earth. In addition, by taking part in such practices, Aghoris are able to eliminate the fear of death within themselves. Admittedly, ordinary people tend to avoid Aghoris because they are shocked by their practices, but at the same time hold them in respect as holy men and women who are going beyond normal boundaries to try to reach the divine.

Sadhus will not normally have a permanent home, but will construct for themselves something akin to an open-sided tent within which they will have a holy fire or dhuna. They live a very basic lifestyle, relying on charity for food. They live outside the limits of conventional society, but there is a reason for this. Their entire purpose in life is to help other people, and they feel that the only way they can do this effectively is by living outside society.

They listen to people's problems and provide them with advice; they are often knowledgeable in natural medicine, providing remedies and treatment for those who are sick and they will provide tuition in yoga, meditation and in the scriptures. Sadhus will normally have received instruction from a guru when they were young, and in their turn will take on disciples. A boy will become a disciple at perhaps the age of nine or ten and will undertake a form of spiritual apprenticeship before being formally initiated in his teenage years. The teaching of the sadhus has a strong element of ethics. Sadhus are aware that if they are to be accepted as moral teachers in the community, then they have to demonstrate that they themselves lead an ethical life.

When Westerners came to India in the 1960s and 1970s, they would generally have joined an established ashram, where the conditions of living would have been closer to those in the West. It would have required great determination to take on the life of a sadhu and receive the traditional teaching, but nevertheless some young Westerners did this, and in so doing, participated in an extremely ancient spiritual tradition (Allsop, 2000; Rampuri, 2010).

Not only were spiritual insights from Eastern religions carried to the West, but cultural artefacts from India also soon became embedded in the hippie counter-culture. The use of strings of beads as an aid in meditation or in repeating holy syllables is common in many religions, but particularly so in Buddhist and Hindu cultures. In India a string of meditation beads is known as a mala. There are normally either 108 beads on a mala or a sub-division of that number, if the mala needs to be shorter. There is one additional bead on a mala, which is tied in a prominent way, so that the user will know when one 'round' of meditation has been completed. The meditator sits in the lotus posture turning the beads one at a time with the thumb, repeating the favoured mantra once for each bead. When the 109th bead is reached, the direction of counting is reversed, and the process repeated. Such repetition of holy syllables or mantra is a very common spiritual technique in India, designed to calm the mind and senses, and is known as japa.

Mala beads can be made from a variety of materials such as stones or wood, although the archetypal mala in India is made from the seeds of the rudraksha tree. The word rudra represents the Hindu God Shiva. The fruit of the tree has a hard seed core, which is the part used as a bead. The seeds are brown with a rough, convoluted surface and are traditionally linked together with a red string.

As there was an increase in the number of different artefacts from India carried back to the West, this opened the way for commercial opportunities. Incense, bells, shoulder bags, kaftans, sarongs and Afghan-style sheep or goatskin coats became part of a counter-cultural hippie style. Entrepreneurs imported these cultural artefacts and found a ready market among the youth sub-culture. Some of these artefacts such as malas were religious in origin, while others were part of a general Indian and Eastern culture. However, the large-scale commodification and marketing of India's religious heritage became a significant element of the 1960s cultural life.

However, it is worth adding that the commercialization of religion is not something which was introduced to India by the West. Hindu organizations in India raise money in many of the same ways as, for example, Christian Churches in Europe. It may appear that sadhus have no means of financial support, but in fact the akharas to which they belong often have considerable financial resources. They typically own land and property, some of which may have been gifted in previous generations by lay people. In addition, people will often give small donations to individual sadhus as a religious devotion. Funeral ceremonies including the actual cremation can be expensive for poorer Indian families. Fees have to be paid to the officiating priest, and the wood for the cremation can be very expensive in an area where there are no large, natural forests.

During the 1960s it was not only Indian gurus who came to the West to establish ashrams and to teach. Occasionally Westerners travelled to India in search of spiritual fulfilment, were initiated by a Hindu guru and then returned to the West to establish their own religious organizations. A well-known example of this is Richard Alpert, born in 1931 into a Jewish family in Massachusetts, he grew up to have a very successful academic career. After obtaining a doctorate in Psychology from Stanford University, he was appointed as a lecturer at Harvard University. He carried out a variety of research at Harvard, but he was particularly noteworthy for his work with Dr Timothy Leary on LSD, Psilocybin and other hallucinogens. The research project began in 1961, but two years later Alpert and Leary were both asked to leave Harvard because of the rather contentious nature of their research. Alpert continued his work with hallucinogens until 1967, when he decided to visit India. There he met the teacher Neem Karoli Baba, otherwise known as Maharaj Ji, who introduced him to a range of Hindu spiritual practice. Maharaj Ji gave Alpert the name Ram Dass, which means 'servant of God'. In 1969 he returned to the United States and became a spiritual teacher himself. He particularly emphasized the role of service to others as an important element in religious practice. Ram Dass also wrote a number of well-known books on spirituality (Dass, 1997, 2000, 2004).

One of the clearest links between Hindu spirituality and the counter-culture to take place during the 1960s occurred at the Woodstock Festival in August 1969. Woodstock became an iconic event representing music and young people of the period, and was opened by an Indian teacher, Swami Satchidananda. The festival took place near the town of Bethel, New York

State, and started on the evening of 15th August. Richie Havens performed the first set, and after that Swami Satchidananda gave a speech and a blessing before the thousands of young people who had already arrived. He sat on a white dias and spoke first about the power and influence of music and sound in the world. He continued to note the enthusiasm for spirituality which he found in the United States, and the strong desire for peace. He argued that people should attempt to find internal peace, and that with the help of music, we could achieve world peace. He went on to urge all people present to work together positively for the benefit of the festival. The Swami then asked the audience to chant the mantra words 'Hari Om' and 'Ram', and then afterwards to have one minute of silence to appreciate the impact of the mantra.

It was a simple and encouraging speech, significant perhaps for stressing the importance of a peaceful state of mind within the individual, and the connection of that with a peaceful state on an inter-personal, macro level. This is a theme which in various forms appears to have recurred with a number of Hindu teachers. Hinduism stresses the importance of achieving a calm state of mind through the use of meditation and yoga, and that it is possible for this individual condition to then influence the world at large. Although this proposition may seem improbable to some, it is worth remembering the role of individuals in initiating world conflicts. In this context, it is perhaps not so unlikely that individual peace could influence world peace. In any case, this idea found a ready audience among young people of the period, no doubt because of the large effect which the Vietnam War was having on their lives.

Swami Satchidananda was born in 1914 in the state of Tamil Nadu in southern India. He married in his early 20s and had two children. He was initiated as a monk in 1949 and given his spiritual name of Satchidananda. Although a traditional Hindu monk, he also showed a sense of affiliation with Western lifestyle, as when, for example, he learned to drive. In 1966 he migrated to the United States and later established an ashram called Yogaville in the state of Virginia. Satchidananda was a strong advocate of the doctrine that in all of the main world religions lay an essential truth. They clearly adopted different religious pathways, but ultimately he felt that they lead to the same spiritual essence. At Yogaville he built a shrine which reflected his respect for different faiths. Young people in particular found a sense of empathy with this philosophy of religious relativism. They were not generally receptive to being told that there were certain truisms which they had to accept. Rather they preferred a philosophy which gave them the flexibility to adapt different religious approaches to their own needs. This relativism was also reflected in Satchidananda's philosophy of 'Integral Yoga' which brought together different yogic approaches to help the individual to further their spiritual growth.

The counter-culture of the 1960s was holistic in the sense that its members and advocates wanted to link together a number of different philosophies into a cohesive whole. These philosophies included a multi-faith approach to society, a respect for the environment, a strong desire for world peace and a more participative, less authoritarian society. In terms of spirituality, young people sought a faith system which was sympathetic to these general goals.

Further reading

Gilmour, M. J. (2009) *Gods and Guitars: Seeking the Sacred in Post-1960s Popular Music*. Waco, TX: Baylor University Press.

Green, M. (2011) *Prophets of a New Age: Counter-Culture and the Politics of Hope*. Edinburg, VA: Axios Press.

Oppenheimer, M. (2003) *Knocking on Heaven's Door: American Religion in the Age of Counter-Culture*. New Haven, CT: Yale University Press.

Pirsig, R. M. (1999) *Zen and the Art of Motorcycle Maintenance*. London: Vintage.

Watts, A. (1999) *The Culture of Counter-Culture*. North Clarendon, VT: Tuttle Publishing.

PART TWO

Hinduism and the counter-culture

4

The philosophy of Hinduism and its attractions for the counter-culture

Summary

This chapter suggests ways in which the philosophical and sociological underpinnings of Hinduism have made them appealing to young people within the counter-culture. These include a broad moral relativism, an absence of rigid structural organization within the religion, no single authority at the head of the religion, the freedom to select one's own teacher and interpreter of the faith and a general absence of theocratic injunctions to control the behaviour of adherents. There is an analysis of the teachings of Hinduism contained within the Bhagavad Gita and the Upanishads, and these texts are related to the work of a variety of well-known Hindu gurus.

Introduction

The young people of the counter-culture were largely brought up and educated within a Christian environment which tended to stress adherence to a range of externally imposed moral constraints. For a variety of reasons such constraints and their accompanying absolutist belief systems were not particularly appealing to young people. Expanding educational opportunities in the post-war period encouraged young people to think critically about twentieth-century history and to analyse how prevalent belief systems, whether religious, political or philosophical, could have influenced world events. Their parents' and grandparents' generations had fought and lost their lives in enormous numbers in two world wars, yet around them the young people of the 1950s and 1960s could see a society driven by social class differences which sustained a range of inequalities. The two world wars appeared not to have changed the considerable economic differentiation in society, and young people saw little justification in seeking to retain the key elements of such a society. Nevertheless they still wanted values to live by, and many sought these in political movements or in what they saw as a more personalized approach to religion. When young people developed a style of living and set of values, different to mainstream society, they often became known as 'drop-outs', a term which became increasingly common from the mid-1960s onwards. On the one hand, it could be used pejoratively within mainstream society to refer to young people who appeared not to be contributing very much to society. On the other hand, it could be used in a more positive way to refer to young people who had made a considered decision to live in a different way to those who were part of conventional society. In this sense, to be a drop-out was synonymous with living an alternative lifestyle. It might involve, for example, living in a non-conventional dwelling such as a tee-pee, yurt or dome (Coperthwaite, 2007; Kemery, 2006; Olsen, 2012). It could involve earning a living not by being employed or salaried, but by producing and selling handicrafts or other artefacts, by growing and selling organic vegetables or by printing and publishing alternative literature.

The 1950s and 1960s was also a time when Europe was undergoing a dramatic industrial reconstruction after the war, and many immigrants from the Indian sub-continent made their way to Europe in search of work (Oonk, 2007; Poros, 2010). Such people brought with them their own religious beliefs, and hence an understanding of Hinduism in the West did not depend upon the return of young Western backpackers, but came with economic migrants from India.

The Hindu religion

The religion of Hinduism is very ancient, having no specific founder or date from which it can be considered to have started (Bhaskarananda, 2002). The tradition was originally an oral one, with the earliest Vedas or religious scriptures being written in approximately 1800 BCE. Towards the end of the Vedas are analytical, philosophical documents called the Upanishads, which reflect upon the content of the Vedas (Easwaran, 2007; Saraswati, 2006). In particular the Upanishads expand upon the nature of the absolute in Hinduism. The closest concept to 'God' in Hinduism is the idea of Brahman in the Upanishads. Brahman is perceived as the source of the universe in the sense that Brahman furnishes the material of which the universe is made, and also the mechanism by which creation functions. Brahman does not depend on any other cause or substance in the universe. Brahman is infinite, eternal and omnipresent. Brahman exists in all living things and hence can be regarded as 'imminent'. Yet Brahman also extends throughout the universe, and hence can be considered 'transcendent'. Brahman is thus the spiritual substance and creative energy behind the universe.

For Hindus there is no purpose in trying to attribute certain qualities to Brahman, nor in trying to allocate human qualities. Brahman is held to be beyond any concept of qualities or characteristics. In all human beings there is considered to be a tiny presence of Brahman, and this is known as the atman. The latter can be thought of as the original true 'self' of the individual human being, or perhaps as the soul. The theory that the atman is an intrinsic part of Brahman is encapsulated in the perspective known as Advaita Vedanta. Its most famous proponent was Shankara, an eighth-century CE philosopher and teacher from southern India (Prabhavananda and Isherwood, 1975). Vedanta proposes that the eternal cycle of birth and death (samsara) is the fate of each individual. However, liberation (moksha) from this may be achieved by understanding and accepting the essential unity of the atman and of Brahman. This level of understanding is normally only achieved through the help and advice of a teacher or guru.

The Upanishads

The word upanishad in the original Sanskrit means approximately 'sitting down next to someone', and carries the implication of being seated next to a guru in order to listen to the teachings. The Upanishads set out to explore the nature of spirituality and of humanity's relationship to the religious life. There is, however, a major difference between the Judaeo-Christian approach to religion and that of the Upanishads. In Christianity God is regarded as the most important element in the universe, the creator of all things and the ultimate interpreter of the cosmos. If a human being wishes to understand the world, then it is to God that s(he) looks. The philosophers of the Upanishads, however, had a very different view. They regarded the individual human being as the central feature of the universe, while at the same time accepting that there was a divine element of Brahman within each person. Individuals created their own world and interpreted reality for themselves. This perspective is reflected in modern sociological thought, and particularly within interpretivism, which considers that each human being interprets the world in their own way. In other words there is no such thing as absolute reality, but rather that it is the function of each human being to create and interpret their own understanding of the social world. The Upanishads thus subscribed to a relativistic world view.

The notion that each human being could make sense of the world in their own way had considerable appeal for the young people of the counter-culture. They were encouraged to use techniques such as meditation and yoga to create a feeling of harmony with the world, but after that they could form their own moral perspective and act in ways which they perceived would benefit humanity. According to the Upanishads, the world was not an ethical void. Brahman existed as the spiritual force which created and governed the universe and which was present in each individual. Nevertheless persons had an obligation to create the world as they saw fit, rather than to subscribe to a set of pre-ordained rules. As there was increased contact between Indian culture and the West during the 1960s, this philosophical perspective would have gradually become more evident, and absorbed into the general world view of the counter-culture.

The school of thought propounded by Advaita Vedanta that the atman is part of Brahman is known as non-dualism (Muller-Ortega, 1989). In other words Brahman is ultimately the only unifying force in the universe. All other phenomena, such as everything which we can observe with our senses, is unreal or illusionary. One might argue that this follows logically from the notion that individuals can interpret and re-interpret the world as they see fit. Hence there are multiple worlds which reflect the particular interpretation of each individual.

The theory that Brahman was present in all living things linked with the doctrine of all life being interconnected. This idea helped to give philosophical support to the counter-cultural interest in the environment, ecology and vegetarianism. If all living things are part of each other through the presence of Brahman–atman, then we would want to do everything possible to preserve the environment. Neither would we wish to kill other animals for food.

This approach, rooted in Upanishadic philosophy, is an example of a holistic approach. Everything and everyone in the universe is linked together by Brahman. The counter-culture put much more of an emphasis upon the ways in which people were linked together rather than in their separateness. Divisions between people and groups of people led to conflict, whereas a holistic approach based on similarities and common approaches led to peace.

The idea that each person can develop an individual perspective on the world leads to the notion that we all need to consider ways in which we can fulfil our potential and 'self-actualize', to use Maslow's term (Maslow, 1976, 1999). Within such a perspective the important issue becomes the personal growth of individuals rather than institutional growth, organizational growth or corporate growth.

Shankara, the principal philosopher of non-dualism, was born in the village of Kalady, near present-day Cochin, in the state of Kerala. Shankara stressed that advaita was not a philosophical theory to be understood intellectually, but rather an approach to be appreciated through day-to-day living. In everyday life according to Shankara, we can see evidence of advaita all around us, if only we are conscious of the evidence. So, for example, we might be sitting next to our pet dog, when we realize that we are breathing in exactly the same molecules, which the dog breathed in a few moments ago. Equally the way in which we conceptualize our dog, as for example, 'a friend' or 'a guardian of the home', depends upon our particular view of the world. Our world view affects how we conceptualize our surroundings. In other words, as advaitins such as Shankara argue, there is no division between the subject and the object in the world. They both are related to and interconnected with each other.

In the case of human relationships, person A interacts with person B and forms a judgement about his or her attitudes and world view. Person B also carries out the same kind of evaluation of person A. Within the perspective of advaita there is therefore no distinct subject or object, as each individual is simultaneously both subject and object.

Generally speaking, the Upanishads were not in favour of the ritualistic formalities of religion and sought to concentrate upon the personal development of the individual. This approach found favour in the counter-culture, where most young people sought to abandon convention in favour of a personal spiritual search.

The Bhagavad Gita

On 16 July 1945 a scientist looked out across the New Mexico desert and saw in the distance an enormous explosion which was to change the future of the world. The scientist was J. Robert Oppenheimer, a leading physicist in the Manhattan Project whose aim was to construct the first nuclear weapon (Pais, 2006). The explosion was part of the so-called Trinity test of the first atomic bomb.

Oppenheimer was a brilliant polymath who in his earlier years had learned Sanskrit. When he saw the first flash of light of the Trinity explosion, he said that he thought of an extract from the Hindu scripture, the Bhagavad Gita which is variously translated as 'I am become death, the destroyer of worlds' (see Hijiya, 2000, p. 123). Robert Oppenheimer died on 18 February 1967, but his recollection of the Bhagavad Gita has become a celebrated event. On the one hand, it would appear that he was probably very proud of his achievement of helping to make a nuclear weapon which would shorten the Second World War. On the other hand, he was no doubt conscious that he and his colleagues had produced a nuclear technology which in theory could destroy humanity.

Along with the Upanishads, the Bhagavad Gita is one of the central scriptures of Vedanta. Although known in the West for some considerable time, it became very popular in the late 1960s through the 1968 translation and commentary by A. C. Bhaktivedanta Swami Prabhupada (see Prabhupada, 1989), the founder of the International Society for Krishna Consciousness (ISKCON).

The Bhagavad Gita is part of the long Hindu epic, the Mahabharata (Narayan, 2000). The essence of the story is that Prince Arjuna finds himself in an army awaiting battle with another army assembled not far away. However, this is an internecine war, with relatives from the same family divided between the two armies. Arjuna is horrified at the prospect of fighting against his own family members, and turns to his charioteer Krishna, a manifestation of the divine, for help and advice in his moral predicament. Arjuna asks Krishna to move the chariot half-way between the two armies so that he can see the relatives and friends who are in each army. Arjuna is overcome with grief. He cannot justify in his mind the killing of relatives simply to gain material assets and wealth. He feels that this is completely unethical. Arjuna feels utterly demoralized and unable to resolve his dilemma. As a prince and warrior he feels the obligation to fight, and yet he cannot accept the advantages of winning the battle if this means killing some of his relatives. Krishna tells Arjuna that he must not sink into despondency, but must act with courage.

At this point it is worth noting that the author or authors of the Gita may have intended that the anticipated battle not be viewed as an actual battle, but as a metaphor for the kinds of ethical dilemma which frequently confront human beings. The Gita thus becomes advice not concerning one particular situation but a discussion on how human beings should address the phenomenon of existence. Arjuna asks Krishna to analyse his dilemma and to advise him on a course of action. Krishna starts by discussing the unreal nature of life and death, of pleasure and pain and indeed of the entire material world. All such phenomena are transitory. The only indestructible element in mankind is the soul, the atman. Therefore, the role of men and women should be to focus on the atman, and not to be distracted by ephemeral things.

Krishna goes on to say that Arjuna should not run from the battle, but should have the courage to fight. To do otherwise would be to act dishonourably. However, this should perhaps not be taken literally. For a man or woman confronted by a major ethical dilemma, Krishna's advice may be taken to imply that we should always act ethically as we see it. We should face up to the problem which confronts us, and take the best moral decision which we can.

Then for the first time in the Gita, Krishna advises Arjuna to face the 'battle' with a peaceful mind. He should not concern himself with victory or defeat. In other words, the outcome of the battle is unimportant when compared with the moral decision which precedes it. For Krishna, true yoga entails acting in an ethical way and doing our duty as we see it. The outcome of this is much less important than the moral decision-making. Importantly, if we act in this way we shall have a peaceful mind. The Gita is composed of 18 relatively short chapters, and in the last section of chapter 2, Krishna expounds on one of the main themes of the poem. He argues that people can still involve themselves in everyday life but should try to avoid being attracted by physical or material pleasures on the one hand, and on the other hand should not be discouraged if they suffer disappointment or things do not go very well. If they can achieve this, then they will reach a state of total peace. It is interesting that Radhakrishnan (1993, p. 11) in the introductory essay to his translation of the Gita points out that it is a book designed to be of help to ordinary people in their daily lives, rather than a complex work of philosophy. Throughout the Gita the advice of Krishna tends to be very practical.

At the beginning of chapter 3 Krishna opens up the question of whether it is reasonable for a person caught in a dilemma or moral problem, to evade the question by not involving himself or herself in the world. Krishna argues, however, that people should act in relation to moral problems, but should dedicate their action to Brahman. In addition they should not think about the outcomes of their action. They should not dwell on supposed advantages of their actions, for then they will become bound by what they wish to happen. People will become entrapped by their desires. When this happens, their mental desires will overcome them and destroy their peace of mind. Ultimately one should act as one sees fit, or in a way one judges to be ethical, but should then disengage from the potential outcomes of that action.

In chapter 5, Krishna advises Arjuna to dedicate all his work to Brahman. The wise person, argues Krishna, is not unduly influenced by pleasure and happiness, for s(he) realizes that such things are fleeting. Equally one should not attach significance to unhappiness or sadness, because these emotions are not permanent. They arise and then they are dissipated. The wise person realizes this and devotes all the products of his or her work to Brahman.

Chapter 6 of the Gita starts with an explanation by Krishna of the characteristics of a truly holy person. The true yogi, according to Krishna, is one who attaches absolutely no importance to the material life, to the outcomes of his work or to his achievements. When a person does this then s(he) achieves peace in the soul. When people attain such peace then they are no longer concerned about personal wealth or possessions. They are able to stay calm under any circumstances and in any type of company or situation. Krishna advises Arjuna that the aspiring yogi should sit and meditate each day to practise making his soul peaceful. Yogis should not aspire to any gains or benefits in life. They should not permit themselves to aspire to any material possessions.

It is difficult to point to a direct connection between social trends in the counter-culture and the philosophy of the Bhagavad Gita. Nevertheless, the Gita was widely distributed during the late 1960s and hence the philosophy of non-materialism would have been fairly well-known. Certainly the counter-culture had no aspirations for material wealth, and this emerged in a variety of ways including simple, rural living, the re-cycling of clothes and other artefacts and the lack of desire among many young people to take up traditional, salaried occupations.

In the final chapter of the Gita, Krishna summarizes many of the themes of the whole poem. He reminds Arjuna against the temptation to seek worldly pleasures and money. He notes also that the rituals of religion are not necessarily helpful in the search for Brahman. Krishna points out to Arjuna that the great moral dilemmas and conflicts of life are in fact inescapable. We may not like the difficulties and conflicts with which life confronts us, but ultimately we cannot avoid them, and must address them in one way or another.

For those who read the Bhagavad Gita in the 1960s, it provided an alternative to the stance of the Judaeo-Christian religions. Where people are faced with a moral dilemma, the Gita does not recommend specific or clearly defined responses. Rather it encourages people to try to analyse the ethical choices clearly and then to take a decision. However, it should be a decision not based on potentially selfish outcomes, but on a sense of duty founded on what appears to be the most morally just line of action.

Hindu philosophy and practice

Before the existence of its written scriptures, Hinduism was an oral tradition. The first written scriptures, the Vedas, were gradually commented upon, and further texts produced. There was hence a gradual elaboration of the original tradition. It is worth noting therefore some of the features of Hinduism which made it attractive to the 1960s counter-culture. The concept of Brahman in Hinduism might be better described as a spiritual and moral force guiding the universe rather than a God. Brahman is not really a theistic concept, and does not issue theocratic injunctions in the same way as a transcendent God in some religions. There is therefore less of a concept that Brahman is a force to be 'obeyed'. This provides a much more liberal framework, and appealed to the counter-culture in terms of providing more freedom. As Hinduism has evolved it has had no specific founder but rather a series of religious teachers and philosophers who have added incrementally to the general corpus of spiritual knowledge. Without either a founder or a transcendent God there has been no clearly specified credo by which Hindus are enjoined to live. There are no key beliefs to which all Hindus are expected to adhere, and no absolute moral principles by which Hindus are expected to live. This provided the counter-culture with a spiritual system which was very liberal, and gave its adherents considerable freedom to search for their own spiritual pathway through life. In fact if there is a unifying characteristic of Hinduism, it is its diversity. There are many different groupings and sects, each with their own rituals and practices. This diversity also enabled members of the counter-culture to reflect their own idiosyncratic tastes and interests. Hinduism thus placed no great demands on the young people who were interested in it. In fact, Hindus themselves tend not to employ the term 'Hinduism' but refer to themselves as followers of the Sanatana Dharma – or eternal way of life. From this perspective it is rather problematic whether one can legitimately speak of 'converting' to Hinduism. Many people, not only in the 1960s, have spoken of so doing, but some may argue that one can only follow the eternal way of life by being born into the tradition.

As Hinduism is so diverse, it tends to be very tolerant and accepting of different religious practices. It is thus very difficult to imagine someone being defined as a heretic within Hinduism. As there is no single code of authority, it is difficult to imagine an act of transgression against the religion.

The extent to which Hindus conceptualize Brahman as a deity or as an impersonal spiritual force depends largely upon the particular branch of Hinduism to which one belongs. Certainly the diversity of Gods and Goddesses in Hinduism are referred to as part of the Sanatana Dharma, and frequently regarded as avatars; that is descended or derived from Brahman.

One aspect of Hinduism which appears to have been very attractive to young people in the 1960s was its iconography and symbolism. The 1960s was a period when young people were seeking to escape from the relative formality of dress and design of previous generations. The Second World War had been a period of great austerity, with few resources available for the aesthetics of life. During the 1950s, for example, there was a general lack of fashionable clothes for the mass market. During the 1960s, however, partly because of an improving economy, and related factors such as travel opportunities, young people started to experiment with clothes and other aesthetic elements in their lives. Contacts with the East and its great variety of cultures probably contributed towards this experimentation. Hindu culture is particularly noteworthy for its colourful iconography and imagery. Temples are very colourful, and many Hindu festivals such as Holi have colour at the heart of their festivities. Both in temples and in their homes, Hindus will have representations or murtis of Hindu avatars such as Krishna. Quite apart from religious contexts, clothes and other forms of decoration are above all else colourful in India. This provided a great stimulus to Western culture, and whether it was in paperback book covers or on record sleeves in the 1960s, there was an emphasis upon colour and decoration. Equally Hindu religious ceremonies were sometimes accompanied by bright music and extensive floral decoration. All in all this was in considerable contrast to the perhaps more sober Judaeo-Christian traditions. Throughout the 1960s the aesthetics of India were a strong influence upon young people in the West, and this was reflected in the number of shops selling imported clothes and religious artefacts such as statues, incense and beads. Such artefacts became an intrinsic part of the 1960s alternative culture.

One further element of Hindu religious life was that it tended to be more integrated with everyday life than was the case with religious life in the West. For example, most Hindus have a small shrine of some type in their home, where they perform devotional rituals, or say prayers and meditate. Such a shrine may only be very small, but it will be part of a daily act of religious commitment. There will probably be a small statue of a deity, which becomes the focus of puja, or devotional offerings and worship. The statue may typically be covered at night, but will be brought to its normal location in the morning, and washed and adorned with flowers. Incense may be burned and small offerings of food placed before the murti. Part of the inherent philosophy here is that the deity itself is believed to actually reside in the statue, which explains the care taken in looking after it. Hindus may not feel the need to attend the temple on a regular basis if they are practising puja before their household shrine.

The awareness of such practices enabled young people in search of the spiritual, to realize that this search could take place during their daily lives. The spiritual and secular lives of people could be much more integrated. In fact one might argue that a point of contrast between West and East is that in the West religion tends to be rather more circumscribed in terms of general life, whereas in the East religion and daily life are much more integrated, indeed often scarcely separable. This may have encouraged some young people to try to find a religious tradition which they could use as the basis for their everyday existence.

The counter-culture was concerned to develop a way of life which was more sensitive to the environment. It wanted a life style which avoided damaging our surroundings. The concept of ahimsa or non-violence is rooted in the Hindu scriptures such as the Upanishads, and influences Hindus to avoid killing living things, and to have a vegetarian diet. Hindus will certainly do their utmost to avoid killing cows, which they regard as holy, and which provide rural Hindus in particular with many basic necessities for their daily lives. Ahimsa is a general concept, advocating also the avoidance of conflict between human beings, and the adoption of a life of peaceful coexistence. The concept of ahimsa thus provided a theoretical basis for the lifestyle choices which were being in the decade of the 1960s.

Besides the ideals of non-violence and peace which were very much in evidence in the 1960s, young people were also very concerned with finding a personal identity for themselves, and the mysticism inherent in the Hindu religion provided a focus for this type of aspiration. In finding that identity young people often tried to cultivate a sense of being 'different' from their peers, and certainly from their parents' generation. They were therefore often attracted to some of the more esoteric aspects of Hinduism. The esoteric elements of a religion (in contrast with the more exoteric features) are those which tend to be available only for the specially initiated. They may require special tuition and may not be mentioned in the more orthodox scriptures. Within Hinduism such elements may include tantric yoga and various related meditational techniques. Such practices might also be described as part of a mystical tradition. The overall aim of such a tradition would be, among other things, to gain a more intimate experience of the divine, and to have a more direct spiritual experience than would be the case with more conventional religious practice. To this end many attached themselves to gurus in the hope of attaining moksha, or releasing from the cycle of birth and death.

The 1960s was a period when many people sought to change society, and through the inspiration of such people as Mahatma Gandhi, young people began to appreciate that religious and moral principles could form a very effective basis for social and political action. Gandhi was an example of an extremely spiritual person, who also lived the life of a lawyer, a social and political activist and worker for community regeneration. Despite a very busy and often stressful life, he maintained a profound commitment to his faith, and regularly consulted the Bhagavad Gita for guidance in how he ought to conduct his life. He demonstrated that it was possible to be involved in the most complex and difficult of political action, while remaining firmly attached to spiritual and moral principles. Many people in the 1960s who participated in various forms of protest and direct social action were able to draw upon the same Hindu principles as Gandhi some 15 years earlier.

Further reading

Adorno, T. W. and Horkheimer, M. (1997) *Dialectic of Enlightenment*. New York: Verso Books.
Davis, R. (2006) *Visionary State*. San Francisco, CA: Chronicle Books.

Devananda, V. S. (1999) *Meditation and Mantras*. New Delhi: Motilal
  Banarsidass.
Iyengar, B. K. S. (2007) *Yoga: The Path to Holistic Health*. London: Dorling
  Kindersley.
MacHovec, F. J. (2005) *Light from the East: A Gathering of Asian Wisdom*.
  Berkeley, CA: Stone Bridge Press.
Williamson, L. (2010) *Transcendent in America: Hindu-Inspired Meditation
  Movements as New Religion*. New York: New York University Press.

5

Transcendental Meditation and the Beatles

Summary

This chapter examines the life and philosophy of the Maharishi Mahesh Yogi and in particular the teachings of Transcendental Meditation. It also discusses the Maharishi's writings on the Bhagavad Gita. This chapter explores the events from the first contacts between the Beatles and the Maharishi in 1967, to their leaving his ashram in Rishikesh the following year. Finally, this chapter seeks to explore the continued influence which Hindu teachings had for the Beatles.

The Maharishi

The Maharishi Mahesh Yogi, an Indian spiritual leader and founder of the Transcendental Meditation movement, was born in 1918 in the Indian state of Madhya Pradesh. His first names and family name were Mahesh Prasad Varma. His father seems likely to have worked as a public servant, and to have belonged to a relatively high, well-educated caste. He was born in the city of Jabalpur, which by coincidence was also the birthplace of another celebrated Indian teacher, Rajneesh, later known as Osho. When he was in his early 20s he was given initiation by a spiritual teacher Swami Brahmananda Saraswati, and became his disciple and assistant. He appears to have conducted a great deal of the Swami's correspondence. Mahesh accompanied Swami Saraswati until the latter's death in 1953. The Swami had encouraged Mahesh to devote his life to the teaching of meditation. To this end, Mahesh decided to move to the town of Uttarkashi, which is situated on the Ganges, high in the Himalayas. It is a particularly spiritual location, with a number of temples, and a long tradition of meditation and yoga. For two years Mahesh lived in Uttarkashi practising the meditation and yoga techniques taught to him by his guru, Swami Saraswati. The outcome of this period of study, practice and reflection was a form of meditation known as Transcendental Meditation (Russell, 1976). It was at about this time that his followers started to refer to him as Maharishi and Yogi. The name 'Maha'– 'rishi' means great rishi or great spiritual teacher, while a yogi is a renunciate or holy man devoted to yogic practice. By the late 1950s the Maharishi had decided that he would definitely devote his life to the transmission of Transcendental Meditation around the world. Transcendental Meditation is a form of meditation which employs mantras, or spiritual syllables which are repeated over and over again (Radha, 2005). The repetition of the mantra has the effect of calming the mind and limiting the flow of extraneous thoughts. When unwanted thoughts come into the mind, the practitioner returns his or her concentration to the mantra. The latter is given to the practitioner by the Maharishi himself or by an accredited Transcendental Meditation teacher. The mantra is repeated regularly during two separate sessions in the day – one in the morning and one in the evening. The mantra itself does not appear to have any particular meaning, but the sound of the mantra is reputed to have an effect upon the meditator. Some criticisms have been made of the process, since payment for meditation tuition in effect involves purchasing a mantra. Many gurus in India will be happy to suggest a mantra to someone without demanding any money. The Transcendental Meditation technique was used extensively for such people as prisoners and former members of the armed forces, on the assumption that it would help them to remain relatively calm, when normally they might feel rather stressed.

The teachings of the Maharishi

In terms of Hindu scriptures the Maharishi gave a particular pre-eminence in his philosophy and teachings to the Bhagavad Gita (Hawley, 2001). He considered that the Gita provided an essential distillation of the overall content of the literature of the Vedas. The Maharishi argued that the Gita contained all of the essential practical knowledge and understanding which enabled human beings to lead a tranquil and fulfilled life. He felt that the key philosophical principles of the Gita provided a basis for organizing society in a positive way. When Krishna and Arjuna debate together on the battlefield at the beginning of the Bhagavad Gita, the Maharishi points out that Arjuna is representing the suffering of humanity, while Krishna represents the highest level of consciousness which can be attained (Yogashram, 2012). On the one hand, in terms of Arjuna, while most people would never confront the exact situation in which they find themselves, nevertheless all human beings at one time or another have to face complex ethical problems. Krishna, on the other hand, represents the most sophisticated and complex judgement which it is possible to imagine. The Maharishi argues that the teachings of Krishna are not simply limited to the particular context of the Gita, but are universal in their applicability. It is this universalism within the Gita, which makes it so important and widely read among religious scriptures.

Moreover the Maharishi points out that in the early verses of the poem, there is in effect a summary of the difficulties experienced by human beings in their lives, and the way in which they may be resolved by means of the Gita. The Maharishi's teachings share something in common with Buddhism, since the eradication of human suffering is at the heart of the two philosophies. In both Buddhism and the Gita, there is the essential perspective that suffering does not exist in relation to specific events, but in the psychological reaction of human beings to those events. Two human beings could experience exactly the same event; one could suffer a great deal from it, while the other could react in a more positive way and experience very little suffering. The Gita, on the one hand, advises us not to be concerned with the potential outcome of events, but simply to carry out our duty in a calm and balanced way, dedicating our work to God. Buddhism, on the other hand, reminds us that all material existence is impermanent, and hence it is futile to work towards a particular end, since the ultimate nature of all material objects and living things is disintegration. The basis of the religious argument may be different, but the overall conclusion in terms of how human beings should relate to the world is broadly the same.

The Maharishi attached great importance to the role of dharma and argued that dharma was the force which enabled human spiritual evolution to take place (Sutton and Randerwala, 2013). By this he appears to have meant that through the process of spiritual development, human beings are able to reach their highest creative potential. He argued that in the universe there exists a dialectic of two contrasting forces, one tending towards destruction and the other towards creativity. Dharma enables these two forces to remain in a state of dynamic equilibrium. In sustaining that equilibrium the action of dharma ensures that all human beings experience karma, or the results of their own actions. On the one hand, if we act morally and for the genuine benefit of other people, then we will experience a sense of well-being. On the other hand, if we act in an unethical manner, then we will experience unhappy outcomes. According to the Maharishi the concept of dharma also applies to the individual person living and working within the parameters of the family, and carrying out the traditional occupation or way of life of that family. By following in this tradition the individual maximizes their opportunity for personal spiritual evolution. It is important for the individual to carry out the occupation and activities which have been inherited as part of the family. Complying with societal dharma in this way will improve the chances of attaining what he termed cosmic consciousness. This type of argument concerning dharma or social duty may be more relevant to a society such as India, where even to this day, there remains a tendency for family members to sustain a traditional occupation within the extended family unit. It is perhaps less relevant in the West, where there is a tendency for individuals to select their own occupations. Nevertheless, however, this view of dharma does point to the importance of a sense of social responsibility, and of the individual contributing to the collective.

The Maharishi also related dharma to the concept of caste, in that he felt people should adhere to the dharma of their caste group. However, he did not perceive of caste as an exclusively occupational grouping in society, but rather as a number of families each with a shared sense of dharma and of spiritual evolution within society.

The Maharishi points out that the war portrayed in the Bhagavad Gita has similar characteristics to other wars throughout history, in that it has arisen as a consequence of one group of people trying to dominate another group. He argues that through the effects of dharma, the desire to dominate and oppress other people ultimately leads to unhappiness. He goes on to assert that unhappiness in society does not necessarily have to result from major actions of ill will. He suggests that the accumulation of small negative actions by people can have consequences. If a number of people act negatively in apparently small and inconsequential ways, there will ultimately be a collective consequence in society. Equally if people try to behave morally, even if those actions are apparently minor, then they will integrate and create an overall ethical effect.

The Maharishi is also interested in the psychological background of Arjuna in the Gita. He suggests that Arjuna experiences so much anguish when confronted with the possibility of doing battle with his close relatives, because by nature he is extremely compassionate and caring towards other human beings. If Arjuna had no real sense of empathy and compassion for others, then he really would not have any feelings for people in the opposite camp. In fact, Arjuna is portrayed as someone, who according to the Maharishi, possesses a deep sense of commitment to other human beings and a deep sense of concern for the welfare of others. Arjuna is thus portrayed in the Gita as a paradigmatic example of someone who has profound concern for other human beings, and thus who is receptive to the moral and spiritual teachings of Krishna.

It is suggested by the Maharishi that the collective consciousness of a society is in effect the sum total of the consciousness of each individual member of that society. Each individual thus contributes to the consciousness of the whole. Even if only one person practises Transcendental Meditation conscientiously, this will have a positive effect on the collective. Moreover, if a group of individuals practise Transcendental Meditation together, then the overall positive effect is enhanced. On the contrary, if a group of individuals do not act ethically, then there may be a negative effect upon the collective consciousness which could ultimately lead to conflict and even war. To sum up therefore, there is a cumulative effect in terms of the lives of individuals and their behaviour, which can either have positive or negative consequences for the collective.

When people act according to the 'natural law', according to the ethically positive way in society, then they have a supportive effect on others. They help develop their own and other's spiritual consciousness, and help people progress towards the highest spiritual development of which they are capable.

Various empirical studies have been carried out to try to demonstrate the existence of higher states of consciousness through Transcendental Meditation practice, although without any unequivocal conclusions. The Maharishi tried to link Transcendental Meditation with modern science and psychology, fusing the two perspectives into a coherent system. There remained doubts, however, that the two paradigms were so distinct, that any kind of merging of the two would not be feasible. Other propositions from the Maharishi include the so-called Maharishi Effect. This argues that if a small proportion of a community population practise Transcendental Meditation, then there are advantageous macro effects which will be detected in that community. It has been suggested that Transcendental Meditation is not really a Hindu practice, but is a form of secular meditation without any spiritual content. Nevertheless there are a wide range of views about Transcendental Meditation in terms of its religious content. On the one hand, some would argue that it is a form of new religious movement which can lead to experiences of a spiritual nature. On the other hand, some point to the absence of scriptures, and of a clear belief system, as evidence that Transcendental Meditation is not a religion in the commonly accepted sense of the term.

The Maharishi was undoubtedly a talented entrepreneur. From nothing at all, he set up gradually an extremely complex and sophisticated organization, with very large financial assets. There is reasonable evidence, however, that accumulating wealth was never one of his primary aims, but rather that his financial success was almost an unanticipated accompaniment of the development of the organization based on Transcendental Meditation. The Maharishi always argued that the financial assets went to support and expand the Transcendental Meditation organization rather than to him personally.

There is also significant evidence that apart from some of the assets of the organization on a personal level the Maharishi led an extremely simple life. He appears to have consistently opposed the use of drugs and to have been a vegetarian. He also never suggested that he was anything other than an ordinary man, and certainly never tried to present himself as someone with metaphysical spiritual powers. Moreover he never tried to take any personal credit for his teachings, but continually paid tribute to the man who had been his own guru, Brahmananda Saraswati. By all accounts he never consumed alcohol or smoked, and adopted a very positive approach to all human beings.

Following his decision to teach Transcendental Meditation in as many parts of the world as possible, the Maharishi embarked on a series of journeys taking him to many different countries. However, he perhaps began to be aware that it would be too great an endeavour for him to teach Transcendental Meditation personally around the world, and realized that he would have to train others to carry out this role. Hence in 1961 he travelled to Rishikesh and commenced a training programme for future teachers of Transcendental Meditation. Rishikesh, in the Indian state of Uttarakhand, is located on the Ganges, and being associated with the God Vishnu, has a number of temples and ashrams. During the following years the Maharishi continued travelling and began to meet a number of celebrities.

The Beatles

Just as people were beginning to notice Indian culture for the sake of its spiritual content, Western rock musicians were becoming attracted to classical Indian music and instruments. In the mid-1960s George Harrison of the Beatles became interested in the sitar, and the playing of its then leading exponent, Ravi Shankar. At the beginning of 1966 Harrison married Pattie Boyd who had a developing interest in Hinduism. Later in 1966 Harrison and Boyd visited Bombay, and Harrison formally asked Ravi Shankar if he would teach him to play the sitar. George Harrison subsequently bought his own sitar in Delhi. He felt that there was much more to life than the considerable wealth which he was accumulating as a Beatle. In August 1966 the Beatles played what was to be their final concert and George Harrison turned his attention to a personal search for spirituality, and for Hindu culture in particular. One of the things which impressed George Harrison about Indian religion was that in India Hinduism is a continual way of life, rather than a set of precepts to which one turns from time to time. Hinduism, as far as Harrison was concerned, was a philosophy and religion which were fully integrated into people's lives.

In 1967 Pattie Boyd heard the Maharishi speak in London and wanted her husband and the other Beatles to meet him. In August of 1967 the Maharishi spoke at a London hotel, and the Beatles listened to the talk. Afterwards they had discussions with the Maharishi and agreed with the suggestion that they participate in a study session in Wales. However, on the second day of their stay with the Maharishi they received news that their manager, Brian Epstein, had died. This came as a considerable shock to the Beatles, and the Maharishi advised them on ways of coping with the bereavement. Over the next few months the relationship between the Maharishi and the Beatles became closer, and this provided invaluable publicity for the Maharishi when he was on lecture tours.

The Beatles decided to visit the Maharishi's ashram in Rishikesh and travelled to India in February 1968. There they met up with other celebrity figures including Mia Farrow, the film actress, and Donovan, the folk singer. The Beatles and other Westerners stayed in the Maharishi's ashram located on the opposite side of the river Ganges from the main town of Rishikesh. The ashram consisted of a range of private accommodation blocks, which were well-furnished and equipped. The buildings were set in ample, pleasant grounds with tree-lined paths overlooking the river Ganges. On the one hand, there was tight security around the ashram, and the Maharishi attempted to keep journalists away from the Beatles. On the other hand, he himself gave a number of interviews to the press.

Besides the meditation sessions, John Lennon and Paul McCartney devoted a great deal of time to writing songs. All of the Beatles looked around the markets and shops of Rishikesh, and became very interested in Indian clothes and fabrics. They often wore Indian-style dress, and in particular had clothes made using some of the extremely colourful fabrics which they found in the markets. When they finally returned to England these clothes and materials had a great effect upon the fashion world, and influenced what was rapidly becoming a hippy cultural style.

The Beatles had arrived in February and by the beginning of March were starting to leave separately. They each cited various reasons, but two issues seem to have been central, even though different members of the group may have reacted slightly differently. First of all there were persistent rumours that the Maharishi had made romantic advances to some women, notably Mia Farrow, and may have had sexual relations with other young women. Nothing was proven and these remained merely allegations. Nevertheless they had deleterious consequences for the Maharishi's reputation. Secondly the Maharishi accumulated considerable financial assets, and this was deemed inappropriate for a spiritual teacher. It appears that the Beatles gained from the meditation process, and other aspects of the Maharishi's teaching, but were sceptical about his apparent preoccupation with acquiring financial assets.

The relationship between the Beatles and the Maharishi brought about an enormous interest in the West in Indian clothing, meditation, yoga and the playing of the sitar. Although the Beatles had apparently left Rishikesh with varying degrees of negative feelings towards the Maharishi, in later life they tended to feel more benign towards him, and to say publicly what a positive effect he had had on their lives.

In 1990, the Maharishi decided to move his home to the Netherlands, where he had previously founded a university affiliated to his teachings. As he approached the age of 90 years, his health gradually declined, and in February 2008 he died naturally.

The period which the Beatles spent at Rishikesh was extremely productive in terms of song writing. They had initially gone to India, partly to learn more about meditation, Indian culture and the Maharishi's philosophy, but it was also an opportunity for a period of rest and reflection after the stress of concert tours. At Rishikesh Lennon and McCartney wrote or sketched out ideas for several dozen songs. These songs then became the core of the Beatles' next album which was recorded mainly at the Abbey Road Studios in the summer and early autumn of 1968 (Southall, Vince and Rouse, 2002). The album is often termed 'The White Album' because it had no design on its all white cover.

The Beatles, and particularly George Harrison, had been aware of Indian music and Indian instruments such as the sitar and tambura, before their visit to Rishikesh in 1968. Their 1966 album, Revolver, has as its final track, the Lennon and McCartney song 'Tomorrow Never Knows'. The lyrics were largely created by John Lennon, who was inspired by the book 'The Psychedelic Experience' (Leary, Metzner and Alpert, 1964). The song has rhythms similar to those found in Indian music, and the recording includes George Harrison playing on a tambura, a type of Indian lute.

Probably one of the first occasions on which the Beatles became acquainted with the sitar was in 1965 while they were working on the film 'Help'. For one scene the director organized a contribution from a group of Indian musicians, and this opened the eyes of the Beatles to the potential of Indian instruments in a Western musical context. However, it was George in particular who appears to have developed a strong enthusiasm for Indian melodies, apparently encouraged by David Crosby who was a member of the group, The Byrds.

Later in the same year the Beatles recorded their sixth album, Rubber Soul, which included the track Norwegian Wood. Although John Lennon was the lead singer on this track, the sound of sitar playing by George Harrison can be heard almost from the beginning. This track may have been the first occasion on which Indian instruments had been used on a Western pop recording, and hence it had an enormous effect on the music industry and on young people who bought the music. It opened up the vast potential of exploring other musical traditions and using them in a mainstream pop context.

During the decade of the 1960s the Beatles had an enormous influence upon the lives of young people in all sorts of ways. Their influence extended not only to questions of hairstyles and fashion, although they were immensely influential there, but also in the world of ideas. At times the Beatles pioneered unconventional ideas which otherwise would probably not have easily reached the ears of people. The young listened to what the Beatles said. They may not have accepted all of their ideas, but at least what they said reached a very wide public. For example, John Lennon spoke a great deal on the question of world peace, and no doubt had a considerable influence on the growing peace movement, even if this influence is difficult to quantify precisely. George Harrison managed to encourage a wide interest in hatha yoga, meditation and vegetarianism. Such was the wide influence of George Harrison, that without his support, such ideas would have been very outlandish. However, once one of the Beatles expressed an interest in them, then this had an effect out of all proportion. George was an avid reader of the Bhagavad Gita, and incorporated some of the Gita's themes in the songs which he wrote.

Prior to the 1960s, people in the West had generally not heard of the term 'guru'. This changed dramatically during the period of the counter-culture. Many Hindu teachers and gurus came to the United Kingdom and the United States in order to extend their organizations overseas.

On the famous Sgt. Pepper's Lonely Hearts Club Band, album of 1967, there was just one George Harrison composition – 'Within you, without you'. The song evolved out of George Harrison's study of Hinduism, and was particularly significant in its critique of Western materialism. It is worth considering that the sitar music on some of the Beatles tracks was in a way a reminder of the then fashionable East, and of India in particular. It was an encouragement to young people to turn to Eastern ideas. Almost as a direct result of the Beatles, their music and their interest in meditation, there was in the 1960s an overwhelming interest in Indian philosophy and culture among the young. Members of the counter-culture returned with stories of Kathmandu, Delhi, Goa and Varanasi, and the many temples and ashrams where they had stayed. Places on the route to India such as Istanbul also became part of the stories of the East. There was an immense feeling of the romanticism of the East, including the language. In particular there were a number of Indian cultural terms such as asana, hatha yoga, dharma, karma, dhoti, mala and puja which became part of the everyday vocabulary of young people. Moreover, aspects of an Indian and Eastern way of life were absorbed into the general culture. It became common to see young people in kaftans and other types of Indian clothing. Indian designs found their way on to greeting cards, wrapping paper and posters. People burned incense in their homes and used Indian fabrics for bed spreads, wall hangings and settee covers. Indian carpets, or cheaper imitations of them, along with Indian jewellery, became seen regularly. As such items were in greater and greater demand, there was a proliferation of shops selling them. Some young people, on returning from a trip to the East, saw a market opportunity here, and imported artefacts for sale in the United Kingdom. There was a strong element of consumerism here, with some people seeing an opportunity to market the 'East' in a form of spiritual capitalism. However, among many young people there was doubtless also a desire to immerse themselves in a colourful and fascinating culture with a strong element of spirituality.

All of the Beatles were interested to some extent in Hinduism and Indian culture, but it was George Harrison who committed himself most deeply to the Hindu philosophy and way of life. He became a very close friend and colleague of Ravi Shankar, not merely through the learning of the sitar, but also in terms of being taught about Hinduism by Shankar (Gautier, 2008). In particular it was Ravi Shankar who first loaned him Paramhansa Yogananda's famous book 'Autobiography of a Yogi' (Yogananda, 1998). This book relates the personal spiritual journey of a Hindu teacher, and it became an inspiration to George Harrison. He aspired to having a genuinely close relationship with the divine. He appeared to want to have a mystical understanding of God, and did not feel that he could obtain this through Christianity. He viewed Hinduism as providing practical methods such as meditation and the use of mantra, so that he could have a direct understanding of God. In Hinduism George Harrison saw a religion which linked everyone together in a cohesive whole. It seemed to him that Hinduism was fundamentally inclusive rather than exclusive. Many of the world's religions, on the one hand, seemed to assert a form of infallibility which almost inevitably lead them in to conflict with other faiths. Hinduism, on the other hand, appeared not to reject other faiths, but actually to seek out the good in them, in order to develop a kind of universal religious harmony. George Harrison was very committed to using his religious beliefs in a practical way to help others rather than simply for his own personal development. An opportunity arose in 1971 when Ravi Shankar explained to him the terrible events taking place in East Pakistan, now known as Bangladesh (Schendel, 2009). East Pakistan wanted to secede from West Pakistan and become an independent country. The conflict between the two countries lead to excessive violence, and many thousands of refugees travelled south from East Pakistan to find safety in India. George Harrison decided to organize a rock concert to try to raise money for the refugees. He arranged the participation of Ringo Starr, Eric Clapton and Bob Dylan for a large concert in Madison Square Gardens, New York. There were two concerts held on the afternoon and evening of 1 August 1971, and they were an unprecedented success. It was probably the first occasion on which a large-scale charity rock concert had been held at a major international venue, and it paved the way for subsequent events. The album and film resulting from the Concert for Bangladesh also raised a very large amount of money to help the refugees. The income from the concert was administered by UNICEF. The concert did a great deal to publicize the situation in Bangladesh, and there was a great increase in donations around the world.

It has been argued that many Westerners have treated Indian spirituality as a product to be purchased rather than as a complex religious philosophy to be studied carefully and mastered slowly. It certainly would appear, however, that George Harrison treated his study of Hinduism very seriously indeed and had a sincere wish to develop a close relationship with God through the traditions of Hinduism.

George Harrison died on Thursday 29 November 2001, in Los Angeles at the age of 58. He had been treated for lung cancer. His ashes were later scattered in the Ganges, near Varanasi (Greene, 2006). Tributes came from around the world, acknowledging not only his musical and song-writing ability but also the extensive work he had done for charity.

One aspect of the interest in Hinduism in the West was that there was a tendency in the United States and United Kingdom to treat complex Hindu philosophical concepts and practices in a rather simplistic way. Hence 'yoga' tended to be perceived as simply a form of rather unenergetic physical exercise. There tended not to be any distinction made between the different types of yoga such as hatha yoga or raja yoga. Everything became merged into a series of exercises. There was possibly a degree of cultural condescension here, with ideas and concepts coming from the East, being regarded as somewhat secondary and inferior to those of the more technically advanced West. Nevertheless, Eastern ideas had come to stay, and even when the immediate fashion for India had declined somewhat, the ideas of Hinduism remained embedded in literature, in the media and in Western cultural life in general.

Further reading

Forem, J. (2012) *Transcendental Meditation: The Essential Teachings of Maharishi Mahesh Yogi*. London: Hay House.

Giuliano, G. (1997) *Dark Horse: The Life and Art of George Harrison*, 2nd edn. Boston, MA: Da Capo Press.

Lapham, L. (2009) *With the Beatles*. London: Melville House.

Tillery, G. (2011) *Working Class Mystic: A Spiritual Biography of George Harrison*. Wheaton, IL: Quest Books.

Yogi, Mahesh Maharishi (1990) *Maharishi Mahesh Yogi on the Bhagavad-Gita: A New Translation and Commentary with Sanskrit Text*. London: Penguin.

—. (2001) *Science of Being and Art of Living: Transcendental Meditation*. New York: Plume Books.

6

Drugs, enlightenment and Hinduism

Summary

The connection between drugs and Hinduism dates back at least to the Rig Veda, and the ritual taking of soma, a hallucinogen possibly derived from psilocybin mushrooms or from cannabis. In the West, the experimentation with psychedelic drugs, promoted by people such as Timothy Leary, became a central element of counter-culture philosophy. It influenced both rock music and the visual arts. The use of cannabis by Hindu sadhus, itinerant ascetics, was and remains an important part of their practice. One of the factors which attracted Westerners to India was no doubt the apparently liberal approach to the use of drugs. Allen Ginsburg, for example, was, it seems, deeply influenced by his meetings with Indian sadhus, and his experience of smoking hashish with them. This chapter analyses the links between Hindu culture and the use of drugs in the counter-culture.

The Vedic ritual

The employment of hallucinogenic drugs within Hinduism would appear to go back to Vedic times. The drug most normally associated with this historical period is 'soma', which is derived from the Sanskrit word indicating the process of squeezing or pressing in order to obtain sap or juice from a plant. Hence, during the soma ritual process, the Brahmin priests who officiated at the Vedic ceremonies probably squeezed certain plant roots in order to obtain the soma. The latter word could have been used to describe the actual process of extraction, the plant itself which was used in the ceremony or the substance which was extracted. The substance soma appears to have been considered to be a form of deity or divinity, which represented eternal life. Soma was probably regarded as an extremely powerful divinity within the Hindu pantheon at this period – certainly an equal of some of the most significant deities of the time.

There are many hypotheses as to the exact nature of soma, although it seems certain that whatever it was, it did have some form of hallucinogenic properties (Spess, 2000). It could have been a type of mushroom or perhaps cannabis. It is also possible that soma was some form of opium derivative, since the opium poppy was widely available in the areas to the north of India, from where the antecedents of Vedic Hindus originally came. There is also the possibility that soma may have been extracted from plants of the genus Ephedra. These contain alkaloid substances such as ephedrine which can have a variety of physiological and psychological effects upon those who take it.

It appears that soma gradually became associated within Hindu rituals, with Chandra, the deity of the moon, and it is at least possible that this was because of the time scale for pressing and extracting soma. It may have been that the pressing of the soma plant was linked to the monthly cycle of the moon. At any rate, soma seems to have been employed by the Brahmin priests to generate mystical visions of the Gods, and hence perhaps to enhance their power and authority over ordinary people.

The use of soma is discussed on many occasions in the Rig Veda and other scriptural texts. It is recorded as having been drunk by the God Indra, and hence it is considered by some to be at least the equal of, and perhaps to exceed in power, the most significant deities of the Vedas. Soma was reputed to induce feelings of immortality in those who took it. Clearly it had a profound effect upon the priests who used it in religious ceremonies, and produced mind-altering states of a spiritual nature.

There is wide evidence of the use of herbal substances in many different religious traditions around the world (Forte, 2012). These seem to have been used for many thousands of years, principally for inducing spiritual states artificially without the use of more conventional spiritual practices such as prayer, meditation or chanting. One of the best-known of these plants is the fly agaric mushroom with its bright orange and white cap, which has been used by shamans and medicine men in Asia for many centuries. Some argue that this mushroom is possibly the plant used in soma. Another example of such hallucinogenic plants is peyote, a cactus growing in North America and Mexico, which contains the alkaloid substance, mescaline. This cactus has been widely employed by the indigenous peoples of North America in order to induce spiritual experiences.

The great attraction of the use of such substances appears to be that they can be used to generate religious-like experience fairly quickly rather than relying upon a much slower process of prayer and meditation. The effects produced by these hallucinogens is essentially mystical; that is they produce feelings of unity with God and with the universe.

The use of these hallucination-inducing plants was also probably related to issues of power and authority within a fundamentally tribal and theocratic society. Those priests, such as the Brahmins who used these plants in Vedic culture, would be perceived as being possessed by divine powers, and this would enhance their influence over ordinary members of the tribal system. The Brahmins would be seen as having a direct means of communication with the Gods, and hence of access to the kinds of factors which might influence the fate and future of the tribe. They would be seen as being able to affect, through the Gods, the welfare of the society. Hence the members of the priestly caste were people above all to be respected, and even feared for the power and influence which they possessed. Finally, by charging fees for access to their esoteric knowledge, a priestly caste member had the potential to become wealthy, thus acquiring secular as well as divine authority.

Gradually, for reasons unknown, it appears that knowledge of the components of soma was lost within Hindu culture. To some degree, however, this may have added to its mystique, and it began to attain a semi-mythic status, particularly among Westerners who were interested in the use of mind-altering substances.

Experiments with hallucinatory drugs in the West

The exploration of the use of psychedelic drugs in the West began almost as an academic exercise on university research projects notably in the United States (Sessa, 2012). Timothy Leary (1920–1996) was particularly instrumental in developing this research and would ultimately influence a great deal of the trend towards the use of such substances during the 1960s. Leary carried out research at the University of California, Berkeley, in the late 1940s, being awarded his doctorate in 1950 for a study on the psychology of personality. After a varied academic career Leary was eventually appointed to a lectureship in psychology at Harvard, where he worked with the eminent psychologist David McLelland, and taught and researched as a member of the Centre for Research in Personality. He became interested in the effects of hallucinatory plant substances, and in 1960 went to Mexico where he experimented with psilocybin mushrooms.

Leary was deeply interested in the effects of the psilocybin mushrooms which he had consumed, and returned to Harvard University to found the so-called Harvard Psilocybin Project. This research study sought to explore the effects of psilocybin or its artificially synthesized derivatives in potentially helping people to amend negative elements in their behaviour, and to have a more positive approach towards life. The overall philosophy of the project was that the taking of hallucinatory drugs such as these could have a positive effect upon people, particularly if the process was undertaken under scientific conditions. It could perhaps be argued that there was an element here of an assumption that there could be a positive effect from the taking of such substances, before any balanced and impartial scientific experiments had been conducted. Dr Leary carried out a celebrated study of young offenders in prison to examine whether the administration of psilocybin might improve their general approach to society, and specifically whether it could reduce the number of offenders who continued to offend after release from prison.

The treatment programme consisted of the administration of psilocybin while offenders were still in prison, followed by a programme of psychotherapeutic support once the offenders had left prison. The experiments were carried out at a prison in Massachusetts called Concord State Prison and took place over a two-year period between 1961 and 1963.

Dr Leary concluded that there was a statistically significant improvement in the rates of re-offending when compared with the normally anticipated rates. However, on the basis of one study it seems very difficult to draw conclusions with certainty. The offenders may have been affected in terms of behaviour by the fact that they were being treated differently from normal expectations, or even from other prisoners who were not included in the sample for the study. It would also appear that the effects of administering a psychodelic drug are so unpredictable, and also so likely to affect different experimental subjects in different ways, that conclusions based on one experiment are relatively uncertain.

There is also the issue of the therapeutic support after prisoners have been released. This may well have affected individual prisoners differently, and it is therefore difficult methodologically to be certain of the efficacy of this treatment programme.

Despite the number of methodological and procedural questions raised by this research programme, not least the ethical issues of giving drugs to prisoners, it did raise the issue of possible therapeutic effects of such drugs. The ethical issues, however, remain very important. The general consciousness in both the public mind and in the scientific community about research ethics was not as sophisticated in the 1960s as it is now. Ethical research questions are always very important where treatments are selectively administered to a sample of research participants in a closed community where they may feel constrained for one reason or another to take part. The essential ethical question is one of genuine informed consent.

The use of psychedelic drugs in the United States was seriously restricted in 1966 when the use of LSD was proscribed. This was so not only for general use, but also by psychologists wishing to examine its effects. Similar measures were gradually taken throughout the world. Nevertheless in the 1950s and early 1960s, many people had tried LSD and acted as advocates for its use. Such people did a great deal to popularize the use of LSD within the counter-cultural movement and the pop culture generally.

One of the early experimenters with psychedelic drugs was the author Aldous Huxley. He took both mescaline and LSD in the early 1950s and his book 'The Doors of Perception' (Huxley, 1954) was an account of his use of mescaline. Throughout the 1940s and early 1950s, Huxley had gradually become very interested in mystical experiences in religion, and had meditated and studied ways in which people tried to obtain enhanced spiritual experiences in different religions. With the help of a psychiatrist friend, Huxley took mescaline in 1953 and the experiences resulting from this formed the basis of his book. He had studied, prior to this practical experiment, the use of the peyote cactus which contained mescaline, among the indigenous peoples of Mexico, particularly in relation to religious ritual.

Huxley discussed his personal visions and experiences in 'The Doors of Perception' and concluded in general that mescaline was an aid to spiritual experience which could help people have a more fulfilled mystical experience. Some people, including leading academics, criticized the book, arguing that the most important thing was that religious seekers have religious experience, using their unaltered consciousness, and not through the medium of drugs.

Aldous Huxley continued using and experimenting with psychedelic substances, in particular LSD. This lead to Huxley and Timothy Leary knowing each other, and collaborating to some extent. As the use of psychedelic substances became better and better known, rock groups of the 1960s became more involved with psychedelia. Groups such as Jefferson Airplane and The Doors sought to use the psychedelic experience to inspire a new form of music. In fact 'The Doors' are reputed to have been named by lead singer Jim Morrison after the title of Aldous Huxley's book on mescaline. This new form of rock music was also considerably characterized by the use of Indian instruments such as the sitar and also some of the complicated rhythms of Indian music.

Writers and literature of the 1950s and 1960s were considerably influenced by the psychedelic and hallucinatory drug movement. Arthur Keostler, the author of 'Darkness at Noon' (Koestler, 2005) experimented with psilocybin in 1960 but was not persuaded that psychedelic drugs contributed positively to his life. He also met Timothy Leary at Harvard University but remained unenamoured by the drug experience.

A psychedelic culture

One of the best-known examples of a writer who was influential in both literary and rock music circles was Ken Kesey (1935–2001). He was educated initially at the University of Oregon and later studied creative writing at Stanford University. While at Stanford, Kesey worked part time as a care assistant at a local hospital and also took part in an experimental project on LSD and other psychedelic drug use at the same hospital. Kesey became very interested in the use of hallucinatory drugs and continued using them long after he had left the project. He was known to host a number of social events where people would experiment with hallucinogens. These events included rock bands such as The Grateful Dead and were mentioned in the writing of Tom Wolfe. Kesey's experience of working in a hospital lead to the writing of his most famous novel 'One Flew Over the Cuckoo's Nest' (Kesey, 2005).

This highly influential novel was published in 1962 and later made into a successful film. The story takes place in a psychiatric hospital where the patients are manipulated and controlled by an all-pervading and insidious administrative system. One patient continually challenges the hierarchy but is ultimately defeated. However, another patient finally escapes from the hospital, in what could be taken as a metaphor for the achievement of ultimate personal freedom. The book was seen among other things as a clear statement of the ethical and political values of the 1960s. The ordinary citizens, and particularly the poor and disenfranchised, were seen as the victims of powerful bureaucratic organizations. The key principle for people was to be aware of the hegemony of such organizations and to be continually prepared to combat these forces of suppression and oppression. The psychiatric patients in a sense were a metaphor for all oppressed people whose freedoms were constrained by society. In a more literal sense, however, they represented themselves, in that society was becoming more and more aware of the way in which people were institutionalized, and in fact could be liberated without necessarily any seriously adverse effects for society. Ken Kesey wrote a book which spoke to many about the nature of personal liberty, and the need to place limits on the power of institutions to control intrinsic personal freedom. To that extent it was an archetypal book of the decade of the 1960s.

By 1964 Ken Kesey had begun to attract an informal group of friends who at various times lived a communal life together, and sometimes set off to travel across the United States. These journeys of exploration took place in a renovated school bus which was painted in psychedelic colours and patterns. The bus was nicknamed 'Further', and the group adopted the name of 'The Merry Pranksters'.

In the summer of 1964 Ken Kesey and the Pranksters set off from California travelling eastwards to New York City. They took LSD themselves, and from time to time offered it to people they met en route. This did not contravene the law, as LSD remained legal until 1966. Ken Kesey viewed LSD as a force for good in society as he felt that it opened up the business mind to a range of possibilities and different ways of looking at the world. He viewed the journey in 'Further' as a metaphor for a challenge to existing American society. He wanted to demonstrate that there were viable alternatives to the existing norms of society, and that this was a way of demonstrating those alternative values.

The Merry Prankster bus journey was a theatrical and artistic way of commenting upon the perceived nature of American society. The main driver of the bus for the different road trips was Neal Cassady, who had travelled so extensively with Jack Kerouac. In fact, as the 1964 trip reached its destination in New York, Neal Cassady introduced Kesey to Jack Kerouac and Allen Ginsberg. Ken Kesey was thus a historical link between the Beat Generation of the 1950s, and the hippie movement of the 1960s, as he had many links with the rock bands of the mid-1960s. Neal Cassidy also remained an important link between the two social movements. He was a leading member of the Pranksters, but from 1967 onwards started to spend more time in Mexico. He travelled there with a small group of Pranksters and continued with his uninhibited life of drinking and drug taking. He collapsed and died the following year at the age of 41 years. Another member of the Pranksters was Carolyn Garcia, who later married Jerry Garcia, the lead guitarist of The Grateful Dead. This group was often present at the so-called acid tests held by Kesey in California in the mid-1960s. These were all night parties at which people consumed LSD.

Links with Hindu culture

The Grateful Dead also played at a number of very significant events in the mid-1960s, including an event known as the Mantra-Rock Dance in 1967 at San Francisco. This musical event was organized to support the recently founded ISKCON. Swami Prabhupada, the Indian teacher who had established ISKCON, had been sent in 1965 by his own guru to try to establish his Hindu teaching in the West. With the assistance of Allen Ginsberg and others, Swami Prabhupada set up the first ISKCON centre in the United States, based in New York City. By this time the counter-cultural movement was becoming very aware of Hindu culture, and several disciples of Swami Prabhupada travelled to San Francisco to try to create an interest particularly among young people there in the philosophy of Swami Prabhupada and in the ISKCON movement. They set up the second ISKCON centre in San Francisco, in the Haight-Ashbury district. This expansion of the new movement required funding, however, and followers of the Swami decided that a rock concert might not only raise funds but could also help transmit Swami Prabhupada's spiritual message and gain publicity. Through a number of contacts ISKCON managed to interest Allen Ginsberg, and the rock groups Big Brother and the Holding Company, and The Grateful Dead, in appearing at the concert, and also to waive their appearance fees, so that concert income could go to the ISKCON movement. There was a slight potential philosophical conflict, however, between the teachings of Prabhupada and the general values of the hippie movement. Swami Prabhupada was against the use of drugs, and yet it was likely that they would be used at the concert among the audience. Despite this, Prabhupada decided to attend the concert and to use the opportunity to publicize his religious philosophy. On the evening of the concert, Swami Prabhupada appeared to have a considerable effect upon the young people present. He was a charismatic speaker, and the event did a great deal to extend the popularity of Hindu culture in the San Francisco area.

It is sometimes difficult when examining the issue of cultural transmission, particularly in a historical sense, to identify specific examples of it happening in practice. We can observe the final result, but it is not always easy to observe instances of it occurring on a micro level. In the case of Hindu culture permeating the counter-culture, however, this concert can be viewed as an example of the process in action. There is the separate question, however, of why Hindu culture excited young people. There may have been a number of factors here, including the rather 'exotic' nature of the religion, its colourful religious symbolism and importantly perhaps, its relatively liberal and tolerant philosophy.

One of the commonest drugs which has been used in a religious context around the world is cannabis. This is particularly true of Hinduism, where cannabis has probably been used since Vedic times. In India, the use of cannabis has always been associated with worship of the God Shiva, and devotees of this God, especially the itinerant holy men or sadhus, smoke cannabis as a form of religious ritual. The normal method of smoking is to use a chillum pipe. This is a form of pipe which probably originated in India and consists of a short tube, slightly conical in shape. The chillum may be shorter or longer, but typically may be about six inches in length. Sadhus place the cannabis resin in the broader end of the chillum. Chillum smoking among sadhus is very often a group ritual event within a spiritual context. The pipe is passed from sadhu to sadhu, who are sitting in a circle. The chillum, however, does not come into contact with the mouths of the participants. It is placed between the middle fingers of one hand, and the hand then cupped and placed to the mouth. On inhalation, a vacuum is created in the hand, and smoke passes down the chillum into the hand. This is a commonly used method of smoking in the Indian sub-continent, and one will often see people smoking cigarettes using this method.

In India chillum pipes are normally made of clay or wood, and may be decorated according to the owner's taste. During the 1960s travellers returning from India took chillum pipes back to the West and even started making them. They became a popular souvenir of a trip to India and became a common sight in hippie communities.

The daily life of the sadhu in India is intimately linked with the smoking of cannabis as part of a ritual for the God Shiva. Although sadhus belong to a number of different denominations, with different histories and to some extent culture, there are many commonalities to the way in which they lead their lives. At some times of the year they may travel around India to holy places, and to meet fellow sadhus. At others they may attend major gatherings of sadhus, the most famous being the Kumbh Mela. For part of the year, however, they may reside in one place, usually somewhere which has some significance for them. This may be a holy place or city, near a major temple, or it may be near the residence of their own guru. This will enable them to visit their guru from time to time to receive teaching and advice. They will probably construct for themselves a small temple or hut in which they will live and cook food. Such 'buildings' may be extremely basic in structure, ranging from a simple tarpaulin stretched between branches to a small one room 'temple' constructed from wood and dried mud or cow dung. Sadhus are supposed to have renounced worldly possessions, and so if they choose to have a 'home' it should be very basic in order not to distract them from their ascetic lifestyle. Some sadhus may not have any kind of shelter at all, while others may sleep and meditate in a natural shelter such as a mountain cave. Some sadhus may live alone, while others will be accompanied by a disciple, typically a young man who is learning the customs and practices of the ascetic life. The disciple will receive tuition from his guru in the scriptures, in yoga and in meditation. In exchange the disciple will do domestic chores for the guru, preparing food and tea, and maintaining the holy fire or dhuni at the guru's living place. Many disciples are relatively young when they attach themselves to a guru. They may be as young as 10 or 11 years. Usually the parents will know the guru to some extent, and their son will have demonstrated an affinity for the spiritual life. There will be an agreement for the guru to take their son as a disciple. From that point onwards, the son will probably not return to his parent's home. He may meet them on the streets to talk and discuss his new life, but the key principle is that on becoming a disciple, his attachment is from then on to his guru and not to his parents.

A sadhu will typically rise at dawn or earlier and make his way to the nearest river or lake to bathe. Most sadhus will live fairly close to a source of water. He will then return to his hut and may rub ashes from his dhuni over his body and long hair. This often gives sadhus a ghostly, other-worldly appearance. He may then offer prayers to Shiva and carry out some yoga exercises. The latter are to maintain the suppleness of his body, and to give him control over body and mind, in particular maintaining a calm mind. At this time he may smoke his chillum, and drink a cup of sweet tea prepared by his disciple. His disciple will have cleaned and swept the hut, and will also have ensured that the holy fire is lit. If the sadhu stays at his hut during the day, he will sit in front meditating and receiving visitors. These may be people simply passing, or they may be members of the local community. Sadhus are often in great demand for advice on a range of family or spiritual issues. People will come to consult them, much as people may consult their family priest in the West. Visitors will leave a donation of money or food at a small shrine in the sadhu's temple. The sadhu may also spend his day touring the local area, meeting other sadhus, visiting people who he knows to be ill or perhaps engaging in more yoga practice.

When evening starts to descend the sadhu will return to his hut or cave. He and his disciple will prepare an evening meal of spiced vegetables accompanied by chapattis. He will prepare sufficient food for the fellow sadhus who will call to eat, along with an indeterminate number of homeless or destitute people from the locality, who will rely upon the sadhu to support them whenever possible. In any case, the vegetables and flour, and money, will have been given as donations, and hence the sadhu acts as the hub of a form of social security system. After the meal people will sit around talking, and the sadhus may smoke a chillum. Finally guests will depart, and the sadhu will settle down for the night.

It is worth noting that the cannabis is not smoked to obtain any kind of drug-induced 'high' but fundamentally to help calm the mind. A great deal of the meditational and yoga practice of sadhus is devoted to attaining a calmness of the mind, so that the sadhus are not disturbed by extraneous events. The smoking of cannabis helps in this process. In reality, there appear to be few practical restrictions on the use of cannabis among sadhus. In some parts of the Indian sub-continent, there are legal restrictions on the sale of cannabis by sadhus. However, there do not appear to be limitations on the use of cannabis by sadhus for personal and spiritual purposes.

Sadhus live a very simple life which one assumes must be physically relatively hard. They have very few possessions, limited normally to a metal or pot jug in which they carry water. They will be minimally clothed and will often carry a pole to steady them on their long walks. They will also often have a shoulder bag, for one or two minor items such as religious images. Such shoulder bags became a key element of the hippy dress style in the West. Many sadhus will also participate in various ascetic practices or penances in order to help focus their minds on God. They may take a vow to stand up for a number of years, never lying down; they may hold an arm in the air for many years or they may hold a particular yoga posture for a very long time. The smoking of cannabis is said to help them in surviving the discomfort of such penances.

The number of sadhus in India is probably declining, affected by many aspects of a post-modern society. However, the sadhu way of life remains a uniquely Hindu institution and contributes to our understanding of the nature of spirituality.

Further reading

Doniger, W. (trans) (2005) *The Rig Veda*. London: Penguin.

Hausner, S. L. (2007) *Wandering with Sadhus: Ascetics in the Hindu Himalayas*. Bloomington, IN: Indiana University Press.

Leary, T., Metzner, R. and Alpert, R. (2008) *The Psychedelic Experience*. London: Penguin.

Rampuri (2010) *Autobiography of a Sadhu: A Journey into Mystic India*, 2nd edn. Merrimac, MA: Destiny.

Storl, W.-D. (2004) *Shiva: The Wild God of Power and Ecstasy*. Rochester, VT: Inner Traditions.

7

Ahimsa, Gandhi and the peace movement

Summary

The doctrine of ahimsa or non-violence is a central concept in Hindu belief and practice. Mahatma Gandhi famously used it as a cornerstone of his non-violent protest movement against the British occupation of India. Gandhi's approach to non-violent political action was not only successful in practical terms but also made a strong moral statement. This strategy was adopted by many of the student and political demonstrations of the 1960s, including the Martin Luther King march on Washington in 1963 and the protests in Czechoslovakia against the Warsaw Pact invasion of 1968. Indeed, Martin Luther King made a pilgrimage to the birthplace of Gandhi and was awarded the Nobel Peace Prize in 1964 for his action against racial inequality. This chapter examines the influence of ahimsa on young people taking direct political action in the 1960s in support of the anti-war movement and in support of civil rights.

Attitudes to peace in the 1960s

The young people who were born in 1946, the year following the end of the Second World War, would not by 1960 have had a great deal of exposure to the reality of war. Their fathers, returning from the war, were understandably not eager to share with their children some of their terrible experiences of the battlefield. In the United Kingdom, military conscription or 'National Service' as it was known ended in 1960 (Shindler, 2012). The last young men to be conscripted entered military service in November of that year. For the 14-year-olds of 1960 there thus appeared little prospect that they would be obliged to shoulder a rifle. They may have heard stories of warfare from older brothers who had served in either the Korean War or during the conflict at the Suez canal. These events, however, had ended in 1952 and 1956, respectively, and were beginning to fade in the memory. In the United States the 1948 Selective Service Act was still on the statute books, permitting young men to be called into military service when necessary. However, in 1960 the political situation in Vietnam showed few signs that it would draw the United States into a large-scale and bitter conflict.

At the beginning of the decade of the 1960s the concerns about peace were largely motivated by the politics of the Cold War and the developing nuclear arms race (Gaddis, 2005). During the Second World War the Allies and the Soviet Union appeared to be working in unison to combat the threat from Hitler's Germany. This was particularly so, once Hitler had opened a 'second front' and invaded the Soviet Union in Operation Barbarossa which began in June 1941. However, this apparent union was one of convenience, motivated by the need to face a common enemy. In reality there was enormous distrust between the Allies and the Soviet Union. Towards the end of the war the distrust was exacerbated when the Soviet Army was allowed to reach Berlin before the Allied forces. The Americans did not consult with the Soviets over the plans to develop a nuclear weapon, although it seems likely that Stalin was kept well-informed through Soviet espionage in the United States. The end of the Second World War saw the development of entrenched positions both from an ideological point of view and also in terms of the increasingly important nuclear arms race. The nuclear age had started with the dropping of atomic weapons on Hiroshima and Nagasaki, ending the war with Japan in August 1945. This initiated a fervent attempt in the Soviet Union to develop their own nuclear weapon, which they succeeded doing exactly four years later in August 1949. This was the start of the true nuclear arms race. Between 1952 and 1964 the United Kingdom, France and finally China developed nuclear weapons. With this came increasing calls for a limitation to be placed on the expansion and availability of nuclear weapons. These feelings grew increasingly stronger in 1962. In that year the United States began to fear that Soviet missile sites were being constructed in Cuba (Dobbs, 2009). The US government felt that the proximity of Cuba to the American mainland constituted a serious threat, and proceeded to place an embargo around Cuba in order to prevent the arrival by ship of Soviet missiles. This lead to a serious confrontation between the United States and the Soviet Union, which lasted from 16 to 29 October 1962. During that time there was a very real threat of nuclear war. Eventually, it was agreed that Soviet missiles would not be kept in Cuba, and in a reciprocal agreement, American missiles which were a threat to the Soviet Union would be removed from Turkey. As a result of these events there was a general realization of the ease with which the world could be brought to the point of nuclear war. The main factor which appeared to be capable of preventing nuclear war was the reality of 'mutually assured destruction'. This hypothesis argued that there could not be a winner in a nuclear exchange. Both sides would suffer such destruction and casualties that the conflict would achieve no purpose. Hence, the hypothesis argued that nuclear war would not be initiated between rationally thinking states. Nevertheless, people around the world had been shocked by the so-called Cuban Missile Crisis, and there were increasing feelings that steps had to be taken to limit the risk of nuclear war.

One of the best-known organizations to campaign against nuclear weapons was the Campaign for Nuclear Disarmament (CND) which was founded in 1957. It argued for unilateral nuclear disarmament and was linked with the famous Aldermaston Marches between the Atomic Weapons Establishment at Aldermaston and Trafalgar Square in London. Among the founders were the philosopher and peace activist Bertrand Russell and the writer J. B. Priestley. The Society of Friends, or Quakers, were also involved in supporting the organization. In 1960, however, Bertrand Russell who was then the president of CND relinquished that role to help establish the Committee of 100. This organization was founded on the principles of Mahatma Gandhi, such as non-violent action. The organization was involved in a range of protests such as demonstrations outside the Ministry of Defence in London, in 1961. The members of the Committee of 100 adhered to the Gandhian principle of peaceful non-cooperation and protest, despite the subsequent arrest of many members. Three months after the Ministry of Defence protest, significant non-violent direct action was also taking place on the other side of the Atlantic. Legislation had been passed making it illegal to have racial segregation on buses which travelled from one state to another. There was every suspicion among civil rights workers that in reality, this would not be enforced in the southern states of America. Hence, so-called freedom riders deliberately rode on the buses in mixed black and white groups to see if there would be any reaction. In fact when blacks and whites rode on the same bus they often encountered extreme violence at a local level in the southern states.

Although the American Civil Rights Movement was not trying to combat the possibility of nuclear war, it was still a peace movement in the sense that it was fighting civil and racial injustice on a very large scale. Moreover, that injustice was ultimately founded upon violence or the threat of violence, often in contravention of national legislation or legal precedent. The fundamental approach of the Civil Rights Movement in America was first to emphasize the ethical issues involved in racial equality, and then to ensure that the practical tactics employed by activists were non-violent in nature. Hence, the overall philosophy of the Civil Rights Movement in America was similar to the anti-nuclear protest movement in the United Kingdom. The tactics of non-violent marches and sit-ins were as difficult for the respective governments to address as had been the case with Gandhian protests in the days of the British Raj. Perhaps the most celebrated peace march in the United States took place on 28 August 1963, with the March on Washington, at which Martin Luther King spoke (Jones, 2013). The claims for racial equality did gather pace during this period, and even though President J. F. Kennedy was assassinated in November of that year, in 1964 the Civil Rights Act was passed under President Lyndon Johnson. This Act made it illegal to discriminate on the grounds of ethnicity, gender or religion.

At the same time as the direct action in favour of civil rights, the war in Vietnam was becoming more intense. The conflict expanded with great rapidity. Towards the end of 1964 there were just over 20,000 American military 'advisers' in South Vietnam. Only three years later, at the end of 1967, there were approximately half-a-million American troops on Vietnamese soil. Arguably the principal factor affecting opposition to the Vietnam War, at least in the United States, was the number of American casualties. These rose from just over 200 in 1964 to well over 16,000 in 1968. The war was beginning to affect many families, across a range of social strata. In addition, the increased potential of television journalism meant that the realities of the Vietnam War could be easily broadcast across America. No doubt, the media did not report all of the incidents of extreme violence, but nevertheless the public in both the United States and around the world were left in no doubt about the real nature of war, and of this war in particular.

There was also an increasing opposition to the morality of the Vietnam War. Politically, one of the main justifications for the war from the viewpoint of the American administration was the possibility that South Vietnam would fall permanently under the influence of communism, and that communism would develop in other countries in southeast Asia. However, those in opposition to the war considered that even if this were true, Vietnam had the right to develop its own political future. Opponents of the war stressed the unethical nature of the military tactics of the Americans. The use of napalm bombs caused terrible injuries, sometimes to civilians. In addition, defoliants were widely sprayed from aircraft in Vietnam. The purpose of this was partly to destroy the camouflage for Viet Cong supply lines, but also to hamper cultivation of crops where these were used to support the Viet Cong. Quite apart from environmental concerns, opposition focused upon the use of defoliants such as Agent Orange, which had very serious effects upon the general population exposed to it, for example in causing birth deformities.

Practical opposition to the war in Vietnam was often associated with the movement for civil rights. For many young people, the issues were linked. On the one hand they perceived black people as being oppressed and disenfranchised in America, while on the other hand America was ignoring the intrinsic rights of the people of Vietnam. Typically, the same young people would be involved in sit-ins and demonstrations against what they saw as related forms of oppression. In addition, the same principle of Gandhian non-violent, direct action pervaded the two protest movements. For example, a common protest action against the war was for young men to burn their draft cards. The draft had become increasingly perceived as reinforcing divisions and injustice in society. The common perception was that young black men, or young men from poorer socio-economic groups, were more likely to be drafted. Some disputed these claims, but perhaps the most significant issue was that they became the received wisdom, and had an adverse effect on public opinion in terms of support for the war.

During the mid-1960s, however, the US government was not the only one to be challenged for its policies. On the night of 20 August 1968 the Soviet Union invaded Czechoslovakia, bringing condemnation from many countries around the world, and even from some Soviet satellite countries (Williams, 1997). The Soviet Union had for some time been unhappy with the policies of the government in Prague, lead by Alexander Dubček. He had pursued a policy of general liberalization, within an overall Communist philosophy. The Soviet Union perceived this as a threat to their authority and concerned that other countries might follow suit. The invasion force was very large, being probably in excess of half-a-million troops from both the Soviet Union and other communist countries. There was no significant opposition to the invasion, and indeed the Dubček government advised people not to resist the troops. However, many people in Czechoslovakia pursued a policy of non-violent action against the Soviet soldiers. On a personal level, they did not assist the soldiers; they used banners and posters to express their feelings, and did their best, short of violent intervention, to make clear their opposition to the invasion.

It was thus clear that during the 1960s, the principle of non-violent direct action was perceived as the most appropriate method to address social injustice. In the early 1950s Martin Luther King had gradually become aware of the history of Gandhi's programme of action against the British in India, and in particular the approach of non-violence which had permeated all of his political action. King began to appreciate that non-violence was not only the most ethical philosophy he could employ in the struggle for civil rights in America but also likely to be the most affective. He became profoundly committed to the principle of non-violence and in 1959 embarked on a visit to India to see some of the results of Gandhi's actions for himself. He was pleased to find out that the struggle for civil rights for black people in America had been widely reported in the Indian media, and that Indian people saw the relevance of their own struggle for freedom and self-determination, to the situation of black people in the United States. While in India, Martin Luther King had discussions with some of Gandhi's family members, and also visited Rajghat in New Delhi, where Gandhi was cremated following his assassination.

The history of non-violence in Indian culture and religion

During his lifetime of political action in India, and since his assassination in January 1948, Gandhi's approach to non-violence became very well-known around the world. Although Gandhi is perhaps the most famous modern exponent of non-violence, this philosophical approach has a very long history in Indian culture. The original Sanskrit term for the approach of non-violence is *ahimsa*. This concept, which dates back to the Upanishads, does not simply mean the act of renouncing warfare or of not attacking someone physically. It takes as its starting point the idea of having respect for not only other human beings but also the entire living world. In terms of human beings, the concept of ahimsa signifies for example, not saying hurtful things to people, treating other people with the same kindness and thoughtfulness with which you would like to be treated yourself and developing a sensitivity and empathy towards others. It thus embraces a psychological dimension as well as a physical dimension. This same philosophy is extended to our dealings with animals, and hence ahimsa is usually interpreted as adopting a vegetarian lifestyle, as the killing of animals for food would clearly be contrary to non-violent principles. One can extend the concept of ahimsa further to our relationship with the environment, which according to this philosophy should be non-exploitative. We should use the natural environment only to the extent that we need in order to survive. The philosophy of ahimsa also discourages human beings from having unpleasant, violent or selfish thoughts about others. Although some may argue that this is unattainable in practice, others see it as an ideal to which to aim.

The Hindu concept of ahimsa has influenced other Indian religions in different ways. Buddhism embraces the concept of mindfulness, which encourages Buddhists to, at all times, act with careful thought, sensitivity and care towards other living beings. The Jain religion has perhaps gone further than most in adopting the principle of ahimsa. Jain monks for example will often use a light brush to sweep the path in front of them in order that they do not accidentally tread on small creatures. Ahimsa has had a great influence generally on Indian culture, and indeed vegetarianism is widely practised throughout the sub-continent. However, it is through the integration of ahimsa with practical political activity that Gandhi brought the concept into the wider consciousness of the world.

Gandhi and ahimsa

Gandhi would have been familiar with the ideals of non-violence and vegetarianism from his childhood in Gujarat. Indeed later, when a law student at the Inns of Court in London, he became very active in promoting vegetarianism. However, it was not until he obtained a post as a lawyer in South Africa that Gandhi came across the systematic racism and discrimination which caused him to develop ahimsa into a practical political philosophy. The Indian community in South Africa were subject to a variety of racist and oppressive measures, consisting for example of incidents of violence against the person, to legislation which treated them adversely when compared to the white population. Gandhi became convinced that any type of violent resistance not only would be ineffective, as it would be suppressed by superior force, but also was not ethically acceptable. He came to the conclusion that a form of non-violent resistance was the best way to both demonstrate opposition to the policies of the South African government and try to convince them of the virtues of his case. However, he drew a distinction between passive resistance and non-violent resistance. He perceived the former as not demonstrating sufficient determination to overcome the unfair and illegitimate actions of others. The latter, however, implied in his view a firm and committed determination to oppose injustice, while at the same time adopting exclusively non-violent methods.

It was in this context that Gandhi developed the expression *satyagraha* to describe his philosophy of non-violent political action. It translates literally as 'a determination to abide by truth', but for Gandhi the concept had a number of nuances of meaning (Fischer, 1997). Those who adhered to this policy of political action were asked to analyse carefully the morality and fairness of their case, and then to advocate that as clearly as possible. When they employed non-violent methods of protest, the satyagrahis, or adherents of satyagraha, needed to accept that such protests might well-attract a violent response. Gandhi asked them to accept the danger and suffering inherent in their actions, and to realize that ultimately they may have to accept death as the ultimate result of their action in a just cause.

Gandhi hoped and believed that acting in this way would in many circumstances win the respect of their opponents. If the satyagrahis continued, even in the most difficult circumstances, to argue their case calmly and non-violently, then they would ultimately win acceptance of the justice of their cause. However, this would not be won without a potential cost. Satyagraha demanded, according to Gandhi, enormous personal courage, even to the point of being prepared to lay down one's life.

When Gandhi returned to India, he embarked upon the political struggle for the independence of his country and employed the strategies of satyagraha which he had developed in South Africa.

Gandhi had returned to India in 1915, and once the First World War had ended there were increasing calls for the independence of India. There were isolated acts of violence against the British, particularly in the Punjab area of northern India. Concerned by the potential for a breakdown of law and order, the British government in London passed the so-called Rowlatt Act in March 1919, which in effect gave them sweeping powers against anyone challenging the Indian government. Some leaders of the Indian independence movement were arrested, and this caused further anger among the Indian population. Gandhi called for his followers to mount a satyagraha movement against the Rowlatt Act. The satyagraha was not entirely supported, but people continued to protest against the introduction of this legislation. On 13 April 1919 a large group of people of several thousands gathered in the Jallianwala Bagh in Amritsar, the principal city of the Punjab. This location was a large open space surrounded by walls, whose only access was several extremely narrow alleys. The date of 13th April is the annual day on which Sikhs celebrate Baisakhi, or the founding of the Khalsa, the community of Sikhs. It is also the start of the Hindu new year. Hence the gathering in the Jallianwala Bagh was of a cultural nature, although no doubt there was plenty of discussion about the demands for Indian independence. However, it appears to have been completely peaceful in nature and intent. Nevertheless, the local British army commander, General Dyer was unhappy about the gathering, and mindful of the recent political situation decided to take action. He took a group of soldiers into the Jallianwala Bagh in the late afternoon and ordered them to shoot into the crowds. The Hindus and Sikhs there were standing closely together, and the result was a very large number of deaths, officially approaching 400. However, it would appear that a more realistic estimate would be in excess of 1,000. As news of the massacre spread, there were incidents of protest and violence in India, and much official repudiation of the action in Britain. So strong was the opposition to the Amritsar massacre, that demands for Indian independence gained a new momentum. Gandhi persisted with his policy of trying to encourage non-violent protest. Not all Indians agreed with his strategy, but gradually it was perceived as an ethical policy which could achieve practical gains.

One of Gandhi's most famous actions in the spirit of satyagraha was his opposition to the British tax on salt. The British had made sure that they controlled the manufacture and distribution of salt in India, and also added a substantial purchase tax on salt, which generated considerable revenue. The humidity of the Indian climate made the consumption of salt essential, and hence all Indians, of all social classes and financial backgrounds, had to buy salt. Yet on the coastline of India, salt often collected through the natural evaporation of sea water. Gandhi sought to demonstrate the oppressive and unfair nature of the British salt tax, by organizing a non-violent protest march to the sea, at the coastal town of Dandi, in the state of Gujarat. The march by Gandhi and a group of satyagrahis commenced in March 1930 from Ahmedabad, and set out for Dandi, arriving on 6th April. On his arrival Gandhi collected a small amount of tax-free salt from the beach at Dandi, thus breaking the law. The march and the ethics of the issue surrounding salt tax had been widely reported in Europe and the United States, and had a marked effect on world public opinion concerning the British policy in India. As a result of the non-violent action at Dandi, there were many other cases of civil disobedience throughout India. Notable was the boycott of British manufactured goods. Instead of purchasing British-made cotton cloth at inflated prices, Gandhi encouraged Indians to spin their own cloth. Other British products were also boycotted. This policy had a tangible effect on the British economy.

Gandhi subsequently encouraged a group of satyagrahis to march towards a salt-making factory to the south of Dandi. The non-violent protesters were met by police who beat them. The satyagrahis, however, did not resist the violence to which they were subjected.

Gandhi's policy of non-violent resistance was ultimately successful in achieving independence for India. It won the respect of many British people, who realized that the British administration would have to withdraw. It was, however, unsuccessful in eradicating violence from Indian society. In 1947 the communal violence accompanying partition which led to the creation of the states of India and Pakistan resulted in a very large number of deaths. Gandhi himself, suspected by a Hindu extremist of favouring too much the new Muslim state, was assassinated in January 1948, in the grounds of Birla House in New Delhi.

Nevertheless, many aspects of Gandhi's philosophy lived on to influence society in the West, particularly during the period of the 1960s. In a world where people were beginning to realize the finite nature of our resources, particularly in terms of the environment, Gandhi's asceticism and vegetarianism provided a model for a more modest and simple style of life. His advocacy of a less consumerist existence, for example in terms of his weaving simple cloth for his own use, and in having few possessions, inspired many young people in the 1960s. Gandhi had a dislike of political systems which tended to oppress people, which were centralized and which tended to take decisions for them. He was thus clearly anti-colonialist, but more than that he favoured systems which distributed power away from central government and gave people power over their own lives. He was more in favour of autonomous or semi-autonomous villages and communes, which placed people very close to the decision-making process. The communal living movements of the 1960s thus looked to Gandhi among others, for inspiration. Above all, his adherence to non-violence was a major influence upon the hippy movement, with their slogans such as 'Make love, not war'.

After his death, Gandhi's ideas continued to have a major effect on freedom and independence movements around the world. A notable case was the fight against apartheid in South Africa. During the 1950s and early 1960s, Nelson Mandela had been influenced by Gandhi's ideas. He subscribed to the principle of non-violence, and felt that it was both an important moral principle and also an effective political strategy. However, he did not feel that on its own, it could necessarily bring about social and political change when confronted by an intransigent government. He felt that at times it might be necessary to resort to violence, but that it was always desirable to place an emphasis upon non-violent methods. However, in 1964 he was convicted of sabotage against the South African government. Nevertheless, he continued to be inspired by the example of Mahatma Gandhi.

As the 1960s progressed, political events often resulted in a challenge to the principle of non-violence. The year of 1968 was particularly significant in terms not only of political change but also of a range of different responses to events. Martin Luther King was assassinated on 4 April 1968, and a number of leading politicians, including Senator Robert Kennedy, called for an adherence to the non-violent methods advocated by King. However, there was also the feeling that non-violent strategies were fundamentally ineffectual against what many saw as the entrenched racism of the United States. The result was that in a number of American cities such as Washington and Chicago, large-scale riots took place. Senator Robert Kennedy was also assassinated almost exactly two months later on 5 June 1968.

The Vietnam War

In early 1968 the war in Vietnam reached a new level of intensity. The North Vietnamese commenced a wide-ranging attack on the south of the country, which became known as the Tet Offensive (Willbanks, 2007). There were many casualties on both sides, with the Americans losing nearly 550 soldiers in a single week in February. In a monochrome photograph taken on 1 February 1968, the Tet Offensive left us one of the most tragically enduring images of warfare. On that day, during wide-scale insurgencies in the Saigon area, a presumed Viet Cong captain named Nguyen Van Lem was captured by the South Vietnamese army, and brought to Nguyen Ngoc Loan, who was then the head of the National Police. The Viet Cong officer was summarily executed by Nguyen Ngoc Loan with a revolver shot through the head. The moment of execution was captured on film by a press photographer. The photograph was seen around the world. There was something about the image of two men caught together at the moment of death, which brought home to people the horrific nature of war, and of the Vietnam conflict in particular. This image alone did a great deal to support the peace movement in the United States.

There was by now a rapidly growing scepticism among the general public in the United States, concerning the portrayal of the war by the government. By 1968 many American veterans of the Vietnam War were beginning to give voice to their opposition to the war. They joined protests, and some returned the medals which they had been awarded for service during the war. One of the most significant protests occurred at the Democratic Party National Convention in Chicago during August 1968. An estimated 10,000 anti-war protesters gathered in Chicago in order to make their feelings felt at the convention centre. However, the protesters did not adhere to peaceful strategies, and the period of the demonstrations was marked by violence on the part of the police.

The Vietnam War in a sense defined the 1960s. It provided a number of important contrasts notably that between the intervention of the most powerful military country in the world and a much weaker, although ideologically committed country. Although many American people probably felt initially that a fight against communism was legitimate, as the war continued there was a gradual change of attitude. Under the arguments of the peace campaigners the ethical basis of the war came to be challenged. The American electorate began to feel uneasy about the level of military force used, and particularly the effects on the civilian population of Vietnam. Images of civilians caught up in the fighting had a particularly potent effect on world public opinion. In June 1972 a little girl named Kim Phuc was badly hurt in a napalm attack on her village. She tore off her burning clothes and ran with other villagers to escape the bombing. The scene was captured on camera and became a defining image of the war. Helped by people present at the time, the nine-year-old was taken to hospital, and survived despite her serious injuries. The photograph was widely circulated in the media, and provided a very strong argument for peace. Just over a year later, on 15 August 1973, American military intervention in Vietnam ended.

The work of Mahatma Gandhi, Martin Luther King and the many young peace activists of the 1960s has not ended war. It has, however, outlined an alternative way of dealing with world problems and shown that non-violence can, under certain circumstances, be stronger than conflict.

Further reading

Gandhi, M. K. (2012) *An Autobiography: Or the Story of My Experiments with Truth.* London: Penguin.

King, M. L. (2000) *The Autobiography of Martin Luther King Jr.* London: Abacus.

Sharma, S. R. (ed.) (2002) *Gandhi: Ahimsa and Non-Violence in Practice.* New Delhi: Cosmo.

Tidrick, K. (2006) *Gandhi: A Political and Spiritual Life.* London: I.B. Tauris.

Wiest, A. (2002) *The Vietnam War: 1956–1975.* Oxford: Osprey.

8

Sexual liberation, tantra and the Kama Sutra

Summary

Hindu culture, with its erotic temple carvings and the explicit advice of the Kama Sutra, has seemed to have a liberal approach to sex. These, along with tantric yoga practices, are in fact more concerned with using sexual energy to attain higher levels of spiritual consciousness. Nevertheless, India offered to the Western counter-culture a view of a society which was more open about sex, and which also offered a more central role for women, as for example, with the importance of female gurus. In the West, the decade of the 1960s started with the first availability of oral contraceptives, and with the Lady Chatterley's Lover obscenity trial. Later in the decade, the first Women's Liberation Conference was held at Ruskin College in 1969. In the same year, the Stonewall Inn riots marked the beginning of a vociferous campaign for gay rights. This chapter examines the influence of Hindu culture on the sexual revolution in the West, and the appearance by the beginning of the 1970s of then rather radical phenomena such as mixed halls of residence in universities.

Life before the 1960s

The change in sexual mores which took place during the decade of the 1960s was arguably not the result of factors exclusive to the 1960s, but perhaps more accurately seen as part of a social continuum of change. War is often perceived as a major factor in social change, and with regard to sexual behaviour, soldiers returning from armed conflict often bring back with them the changes in habits developed in a war zone. As these shifts in moral values begin to permeate society, one sees changes not only in personal mores, but also in artistic expression such as in literature. After the First World War, the writing of D. H. Lawrence and of Henry Miller began to give voice to such social changes, although there were continued challenges to the open publication of their work. The effects of the Second World War were probably even greater, given the much broader geographical scope of the war. As people tried to resume their lives after the war, economic restrictions were a major factor, and certainly the early 1950s was a period of considerable austerity. Throughout the 1950s the overall social atmosphere was one of adherence to social conventions. Marriage was the social norm, and sexual relationships outside marriage tended to attract social hostility. There was little discussion in the media of questions relating to sexuality, and the topic was not regarded as a suitable one for conversation in normal society. Images in advertising or on television only hinted in the vaguest way at a sexual content. Where sexual relationships took place outside marriage, they were in the large part restricted to couples who had every intention of getting married. Nevertheless, as the children of the baby-boomer period grew into adolescence, they became a considerable force for social change. By the beginning of the 1960s, evidenced, for example, by the Lady Chatterley's Lover trial, there were signs that change was developing in society. Perhaps the most important changes were those in the legal and medical spheres.

The changes of the 1960s

An important example of the transition which took place between the 1950s and the 1960s was in the legal status of abortion. During the 1950s and until 1967, abortion was illegal except in certain very narrow circumstances. The Infant Life (Preservation) Act of 1929 created a criminal offence of 'child destruction' which made it, to all intents and purposes, illegal to obtain an abortion. However, the Abortion Act of 1967 changed the legal framework. Abortion was still formally illegal, but the 1967 Act created a wide range of circumstances which could support a legal defence for abortion. The Act changed the legal and ethical focus, placing much more emphasis upon the legitimacy of a woman taking decisions about what should happen to her own body. A similar situation happened in the United States six years later, with the Supreme Court judgement of 1973, citing the 14th amendment of the United States Constitution. This judgement became known as the Roe v Wade case. Many people of course opposed abortion on both moral and religious grounds. However, one can view the legalization of abortion as part of a trend away from unchallenging adherence to social norms in the area of sexuality, towards a position of much more autonomy and self-determination for women. During the 1950s the risk of unwanted pregnancy had been the major restraint on sexual behaviour, and the legalization of abortion was one factor in creating a more liberal social context. The other factor was in the development of effective contraception.

After a great deal of clinical research during the 1950s, an oral contraceptive pill to be taken once a day, became available in 1960 in the United States, and in 1961 in the United Kingdom. The contraceptive pill became almost immediately, very widely taken, and it revolutionized many aspects of life in terms of marriage and sexual activity (Watkins, 1998). Within marriage, it enabled young couples to delay having children until they felt that it was appropriate for them. They could wait until they were more economically stable, in terms, for example, of having a house. In addition, it enabled young women to become established in a professional career, which they would be able to resume after having children. In the 1950s, young women normally had children at an age before they had either extended their educational qualifications or developed a career. This made it very difficult for them to gain professional employment once they were able to return to work. The contraceptive pill was thus very influential in enhancing the employability of women, and enabling them to compete in the job market.

The 'Pill', as it became known, also separated the emotional and sexual lives of young women from the contract of marriage. In a world circumscribed by the institution of marriage, women were dependent upon men for economic and emotional security. With easy and effective contraception, which moreover was under the control of women, the latter could establish themselves as independent, free and autonomous beings. They could choose their sexual partners, whether one or many, and do this independently of any need to rely on men for financial security. The latter factor also had the result of making it much easier for a woman to leave a relationship within which she was unhappy, or in the case of marriage, to seek a divorce. A woman need no longer necessarily remain in a relationship for purely economic security, as had been the case in the 1950s.

The newly found freedom in the 1960s for women to treat sexuality as something separate from the institution of marriage became reflected in other areas of society. It became much more acceptable in the 1960s for women to display their bodies in different ways, without necessarily attracting accusations of lewdness or vulgarity. Dress designs for young women became simpler and freer throughout the decade, culminating in the miniskirt of the mid-1960s. This initially attracted considerable criticism, but very rapidly became popular. It could be seen as a general trend towards the liberation of the female body, and the right of women to display their body if they so wished. Topless bathing was possible in some parts of the world, notably at resorts such as St Tropez in the south of France, but did not spread very widely because of the threat of prosecution for indecent behaviour.

A new sexual liberalism also began to slowly pervade the arts during the 1960s. In the theatre, perhaps the most celebrated example was the musical 'Hair', which was performed in New York in early 1968. Many of the key ideas of the counterculture were included in the story line for this musical, notably the Vietnam War protest movement. However, the most contentious aspect of the musical was a very short nude scene. Censorship still existed in the English theatre in early 1968. However, later in the year Parliament passed the Theatres Act, considerably reducing the level of censorship, and enabling the play to be performed. Newspapers gradually liberalized the images which they were prepared to publish. The Sun, for example, was first published in the United Kingdom in 1964, and in 1970 it published its first photograph of a girl topless.

The cinema also became dramatically more liberal as the decade progressed. In fact, even during the 1950s there had been films which exceeded the norms of convention. The French film 'Et Dieu créa la femme' directed by Roger Vadim was released in 1956 and featured the first scenes of Brigitte Bardot naked. She and her co-star Jean-Louis Trintignant became famous around the world. In 1965 John Schlesinger directed the film 'Darling' about the life of a model in 'swinging London'. It made a star of Julie Christie. The film examined the amorality of some aspects of London society in the mid-1960s. A year later, Michaelangelo Antonioni directed 'Blow-up' a film about a London fashion photographer. It included an erotic scene involving the photographer and two young women at his studio. The French New Wave movement (La Nouvelle Vague) often reflected the new liberalism in the cinema (Sellier, 2008). The 1966 film 'Trans-Europ-Express' directed by Alain Robbe-Grillet included erotic scenes, and was perhaps typical of the New Wave in general. The Surrealist movement in cinema also explored the new boundaries of sexuality (Richardson, 2006). 'Belle de Jour' directed by Luis Buñuel in 1967 was avant-garde in imagery and also in theme, dealing as it did with the existence of a middle-class woman who worked as a prostitute for several hours each afternoon.

The developments in the media and in fashion reflected a growing independence among young women. The impact of the contraceptive pill enabled women, if not to gain, at least to move towards a form of economic equality with men. With this went a desire for emotional and sexual equality. Young women were no longer prepared to permit men to define the nature of their sexual lives. They were able to select sexual partners irrespective of any economic ties. The new generation of the 1960s was not prepared to accept what they saw as the sexual repression of the previous decade. The new sexuality was linked to a philosophy of naturalism. Sex was increasingly perceived as a natural human activity, not something to be hidden away and of which to be ever so slightly ashamed. Sexual pleasure was perceived as entirely legitimate and something to which human beings were entitled. The human body was not something to be concealed, but rather something to be celebrated. Nevertheless, the 1960s was not a decade of uninhibited sexual activity for all. Many people remained in monogamous relationships, which however were somewhat changed by the social trends mentioned earlier. This was the first generation in which young women could delay having children until they had travelled abroad, developed their career or fulfilled themselves personally in whatever way they wished. The baby-boomer generation also had the advantage that the 1960s was a period of relative economic prosperity, providing the possibility for such personal development.

It is also worth noting that during the decade, although sexually transmitted diseases of course existed, they could be clinically treated, and did not dissuade people from sexual activity. Importantly, the AIDS epidemic had not then developed. The HIV virus may have existed in humans in central Africa, in the late 1950s, and could have spread to the United States and Britain perhaps by the late 1960s. However, it had not developed into a significant problem until the early 1980s (Whiteside, 2008).

During the 1950s it was very difficult for people to obtain accurate information about sexual matters. Sex was not considered a subject for polite conversation, and young people in particular found it very difficult to obtain information. Schools provided virtually no sex education, other than mechanistic accounts of reproduction, normally set within the context of a biology lesson. Parents were probably generally reluctant to discuss sexual matters with their children, and had no access to published material to help them with the task. The information to which adolescents had access was limited to medical tomes in libraries, which dealt with pregnancy and birth, or with sexually transmitted diseases and their consequences. There were certainly no books available on the techniques of love-making.

The situation gradually began to change in the 1960s. The liberalization of sexual matters created a need for reliable advice on the practice and techniques of sex, and lead ultimately to the publication of a range of sex manuals. However, it was not until towards the end of the decade that detailed sex manuals such as Reuben (1969) became available, although even in this case there were no detailed illustrations. During this period publishers were still nervous about books which had illustrations of love-making, even if specifically aimed at public information. It was not until several years later, with, for example, the book by Comfort (1976) that illustrative matter was available in a sex manual.

The contribution of Hindu culture

Despite the reluctance during the 1960s to making sex manuals widely available, historically this had not always been the situation. Many centuries ago, books were published on the subject. However, it was often the case that such books widened their scope to include the art of relationships between men and women, with love-making being one element in this. A song in the musical Hair makes reference to a book which has long been regarded as an authoritative statement on the art of love-making – The Kama Sutra. The author of the Kama Sutra was a Brahmin named Vatsyayana who probably lived some time between the third- and sixth-century CE. Contrary to the popular myth that it is exclusively concerned with techniques of love-making, it is in fact a much more complex and sophisticated book. It is a guide to living in a sensitive way with the opposite sex, of how to live within a framework of physical and psychological love, of ways to develop affection and mutual respect with one's partner and of different approaches to the pursuit of physical pleasure.

Vatsyayana argues strongly that his book should not be used entirely as a sex manual. A person who seeks to have a balanced life should devote him or herself to moral conduct, religious duties, the pursuit of an occupation and income and finally physical pleasure. He or she should certainly not become obsessed with the idea of physical pleasure. In this way, each human being will have a balanced and fulfilled life.

The Kama Sutra was first translated into English by Sir Richard Burton and colleagues, and published for private circulation in 1883. More recent translations have been carried out by Daniélou (1994) and by Doniger and Kakar (2002). At the time of Burton's translation, Victorian society was very much opposed to the publication of any work with an erotic content, and the book had to be privately published and distributed. One consequence of this for Burton and his colleagues was that it was not possible to copyright the translation, and hence it was copied many times since 1883, and circulated privately by people. Legal restraints meant that it was not possible to publish and sell it publicly. In the 1960s, however, the situation became much more liberal in terms of the publication of such works, and Burton's translation became widely available (Vatsyayana, 1962, 1963). The 1960s counterculture thus finally had access to probably the oldest, yet most comprehensive manual on sexuality which was available.

It is also worth noting in parentheses, the enormous achievement of Victorian scholars such as Richard Burton (Rice, 1990). He travelled in many parts of the world, including India and the Arab world. He was physically extremely resilient, being the first European to see Lake Tanganyika, during an African expedition on which he became very ill. As a linguist he learned many languages, including many Indian languages and dialects. He produced well-known translations of 'The Arabian Nights' and of 'The Perfumed Garden'. Burton was an iconoclast, and challenged many of the conventions of society at the time, being in many ways a forerunner of the spirit of the 1960s.

Other travellers and writers brought back to Europe, detailed accounts of Hindu culture, and notably scholarly records of the link between eroticism and Indian religion. Notable among these was Alain Daniélou (1907–1994) who was born near Paris. He travelled to Afghanistan in 1932, and two years later to Calcutta. After numerous journeys in the East, he lived in Benaras for many years, making a detailed study of Hinduism and of Indian languages. He became fluent in speaking Hindi, and learned Sanskrit. He ultimately became a professor at Benaras Hindu University, and also made a particular study of the God Shiva, and his place in Hindu culture (Daniélou, 2003). Along with a colleague he visited the temples of Khajuraho, and made a detailed study of the erotic sculptures on the temple walls, which have now become very famous. In the mid-1950s he became head of the Library of Sanskrit documents at Madras. From the early 1960s onwards he spent much more time in Europe, and was a major figure in disseminating an understanding of Indian religion around the world.

Daniélou's knowledge of the erotic sculptures of Khajuraho ensured that they became well-known in Europe. Khajuraho is a small town in the Indian state of Madhya Pradesh. Its name is said to derive from the Sanskrit word for 'date palm', and many of these grow in the region of Khajuraho. Despite all the publicity about the sculptures, the town has remained small, having a present-day population of about 20,000. Nevertheless, the town now has an airport and several large hotels, to cater for the many visitors who come to see the temples and sculptures. The temples were probably constructed over a period of about two centuries, from approximately 950 CE to 1150 CE when the rulers of the Chandela dynasty held power in the region. For a long period of time the temples were left to decay and crumble, but in modern times the intervention of the Archaeological Survey of India has ensured that at least some of the temples are preserved. There were originally over 80 temples, although now only 22 remain in a state of reasonable preservation. The temples of Khajuraho have been declared a UNESCO world heritage site. Most of the temples are Hindu or Jain in origin. Of the numerous sandstone sculptures which adorn both the interior and the exterior of the temples, only perhaps one-tenth can be classified as erotic, and virtually all of these are on the exterior walls of the temples. Many of the sculptures simply portray everyday life in the area, during the period when the temples were being built.

The original purpose of the erotic sculptures is not known. Equally it remains somewhat unclear why the rulers of the area should decide to construct such grand temples in what was then also a relatively small town. As the sculptures with an erotic content are usually found on the outside of the temples, while sculptures of deities are normally in the temple interiors, this may suggest a distinction between the pleasures of an earthly existence and the virtues of the spiritual life. As people approach a temple they are first reminded of the pleasures of the body, but as they enter the temple to pray, they symbolically leave these behind to concentrate upon the religious life. It may also be that the erotic sculptures are a representation of the process of creating life and of the cycle of being. Alternatively, as the erotic sculptures are only a minority of the total sculptures, it may simply be that the totality of the art work represents all aspects of daily life, and the sex is but one element of that. It is also possible that the sculptures were originally related to the teaching role of the temples. The temples would originally have housed groups of young trainee monks, who were bound by a celibate life. The sculptures may have been a reminder of what they had vowed to leave behind, and of their commitment to the spiritual life. A final hypothesis is that the rulers who committed to many resources to the building of these temples may have been devotees of tantric practice. With this tradition, sexual practices are sometimes seen as a route to higher spiritual achievement.

In any case, the sculptures of Khajuraho made available to the West by such scholars as Daniélou, along with the publication of the Kama Sutra, provided young people of the counter-culture with information on sexual practices which was lacking from Western sources at the time. Perhaps ironically, however, these images represented an Indian culture of antiquity rather than the nature of Indian society in the 1960s. At the time, contemporary Indian society required adherence to very strict social norms in terms of the depiction of, and attitudes towards sex. It was in many ways much stricter than the corresponding Western cultures. Only now, particularly with the advent of the Internet, is Indian society beginning to become more liberal in Western terms.

The other main source of ideas on sexuality derived from India was the tradition of tantra (Van Lysebeth, 1995). The latter constitutes a complex set of teachings, elements of which are found in all the major religions deriving from India, particularly in Hinduism and Buddhism. Tantra began to develop during the first 300 to 500 years of the Christian era. It seeks to make use of the energy which permeates both the universe and individual human beings and to utilize this so that a person can understand the true nature of the divine and gain spiritual liberation. It is probably more accurate to view tantra, not as a single religion, but as a spiritual tradition which can be incorporated into other faiths. There is no single set of teachings, and to some extent tantra has taken on some of the features of the religion in which it is located. In order to train as an exponent of tantra, one has to become a disciple of a tantric guru and submit to an often very long period of training. Tantra has a perhaps justified reputation of being an esoteric tradition, characterized by a certain degree of secrecy in terms of the knowledge which is transmitted. It is also a tradition which is not as male-dominated as many religions, and includes a number of female gurus. Much of the training in tantra involves gaining an understanding of the diversity of rituals which are used. It is interesting that the tantric tradition is not as linked to the caste hierarchy as is mainstream Hinduism. Tantra is particularly concerned with worship of the ascetic God Shiva. It employs a variety of techniques, but yoga, meditation, mantras and the use of mandalas or religious diagrams are among the most common.

Tantra has been particularly well-known because of it approach to sexuality. Tantric practice has sometimes advocated sex as a means of attaining liberation and enlightenment. Perhaps the most famous advocate of this approach to sex was Bhagwan Shree Rajneesh (known later as Osho). In the late 1960s he publicly advocated a much more relaxed approach to sex, which brought him considerable notoriety. He also published a number of books on tantra (Osho, 2009, 2011).

Thus, during the 1960s, young people had access to several sources which espoused different and much more liberal approaches to sexuality. The material from India was, as we have seen, often historical, and did not reflect the rather conservative attitudes of the then Indian society.

The equality of women

In the West, as the 1960s progressed there was a gradual liberalization in terms of sexual attitudes. The first Playboy club opened in the United States in 1960. It gradually became more acceptable for young women to wear skimpier clothes in public. There were fewer restrictions upon the presentation of the female form in film, television, newspapers and in advertising. The Miss World contest first appeared on BBC television in 1959, to considerable enthusiasm. However, a decade later in 1970 there were protests by feminists when the contest was held at the Royal Albert Hall in London, reflecting a gradual changing of attitudes towards the end of the 1960s. Earlier in the decade, it is probably true to say that the new liberalism in female dress had been broadly welcomed and had led to an entirely new approach to fashion. However, towards the end of the decade some women began to view the new liberalism as not entirely positive for women. They began to argue that women were often presented in ways which focused upon their appearance rather than upon their intelligence, careers and achievements. Attitudes to sexuality, could they argued be perceived as a form of male oppression which ultimately exploited rather than liberated women. The increasing emphasis upon freedom for women resulted in the first Women's Liberation conference at Ruskin College, Oxford in 1970.

However, earlier in the 1960s there had been important initiatives regarding women's equality. In the United States, President John F. Kennedy established the Commission on the Status of Women in 1961. During the Second World War women had of necessity needed to take a more proactive role in the economy, and had worked more than effectively in areas normally considered the exclusive province of men. This progress had been somewhat lost after the war, yet the United States and the United Kingdom were now beginning to appreciate the potential contribution of women to the workforce, quite apart from the ethical arguments for women's equality. The Commission reported in 1963 on the widespread inequality experienced by women in the United States, and argued strongly for legislation and strategies to work towards the equality of women in society.

In the same year in the United States, the Equal Pay Act was passed, establishing the principle that men and women should receive the same remuneration, when they were performing similar work. In the United Kingdom, Parliament passed an Equal Pay Act in 1970, which set out to achieve similar goals. In the United States, 1964 saw the establishment of the Equal Employment Opportunity Commission which set out to tackle the issue of race and gender discrimination in the general field of employment. A decade later, the Sex Discrimination Act 1975 was passed in the United Kingdom. At the same time, the Equal Opportunities Commission was formed with a statutory responsibility to promote gender equality.

Gay equality

Although the 1960s saw a liberalization generally towards sexual matters, this was less so in relation to homosexuality. The overriding picture in the United States was one of antipathy towards gay people, and of, for example, police raids on bars which were popular with the gay community. Society often appeared to want to marginalize gay people, so that they were unseen and not heard. In the months preceding the 1964 World's Fair in New York, strenuous efforts were made to close down gay bars, and to make the gay community much less visible. This general approach broadly continued throughout the decade, until the Stonewall Inn riots in June 1969 marked something of a change in attitudes. One year later, on 28 June 1970, the first anniversary of the riots, a Gay Pride march was held for the first time in New York City. From then on, there was a gradual, although slow, liberalization of attitudes towards the gay community.

In India, the general reluctance to talk about sexual matters throughout the 1960s and onwards applied equally to homosexuality. Nevertheless, there is evidence that in ancient societies in India, attitudes to homosexuality may have been as accepting as they were to other forms of sexual activity. There are references in some Hindu scriptures which note the existence of homosexuality, and there are some images at Khajuraho which clearly show same-sex love. The Kama Sutra acknowledges that men may have profound feelings for each other, and that this may indeed lead to marriage. These references therefore suggest that in ancient Hindu society same-sex relations were considered as simply another form of sexual activity to heterosexual relations. Some of these references may have come to the attention of members of the gay community in the West, although the fact that they were not particularly publicized in India suggests that their distribution would have been on a limited scale.

However, what may have been more influential for visitors to India in the 1960s was that India has for many centuries supported communities of gay men who have a distinctive lifestyle, albeit on the margins of Indian society. Probably the best-known of these groups are the *hijras* who live predominantly in northern India. These men, who dress as women and wear makeup and jewellery, earn a living as dancers and musicians and also as sex workers. Some decide to undergo voluntary castration when they join the community, although this is apparently not a universal practice. They all belong to a single, identifiable caste, and are a recognized, although not socially accepted, group in society. They have, over the years, been subjected to quite extensive discrimination and indeed hostility and aggression. Nevertheless, they continue to exist as a distinct social group and have won some concessions from formal Indian society. In contemporary India, when completing some administrative forms, for example, they are permitted to define themselves as a 'third gender' rather than to restrict their self-definition to being either male or female. There are signs that Indian society is slowly becoming more accepting of the gay community, and a major event in this regard was the 2009 decision by the Delhi High Court to make homosexuality between consenting adults legal.

The 1960s was thus a time of beginning to explore new gender roles, and of challenging existing social norms. For some, progress in society may have seemed painfully slow, but those early changes enabled people today, for example, to be openly gay in the media, and for us to have what are now taken-for-granted institutions such as mixed halls of residence in universities.

Further reading

Feuerstein, G. (1998) *Tantra: Path of Ecstasy*. Boston, MA: Shambhala.
Giardina, C. (2010) *Freedom for Women: Forging the Women's Liberation Movement, 1953–1970*. Gainsville, FL: University Press of Florida.
Pechilis, K. (ed.) (2004) *The Graceful Guru: Hindu Female Gurus in India and the United States*. New York: Oxford University Press.
Vatsyayana (2012) *The Kama Sutra of Vatsyayana*. Los Angeles: Empire Books.
White, K. (2001) *Sexual Liberation, or Sexual License?: The American Revolt against Victorianism*. Lanham, MD: Ivan R. Dee.

9

Ashrams, communes and the hippy lifestyle

Summary

There is clearly a long history of communal living in the West, whether monastic, or utopian such as with Winstanley, but in the 1960s there was an expansion of the self-sufficiency movement, as a reaction to urban consumerism. This was often, although not exclusively, associated with a hippy lifestyle. The same period saw the establishment of a number of religious movements in India, such as the ISKCON in 1965, and the growth of the Rajneesh (now Osho) movement from the early 1970s onwards. Such groups established religious communities or ashrams both in India and the West, and often sought to recruit young Western members. Other longer established groups such as the Swaminarayan movement founded temples or ashrams in the West, for example, the first London Swaminarayan temple in 1970. This chapter examines the expansion of Hindu organizations in the West in the 1960s and 1970s, and the impetus which that gave to the commune movement.

Introduction

One of the key features of Hindu culture is its diversity. It encompasses a very wide range of schools of thought and of philosophies. Religious rituals and practices range from many different types of asceticism which are physically harmful to the body to extended periods of meditation. Religious practice is accompanied by many different types of bodily adornment and dress, which usually indicate a particular religious denomination or affinity. Some Hindus live completely solitary and isolated lives for many years at a time, while others live in small groups or in monasteries or ashrams. Many Hindus live a conventional householder life. Some attend a temple regularly, others do not. Some read the scriptures regularly, while others do not. Some go on long pilgrimages to holy places, while others do not. In addition, there is no religious hierarchy which operates across Hinduism, to ensure an accepted body of knowledge or norms of behaviour. People will tend to follow their caste rules, or the norms associated with the particular sect to which they traditionally belong. Although such caste or sect strictures impose some limits, there remains a great deal of potential variety of religious practice for the Hindu.

This was very different from the type of society found in Western Europe and the United States in the 1950s and early 1960s. Here the norm remained the nuclear family, with the expectation that this would be perpetuated in subsequent generations. However, the developing counter-culture of the 1960s rejected this type of formality, and particularly sought the kind of communal life which was found in India. Communal life, whether in urban squats or in rural communes, had a number of attractions for young people in the 1960s. They were first of all cheaper, enabling members to share resources and food, and in the case of rural communities, growing their own vegetables. Importantly, they offered the opportunity to organize the community in a completely democratic way and to avoid the less-desirable consequences of a traditional hierarchy. Communities could take advantage of the different skills of members in order to avoid the necessity of having to sell their labour in a traditional work relationship. Communes offered the possibility of a simpler, non-exploitative lifestyle which appeared to link well with the other values of the counter-culture.

When young people travelled to India they often managed to find accommodation in religious communes or ashrams, and were clearly influenced by the style of life. These no doubt helped to shape some of the communities which then arose in the West.

The ashram

Ashrams in India vary enormously from consisting of a religious teacher sitting under a rudimentary shelter to a large and complex, bureaucratic institution with very large financial resources. As there is such diversity among ashrams in India, it is probably useful to try to describe what Max Weber termed the 'ideal type' of institution. In this way we can attempt to identify the key characteristics which most people might associate with an ashram.

To start with an ashram has a social function. It may exist in a fairly isolated location, but it will be sufficiently near a village or other form of habitation, in order to provide a service to those living in the vicinity. An ashram will always have one person who is the spiritual head of the community. This is true whether there is simply one guru living in a cave, or several hundred people living in a fairly complex community. The guru will normally act as a spiritual adviser to the local communities, but will also provide advice on a range of secular matters. People will visit the ashram in order to consult the guru, or to make an offering of food or flowers to the deity associated with the ashram. The guru receives the offerings on behalf of the deity, but clearly the offerings enable the guru to sustain his or her existence at the ashram. This is particularly so in the case of a guru who lives in solitude. In this way, there is an existence of mutual support between the guru and the local community.

As ashrams developed during the 1960s in order to cater for the increasing numbers of Westerners who were interested in Hindu spirituality, many became wealthy organizations. This was not in itself a bad thing, as long as the money was used for charitable purposes. The spirit of an ashram is that income should either be used to further religious activities or to improve the quality of life of people living near the ashram. This might include improvements in educational or medical facilities.

As ashrams expanded, sometimes more and more money was spent on the infrastructure, making visitor accommodation, for example, more and more luxurious. The spirit of an ashram is that it should be a simple, unpretentious environment, so that there are no distractions from the spiritual life. Tobacco and alcohol would not be permitted, and the meals would consist of simple, vegetarian food. There is also an argument that ashrams should not charge fees either for religious instruction, yoga classes or for accommodation. Rather a voluntary donation system should be adopted, whereby residents can make private donations according to their means. They would also be invited to spend part of their day in carrying out work around the ashram, such as preparing meals, tending the vegetable gardens or cleaning premises.

Traditionally in India, when a religious teacher established an ashram, it would normally be in a location recommended by his or her own guru. This would very often be near a river or a lake, since it is the custom for a guru to rise in the morning and immediately bathe. This would then be followed by the practice of yoga asanas, meditation and the offering of prayers to the rising sun. The early morning hours are considered particularly auspicious and appropriate for spiritual practice. The organization of the ashram would usually be linked to the cycle of day and night. Activities begin before dawn, and ashram members would sleep shortly after sunset. It is the tradition in yoga practice to manage with only a few hours sleep.

The guru would normally have a chela or disciple to assist him in the ashram. Many ashrams simply consist of the guru and his chela. The latter looks after the day-to-day needs of the guru, preparing food, cleaning the ashram and bringing wood for the dhuna or ritual fire which is usually present in all ashrams. Importantly, the disciple is also serving a form of religious apprenticeship, so that eventually he will leave his guru, and become an independent teacher.

Nowadays some ashrams may be sufficiently large to support a religious hierarchy, with a senior teacher, and a number of other gurus to assist the principal guru. A large ashram may organize yoga sessions, religious education classes for children of lay members, prayer services and religious tuition of various kinds. The gurus may be in demand to visit other ashrams to give talks, or to visit secular institutions to give lectures or seminars.

However, in the simplest type of traditional ashram, the guru would live in say, a cave in a hillside above a village, or in a basic self-constructed hut. Nevertheless, in all ashrams, the basic principles should apply. These are the giving of spiritual tuition, and the providing of service to the community, in exchange for the guru receiving simple donations of food to sustain his or her life. Even the most simple of ashrams was, however, part of an informal network of lay people and other gurus. The guru might not remain in his ashram all of the year but may depart on a pilgrimage or a visit to his own guru, in order to sustain and renew his spiritual life. Equally he would receive visitors who may stay for a few days, to pray or meditate together, and to hold religious discussions. Although a guru may spend a good deal of time alone, he or she would remain part of an informal network of members of the same religious denomination.

The Hindu teacher

It is worth noting that within this Hindu system of a guru teaching within an ashram, there exists a significant difference from the religious life of the West. In India there has not traditionally been a figure such as the Archbishop of Canterbury or the Pope, who acts as an administrative and spiritual leader of an entire church and often interprets the teachings of that church. The Hindu system is much more fragmented, with each guru offering their own unique insights into Hinduism, albeit within the same broad scriptural context. Hindu teachers can thus be very different in terms of style and emphasis (Forsthoefel and Humes, 2005). Most gurus are part of a spiritual lineage. That is they would have been initiated and taught by their own guru, and he or she in turn would have been taught by their guru. This lineage may also exist within a particular Hindu sect or denomination, which is named after a specific historical teacher of note.

For Westerners coming to India in the 1960s and searching for a guru, it was somewhat difficult to select an ashram and a teacher. Some gurus specifically set out to attract Westerners to their ashrams. However, there was always the danger that a cult of the guru developed, perhaps to the exclusion of concentrating on the teachings. Some Westerners, perhaps in a desire to absorb the teachings of Hinduism, became overly committed to a guru and his organization, with the resultant danger that they might become indoctrinated or indeed vulnerable to the demands of the organization.

This by no means, however, represented a universal picture of the relationship of Westerners with Indian gurus in the 1960s. Some teachers rejected the notion of a guru who transmitted a particular doctrine, and placed themselves at the head of an organizational hierarchy. Notable among such teachers was Jiddu Krishnamurti (1895–1986). As a child and then as a young man, Krishnamurti was reared and educated within the confines of the Theosophical society, members of which believed that he was destined to become a world teacher. He was educated in the hope that he would take on this role. However, in 1929 he found that he could no longer accept this notion of his destiny, and he decided to sever his formal links with the Theosophical Society. From then on, he became an independent spiritual teacher, who eschewed all links and association with any particular religious group.

This was a fundamental element in Krishnamurti's teaching. He did not believe that spiritual insight and truth could be gained by a human-created organization. He felt that 'truth' as a concept was so complex and universal an idea that mere human beings were incapable of devising an organization or a method which could aspire to identifying it. It was thus both inappropriate and futile to create a 'religion' or 'spiritual system' which could purport to finding truth. Equally, a mere human being could not purport or aspire to being a spiritual guide for finding the truth. This would be a false claim. Hence, he argued that the whole concept of a guru was intrinsically flawed. Krishnamurti himself certainly did not wish to be thought of as a guru. Moreover, he did not want people to think of themselves as his disciples. Those people who sought spiritual insights should not in his view subscribe to a particular set of teachings or follow a particular teacher. They should simply reflect upon what they see as 'truth' and do their best to understand it. Ultimately, he saw his principal purpose as helping human beings to be free (Krishnamurti, 1995, 1999, 2010). This he interpreted as not attaching themselves to any one ideological or religious perspective, but remaining independent and autonomous in terms of their view of the world. He carried this perspective over into his concept of education. He wanted children and young people to be intellectually free to see the world in whatever way they wished. He did not want them to feel trapped within one particular world view, which would limit their vision and potential to see the world in new and novel ways. He established a number of centres for the study of his work, such as at Brockwood Park in England and at Chennai in India. However he was adamant that these centres should encourage people to think autonomously, and that neither his teachings nor he himself should develop into any sort of cult or religious doctrine.

A rather different type of ashram was established under the auspices of the Bengali mystic, Aurobindo Ghose (1872–1950). He spent most of his formative years being educated in England, notably at Cambridge University. When he returned to India he became influential in the Indian independence movement, before settling in the former French colony of Puducherry. It was here in 1926 that Sri Aurobindo established the Sri Aurobindo Ashram which was devoted to the practice of his teachings known as Integral Yoga. He was aided in the gradual development of the ashram by one of his followers, a French woman named Mira Richards (1878–1973). Aurobindo named her 'The Mother', and this was how she was subsequently known. In 1968, with the support of UNESCO, The Mother founded what was to become a spiritually based community called Auroville, a few kilometres to the north of Puducherry. It is not an ashram as such, although Sri Aurobindo's teachings permeate the community. Auroville has approximately 2,000 current residents. It is organized with a 'green', environmentally sustainable philosophy in mind, and has a number of small enterprises and businesses within its confines.

Aurobindo's concept of Integral Yoga started with the premise that all existence in the universe can be regarded as part of the same spiritual force (Aurobindo, 1993, 2006). He considered that there was one force controlling the universe, and that the ultimate purpose of humanity was to re-integrate themselves with that force. Aurobindo's goal was that every human being should be helped to transform their consciousness, and become merged with the universal spiritual force. Importantly, Aurobindo felt that his methods would enable people through a process of spiritual evolution to achieve this goal.

A number of study centres were established around the world, inspired by, or related to the teachings of Sri Aurobindo. In 1950, for example, Frederick Spiegelberg, a professor at Stanford University, and Alan Watts wanted to establish an institute of higher education in California which would be devoted to the study of Asian religions. They asked Sri Aurobindo if he could suggest a noted authority on Indian religions, who might be willing to support them. Aurobindo suggested Dr Haridas Chaudhuri, who was then the head of the philosophy department at a college in Bengal.

Dr Chaudhuri subsequently established the Cultural Integration Fellowship, which in 1968 became first the California Institute of Asian Studies, and then the California Institute of Integral Studies. The latter is now an accredited higher education institution and has diversified from its original rationale into a range of subject areas.

The key principles of Sri Aurobindo, namely a respect for the values inherent in different cultures and faiths, and the idea of gradually developing oneself spiritually were very attractive to young Westerners in the 1960s, and the Puducherry ashram acted as a magnet for many young travellers at that time. This idea of an informal community of people linked together by adherence to a set of moral, religious or other ideals, and trying to sustain a communal, cooperative and democratic lifestyle, was something taken back to the West by early visitors to India in the 1960s.

Another example of an ashram in India, which gradually developed into a worldwide Hindu organization, was the Divine Life Society established in Rishikesh. This ashram was founded by a spiritual teacher named Swami Sivananda (1887–1963). He originally trained as a doctor and worked for a number of years in Malaysia, where he cared for the large community of poor Indian migrant workers. Swami Sivananda tried to combine the key teachings of a variety of schools of yoga and to integrate them into his personal approach to yoga. He was also a prolific author, writing many books on yoga and spirituality (Sivananda, 2005).

In 1957 he suggested to one of his disciples, Swami Vishnudevananda (1927–1993), that he travel to the United States and Europe in order to try to establish ashrams there. One of the results was the Sivananda Yoga Vedanta Centre in London. Other centres were established in different parts of the world. Swami Vishnudevananda (1960) published the best-selling book 'The Complete Illustrated Book of Yoga'. In 1969 he also initiated a course of training for yoga teachers. The Sivananda centres around the world now offer a range of activities, including tuition in yoga and vedanta, with some centres offering opportunities to go on pilgrimages to holy sites in the Himalayas.

Communal living

The rise of the counter-culture during the 1960s saw an increasing critique of the institution of the family. The essence of the argument of many young people was that the nuclear family was seen as being a product of the capitialist system of work. The concept of the family as seen by the young people of the 1960s was of a father who went out to work, often trapped within a job which he did not like, and of a mother who stayed at home to look after children and felt trapped within a role which offered no opportunities for personal development. In the view of those young people, the family created the kind of environment within which there were few opportunities for their parents to self-actualize, and generally young people were rather reluctant to place themselves in the situation of their parents. Equally, with the rise of a feminist consciousness, the family was seen as an environment which was potentially oppressive for women. There tended to be such strict role differentiation within the typical family that husband and wife often did not appreciate the nature of their partner's role. Men often did not involve themselves in domestic chores or childcare, and women may have had little experience of the pressures and frustrations of working life outside the home.

Young people also often saw the family as obsessed by what they considered to be limited and restricted goals. To them, the over-riding goal of the family appeared to be to acquire more material wealth, often conceptualized as greater wealth and more material possessions than one's neighbour. Many young people perceived this as a very limited horizon, ultimately pointless and destructive of any possibility of people fulfilling their true potential. Many young people therefore sought to experiment with other forms of relationship, whether a variant of the established family pattern, of an entirely different structure such as a commune.

The different types of ashram in India offered a stimulus to this type of development, demonstrating a range of models around which human relationships could be structured. Most communes which developed in the West during the 1960s evolved around a particular theme. Many young people were conscious that it should in principle be less expensive to live communally, and hence economic factors were important. Other communes were structured around spiritual or political ideas, while some placed ecological and environmental factors at the centre of their lifestyle. Sexual liberation and peace were other important factors, while some young people simply wanted to live out what they saw as a counter-cultural existence of psychedelia and drug taking.

There were, however, some principles which were found in many communes in the West. Many young people had experienced the nature of paternal autocracy in a nuclear family, and wanted to live in a more democratic and participative organization. Instead of living in a competitive environment where each family often tried to exceed their neighbours in a capitalist culture, many young people wanted to live in an organization where resources were communal. Finally, there was already in the 1960s the beginnings of an environmental consciousness, and an awareness that unrestricted industrial expansion would harm the ecology of the planet. Young people were beginning to see that there were alternatives, and that one of these was to live in a communal setting which was in harmony with its natural surroundings.

One of the earliest communes established in the 1960s was 'Drop City' in southern Colorado, USA. It was founded in 1965 and was well-known for its accommodation which consisted of domes made from discarded and waste materials. The domes were influenced by the philosophy of Buckminster Fuller (Fuller, 2008; Sieden, 1989). The commune was never large, having about 20 people as permanent residents. The commune members were involved in creative projects of various kinds, including art and theatre. There were also projects emanating from their experience in building domes for residential purposes. Drop City received a lot of publicity in the media, and many hippies and others visited the site. This proved to be counter-productive for the commune members, as they had set out to establish a secluded and peaceful community. The number of visitors probably lead to the ultimate demise of the community, and the commune closed in 1973.

The Twin Oaks Community was established in Virginia, USA in 1967 and still operates today. It has an optimum number of about 100 residents, and there is a carefully thought-out strategy to ensure that everyone contributes to the work programme needed to ensure the survival of the commune. The community has established small business enterprises such as the manufacture and selling of hammocks, which create a regular income for the upkeep of the commune. Twin Oaks has not been created around any specific religion or belief system, and members are attached to a variety of different faiths. The main themes which can be identified within the organizational structure include non-violence and participative decision making. Twin Oaks is an experiment in living within which green issues and self-sustainability are very important. Calculations have shown that commune members do not use as much energy and other resources as is typical in the United States. The commune maintains contact with the external society, but tries to sustain a simpler, rural lifestyle, by for example, not having access to television. While the governance of the community is participative and democratic, there are also detailed regulations governing, for example, the admission of new members to the community.

One of the most celebrated Hindu ashrams and temples in the West is Bhaktivedanta Manor near Watford, in Hertfordshire, England. This grand house set in 17 acres of land, was originally purchased by George Harrison and then donated to ISKCON in 1973 as a headquarters in the United Kingdom. After the Beatles visited Rishikesh in the Himalayas, George Harrison continued his interest in Indian mysticism and wanted to help ISKCON as their former headquarters in central London had become too small for their purposes. Swami Prabhupada, the founder of ISKCON, had first come to England in 1969 to support the organization. The subsequent expulsion of the Asian community from Uganda in 1972 resulted in many new members of the organization, and the opening of Bhaktivedanta Manor the following year provided a base from which ISKCON could grow.

ISKCON is part of the Vaishnava school of Hinduism and is famous for its members chanting the so-called Maha Mantra or Hare Krishna Mantra. Bhaktivedanta Manor arranges numerous events on Hindu festival days, puts on many courses including long-term training for monks who want to become priests and organizes tuition in Hinduism. In daily life it adheres to the key principles of Hindu culture such as vegetarianism. This is based on the doctrine of ahimsa or non-violence. This philosophy argues that it is morally wrong to terminate the life of an animal, before it has died naturally. If an animal were to be killed then according to the principle of karma, it would need to find a similar animal in which it could be reincarnated, so that its soul could continue its natural evolution to a higher state.

The community at Bhaktivedanta Manor also keeps a number of cows, which are regarded as sacred in the Hindu tradition. The cow is considered holy because in an agrarian society such as rural India it produces milk and other products which sustain life. In a society increasingly concerned with having a bio-sustainable lifestyle, the use of cows and oxen have some advantages over mechanized agricultural methods.

Bhaktivedanta Manor tries to maintain a traditional Vaishnava approach to life, including the practice of meditation and the study of the Vedas. Other ashrams adopt a more multi-cultural and multi-faith approach to their spiritual life. The Community of the Many Names of God lives at the Skanda Vale ashram in Wales. The principal religious orientation of the community is Hindu, but there is an acceptance of the validity of other religious traditions to practise at Skanda Vale. The approach of the community is that all the world's main faiths are part of, and point to a universal spiritual experience. The Skanda Vale organization was founded by Guru Sri Subramanium who was born in Sri Lanka in 1929. The scripture which inspires much of the work of the Community is the Bhagavad Gita, and Krishna's approach to bhakti yoga. The Community established its own monastic order in 1976, and in 2004 it founded a hospice. A strong moral element permeates the activities at Skanda Vale. The ashram does not charge for food or accommodation for visitors, but there is a system of anonymous donations whereby people can contribute what they feel appropriate. The ashram, in keeping with the philosophy of ahimsa looks after different animals, many of which have been rescued from unfortunate circumstances. A considerable amount of food is donated to Skanda Vale, and a proportion is often given to food banks or donated to Third World countries.

Some Hindu organizations which have become well-established in the West can trace back their lineage over 200 years. Such is the organization built around the teachings of the man who became known as Swaminarayan.

He was born in Uttar Pradesh in 1781 and died in 1830. He wrote a book on ethical behaviour, called the Shikshapatri, which is still widely read among the present-day Swaminarayan organization. During his lifetime he was a major social reformer. Most notably he argued strongly for the rights of women and girls, and drew attention to many inequalities inherent in their lives. Female infanticide was unfortunately widely practised, largely due to the excessive cost of dowries. Swaminarayan contributed towards this cost in order to try to minimize the fundamental cause of female infanticide. He also created almshouses to help the large numbers of poor people in his area.

The organization which Swaminarayan founded is now known as Bochasanwasi Shri Akshar Purushottam Swaminarayan Sanstha (BAPS) and its leader is Pramukh Swami Maharaj. The organization has something in the region of 20 million members. The first distinct BAPS temple was opened in 1970 in Islington, London. However, during the early 1990s planning and work commenced on the construction of a purpose-built Hindu temple, which would become the Shri Swaminarayan Mandir, at Neasden, London. This was opened in 1995. This temple was the first to be constructed outside of India on this scale, and employing traditional stone-carving techniques. Specially selected limestone and marble were transported to India from Europe, and carved by expert craftsmen. The many thousands of individual pieces were then coded, before the transportation to England. The temple, including an ashram, reflects traditional Hindu designs and patterns of worship.

Patterns of Hindu ashram life thus provided one model which influenced Western experiments in communal living in the 1960s. Many young people in that decade were keen to break away from the patterns of life established by their parents, and communes appeared to be one way in which this could be achieved. Nevertheless, many young people were to discover that communal living was not necessarily utopia. Any group of people living together had to take decisions about organization, management and indeed political structures. On the one hand, if a commune opted for a decentralized anarchistic model, then it often proved difficult to sustain any form of workable organization. On the other hand, if a commune submitted itself to the whims of an autocratic leader, whether religiously inspired or not, then it was also frequently difficult to sustain. The alternative was to attempt to recreate a range of political structures and mechanisms, which would ensure efficient governance, with at the same time participative decision-making by community members. To attain this normally required sophisticated political skills on the part of members. Some of the potential problems of hippy communes in the 1960s are alluded to in part of the 1969 film 'Easy Rider', directed by Dennis Hopper, where visions of a rural, communal idyll prove somewhat problematic to achieve.

Further reading

Dwyer, G. and Cole, R. J. (eds) (2007) *The Hare Krishna Movement: Forty Years of Chant and Change.* London: I.B. Tauris.

Eugster, S. L. (2007) *Notes from Nethers: Growing up in a Sixties Commune.* Chicago: Academy Chicago Publishers.

Goldberg, P. (2010) *American Veda From Emerson and the Beatles to Yoga and Meditation: How Indian Spirituality Changed the West.* New York: Harmony.

Guest, T. (2005) *My Life in Orange: Growing Up with the Guru.* Boston, MA: Mariner Books.

Krystal, P. (1994) *Sai Baba: The Ultimate Experience.* San Francisco, CA: Weiser Books.

Matus, T. (2009) *Ashram Diary: In India with Bede Griffiths.* Ropley, UK: John Hunt Publishing.

Williams, R. B. (2001) *An Introduction to Swaminarayan Hinduism.* Cambridge: Cambridge University Press.

10

Ayurvedic medicine and naturalistic well-being

Summary

In the 1960s, there was a growing interest in the environment, in ecology and in a return to a way of life which was more in harmony with nature. Many people in empathy with the counter-culture wanted to move from an urban to a rural lifestyle, to adopt a more holistic approach to life and to embrace such ideas as vegetarianism and homeopathic, herbal remedies. Quite apart from a long tradition of natural herbal healing in Europe, they found a natural affinity with the long-standing approach of Ayurvedic medicine in India. This chapter examines the nature of Ayurvedic medicine and the influence it had on the naturalistic philosophy of the counter-culture.

Introduction

There are often two consequences in society following major conflicts. On the one hand there is usually an expansion in industrial activity to help the reconstruction of urban areas, and on the other hand some people react to the urban destruction of warfare by re-locating to the peace of the country. In 'Goodbye To All That' Robert Graves describes such a move, partly motivated no doubt by the need for tranquillity, following the psychological trauma of the First World War trenches (Graves, 2000).

During the transition from the 1950s to the 1960s, a similar rurally oriented movement gradually gathered pace. After a long period of food rationing, it was motivated by such ideals as self-sufficiency in food, natural organic farming without the use of fertilizers, a 'whole-food' diet and a lifestyle which avoided the pollution of the environment. It was sometimes described as a 'back-to-the-land' movement. As the decade of the 1960s moved on, there was an increasing realization that all human beings have a vested interest in the state of the planet, and that as such we have a shared responsibility for our ecosystem. It is perhaps no small coincidence that the word 'flower' figured in the description of the 1960s hippies as 'flower children' and their philosophy as 'flower power'.

It is also interesting that where young people sought to live out a rural lifestyle, the role of men was naturally transformed. Instead of men disappearing to a factory for the working day, leaving women at home with the children, men and women needed to work together, sharing responsibility for agricultural and home chores. The alternative lifestyles of the 1960s would thus help to create a paradigm within which it was much more acceptable for men to participate in home duties, and even to take full responsibility for them. Within such a paradigm men would take a full role in the rearing of children, being seen as a supportive figure in the family rather than as an aloof and distant figure of authority.

Thoreau, 'Walden' and Hindu philosophy

When people look back through history for inspiration to guide them on a return to a rural lifestyle, it is rarely that the writing of Henry David Thoreau (1817–1862) does not occupy a central position. Thoreau was born in Concord, Massachusetts and was one of the early advocates of the importance of respecting the natural world. He had a very spiritual outlook on life, and interestingly was very attracted to the philosophy of the Bhagavad Gita. Thoreau's philosophy of life, and in particular his political philosophy, had, in their turn, a great influence upon Mahatma Gandhi.

At the age of 28 years, Thoreau decided to fulfil his interest in nature and the simple, self-sufficient life, by living a solitary, reclusive life in the forest. He constructed a small, simple dwelling near Walden Pond in Massachusetts, and then lived there for just over two years, as a form of exploration of a simple, naturalistic existence. Then, in 1854 he published 'Walden; or Life in the Woods', an account and analysis of that period. The book contains elements of autobiography, in addition to much reflection upon nature, spiritual matters, vegetarianism and basic living (Thoreau, 1962). In the book Thoreau mentions the Hindu scriptures, and is clearly familiar with yoga and some of its practices.

Thoreau, along with Ralph Waldo Emerson (1803–1882), was a key member of the philosophical movement known as 'Transcendentalism'

(Buell, 2006). This school of thought developed in the United States in the early part of the 1800s and emphasized the need for people to develop their own individual destiny. The Transcendentalists were generally opposed to the effects of corporate society, organizational structures and organized religion.

As a confirmed individualist Thoreau firmly believed that people should protest peacefully when they came across what they perceived as injustice. In political terms he was a strong believer in the capacity of individuals to order their own lives. In 1849 he published 'Civil Disobedience', an essay in which he argued that the citizens of a state should maintain a sense of their own conscience, despite any policy which their government might be promulgating at the time. He was motivated to propose such a policy because of his own firmly held views in opposition to slavery. This essay was read by Mahatma Gandhi, and strongly influenced him in his campaign for Indian independence.

The American poet Walt Whitman (1819–1892) was very much in sympathy with the philosophy of Transcendentalism and had a deep sense of empathy with the natural world. Like Thoreau, he was also familiar with Hindu philosophy and ideas. In his book 'Leaves of Grass' was included the poem 'Passage to India' which made mention of the Ganges, Brahma, Sanskrit and the Vedas.

Sustainability

After the death of Thoreau, the ideals developed in his cabin beside Walden Pond were not lost, but re-developed by others in succeeding generations. In 1954 Helen and Scott Nearing published a book which was to act as an inspiration for the back-to-the-soil movement of the 1960s. It was called 'Living the Good Life', and discussed the kind of principles which supported their self-sustaining existence on a farm in Maine (Nearing and Nearing, 1973).

An idea which became more and more popular in the 1960s was that of holism. The younger generation, in particular, was beginning to accept the idea that all human beings contributed towards our collective existence. Although it was theoretically possible to analyse any organism or even inorganic system into its constituent elements, ultimately it was the collective function of the whole which was important. This idea was not unconnected with the spiritual approach of Vedanta, within which each human being is perceived as possessing a fragment of the total divinity of the universe.

The Gaia hypothesis, first proposed by James Lovelock in the mid-1960s and developed further by Lynn Margulis, suggests that the earth is a large homeostatic system (Lovelock, 1995). Over many millions of years, the different biological, chemical and physical systems of the earth have reached a position of dynamic equilibrium which is capable of supporting life. When one of these systems is caused to change in some way, the homeostatic balance is threatened. The system has to re-adjust in order to continue providing the basic supporting elements for life. This argument provides a means of understanding the importance of not threatening the balance of the earth's biological system. In particular, it points to the inadvisability of consuming or changing one's aspect of the earth's natural resources with the concomitant homeostatic imbalance.

As the human body was also a refined, homeostatic system, it seemed to many in the 1960s that the most appropriate type of medical treatment was one which disturbed the equilibrium of the body as little as possible. While the development of new types of pharmaceuticals, and surgical advances such as the first heart transplant by Dr Christiaan Barnard in 1967, seemed to support the scientific-interventionist approach to medicine, some felt that there were alternatives. There were those who began to advocate lifestyle changes as a better approach to health and the use of more natural remedies. There was thus a gradual movement in favour of naturopathy, homeopathy, yoga practice, vegetarianism and herbalism. Among these 'alternative' approaches to health, one of the most popular was Ayurvedic medicine (Lad, 1999).

Ayurveda

Ayurveda, like many other aspects of Indian culture, started to become better known in the West following post-war immigration, and the increasing numbers of Western travellers returning from India in the 1960s. The term may be translated from the Sanskrit as approximately 'knowledge about life' and embraces the totality of traditional medical techniques which have evolved from Vedic culture. Much of the medicine practised in the West consists of trying to diagnose and treat illnesses and disease once they have arisen. Traditional Indian approaches, however, focus much more on encouraging a balanced lifestyle as a means of sustaining health.

Ayurveda can thus be considered a holistic approach to health and medicine. It considers all of the main aspects of the life of a person, when diagnosing and treating a problem. This might typically involve psychological, emotional and social aspects of a person's life, as well as physiological or metabolic issues. In some university medical courses in India, Western conventional medicine and Ayurveda are taught alongside each other as complementary approaches.

Many of the techniques of Ayurveda appear rather unconventional when compared with Western medicine. They include rinsing the mouth with coconut oil; the pouring of oil or coconut water on to the forehead (a technique known as shirodhara); dropping liquids into the navel and head massage, known as champi (Dalgleish and Hart, 2007). The general nature of these techniques and treatments makes it more difficult to investigate them empirically when compared with the approaches of Western medicine.

Ayurveda has been studied and practised for over two millennia. Two main written works, the Sushruta Samhita and the Charaka Samhita, are in effect textbooks of Ayurveda, and date from approximately 200 CE. However, they were probably originally written at least several hundred years prior to that. The Sushruta Samhita is based upon the work of an Ayurvedic doctor named Sushruta, who lived in Varanasi.

The Sushruta Samhita covers a wide range of medical practice, including much information on what was known about surgery at the time. It details treatments for disease, and medication, and lists a number of surgical techniques including the stitching of wounds. Sushruta appears to have tried different types of anaesthetics including alcohol and cannabis for use during medical operations. The Sushruta Samhita was translated into Arabic and was known in Europe during the Renaissance.

The Charaka Samhita includes information on anatomy and strategies for improving one's general health. It places great emphasis upon the empirical analysis of diseases, based upon visual data, and upon information provided by the patient. It emphasizes the importance of encouraging the patient to provide as careful a description of their medical problem as possible. During treatment, the Charaka Samhita places a great deal of stress upon cleanliness, and upon medical staff demonstrating empathy for the patient.

Ayurveda tends to treat the human body as an integrated whole. In a healthy person there is the assumption that the physical and psychological systems of the body are working effectively in unison. Ayurveda postulates the existence of three main energy sources or doshas, which normally work together in harmony, and help to maintain the equilibrium of the body. The three doshas are the vaadham, pittham and kabam. A skilled practitioner can analyse whether any one of these doshas does not exist in the correct proportion, and hence is causing a disequilibrium, or 'dis-ease' in the body.

As part of the approach to preventative medicine, the philosophy of Ayurveda advocates a diet which contains natural foodstuffs such as whole grains, fresh vegetables and yoghurt (Lad and Lad, 1997). Such food is described as a sattvic diet, as according to Ayurveda it contains a high proportion of what is termed the sattvic guna. The word guna may be translated approximately as a thread, and in the Samkhya School of Hindu philosophy, there are three gunas or ways in which the world functions. These are the sattva guna which is particularly concerned with the process of creation; the rajas guna which concerns the process of preservation and the tamas guna which involves the process of change. Foods containing sattvic guna lead the individual to having a balanced mind. These three concepts are used within Samkhya philosophy to analyse the universe, and in Ayurveda to analyse illness and its treatment. The three gunas are present in all people, but the balance of the them within the body affects how we act and feel.

Sattvic food which is suitable for the practice of an Ayurvedic lifestyle should be food which has been obtained peacefully. That is, it should have been obtained without any harm being done to another living creature. Sattvic food should be vegetarian since eating meat or fish inevitably involves the killing of other organisms. Even in the case of a vegetarian diet, a devotedly sattvic person would normally try to cause as little damage to plants as possible. For example, in the case of eating fruit, wherever possible fruit would be eaten which has fallen from a tree naturally rather than picking it from the tree. It is permissible for those following an Ayurvedic philosophy to drink milk from cows, goats or other domestic grazing animals, as long as the animals lead a healthy, natural outdoor life and are well cared-for.

Leading an Ayurvedic lifestyle, and following a sattvic diet, helps a person to be relaxed, well-balanced and well-adjusted to life in general. The person with a high proportion of sattvic guna is not concerned with the outcomes of actions in life, but behaves ethically, spiritually and with concern for fellow human beings.

The history of the importation of Indian culture to the West from the 1960s onwards has to some extent been a history of selectivity. Indian culture, philosophy, spirituality and literature are complex when taken in their totality. In addition, as much Indian culture is written in the religious language of Sanskrit, this has often posed a barrier to the Western appreciation of Hindu concepts. One of the results is that there has often been a selection of those elements which were likely to be of interest in the West. An example is the case of yoga which represents a very wide range of interwoven ideas and spiritual philosophy. Yet, in terms of introducing yoga to the West there has been an emphasis upon hatha yoga and the use of postures to improve the suppleness, flexibility and general health of the body. This has often been at the expense of other forms of yoga practice.

In the case of Ayurveda, the situation has been exacerbated somewhat because of the difficulty for many Westerners of understanding the exact nature of Ayurvedic practice. From a Western perspective Ayurveda often seems rather difficult to define. On the one hand it may appear to be a philosophy of living, and on the other hand being a system of preventative health involving herbalism and nutrition. Equally it may be perceived as a system of medicine devoted to providing cures for illnesses. Even as a system of medicine it may be defined in different ways. Some may view it as an 'alternative' therapy, so radically different from Western medicine that it is not considered as a fully legitimate system. Others, however, may define it as a fully valid system of medicine, different but equal to any other medical system.

Given these differences of perception and definition, it is perhaps not surprising that different elements of Ayurveda tended to be emphasized in the West, without necessarily relating them to the entire system. These separate elements were very often commodified and marketed as individual elements under the general descriptor of Ayurveda. Examples include Ayurvedic diet, Ayurvedic massage, Ayurvedic detoxification and Ayurvedic stress reduction. One can appreciate something of the process whereby this happened, and the resulting use of 'Ayurvedic' as a commercial brand, but this does not do justice to the sophistication of Ayurveda as a system. The process is reductionist in the sense that it takes a complex system of philosophies and practices, and attempts to separate them into much simpler ideas, which do not reflect the true nature of the whole.

As Ayurvedic treatments became more common in the West, there has been a tendency to judge the treatments according to the same sort of scientific, analytic criteria which are employed for Western medicines. For example, there has been some debates about the metallic content of certain Ayurvedic treatments used in, and imported from India. One of the related issues about the practice of Ayurveda in India, and by implication in the West, is that there is no central regulatory system which covers all of Ayurvedic practice. Hence, such practices are not necessarily consistent throughout India, and different types of treatment may be exported to the West, depending upon their origin in India. However, we are now seeing the development of university degree course in India, both in Ayurveda as a single course of study and of Ayurveda combined with the study of Western medicine. As more and more practitioners of Ayurveda gain university-level qualifications, there is likely to be a greater consistency of practice across India.

When Ayurvedic treatments first became popular in the West during the 1960s, there was a tendency to use herbs, plant extracts, spices and oils which were indigenous to India in the treatments. This was because it was considered important by practitioners to try to replicate the cultural ambience of India during the treatment, and also because it was felt that if the substances employed did not originate in India, then the treatment was not a legitimate Ayurvedic treatment. There was also the question of trying to ensure that the treatments used were as close as possible to those prescribed in the Vedas.

However, as Ayurveda became more and more common in the West, some practitioners started to question whether some Western products could be used in the treatments instead of imported components. For example, in a massage treatment, the question was raised as to whether an oil available in the West could be equally as effective as one from India. This type of question required an analysis of which aspects of Ayurveda were absolutely pivotal to the treatment and philosophy, and which were simply cultural accretions. Something of a compromise on this question is probably developing, although no doubt some patients do prefer a treatment and Ayurvedic experience which clearly possesses an Indian ambience.

One perspective on this general question is that Ayurveda can be thought of as transcending cultural boundaries. Although it has evolved in an Indian cultural and spiritual milieu, it can be argued that its principles apply anywhere. Ayurveda tends to treat the person holistically, reflecting and analysing the extent to which the metabolic aspects of the individual interact with the psychological processes, and in which both of these are integrated with a spiritual dimension. While Western medicine tends to be very specific in its approach, focusing on a specific ailment, there is no reason in principle why Western methods should not be more holistic.

In Ayurveda, one of the overarching concepts is that of equilibrium. Whether one considers the micro level of the individual organism, or of a large ecosystem, or indeed of the universe as a whole, one of the central concepts is the extent to which these exist in a state of equilibrium. All equilibria are dynamic. That is the state of balance can be altered at any moment by a change in the surroundings. We are becoming increasingly aware of this in relation to the natural world, where the intervention of human beings is altering the environment for other living creatures, often for the worse. Deforestation and pollution are bringing about such adverse changes. When an equilibrium becomes unbalanced, because of external factors, it will eventually create a new equilibrium, although that may not be as favourable to life as the previous one. The same process takes place at the level of the human body. If we ingest too much of the wrong types of food, or we are too sedentary, or we are under psychological stress, then our natural equilibrium will be disturbed, and we will not be healthy. We may very well develop an illness. The natural condition of the human body is to be in a state of equilibrium, while the unnatural condition is to be in disequilibrium. The former equates to being healthy, while the latter relates to being unhealthy.

The ultimate purpose of Ayurvedic philosophy is to help the individual person retain a state of equilibrium, and if that balance has been disturbed, to adopt measures in order to return to a state of equilibrium. For this reason, Ayurveda should not be viewed as a treatment designed to 'cure' a particular ailment. Rather it should be viewed as a continual practice designed to help the body and mind maintain the best possible sense of balance. While there are treatment techniques within Ayurveda which are designed, for example, to detoxify the body, the overall Ayurvedic approach is to try to prevent those toxins accumulating in the first place.

The idea of maintaining an equilibrium is also connected with the spiritual dimension of life. Spirituality can be thought of as a state in which we are in the greatest harmony with our own natural selves and also with the natural world around us. Hence, Ayurveda can be viewed as supporting and enhancing our sense of spirituality. The purpose of meditation within Ayurveda is to try to calm the mind and stop it being obsessed with the random thoughts which continually enter it. Meditation helps the person let go of those thoughts, allowing the mind to be more relaxed and at peace. In this condition, the person can be more in harmony, and closer to their original spiritual self.

The concept of a spiritual dimension to health or medical treatment is not part of mainstream Western medicine, and this is probably one of the reasons why Ayurveda has not been embraced by the scientific Western tradition. Nevertheless, there is no reason why the Western and Indian systems of treatment cannot co-exist, or even be used together to help people. Each method has its own logic within its own parameters, but it is sometimes difficult to transfer the method of reasoning from one approach to the other. There is, for example, an increasing tendency to analyse some Ayurvedic herbal treatments according to Western scientific criteria. Whether this is entirely appropriate is, however, a matter of debate. The Ayurvedic system of health is to a certain degree intuitive, while the Western system is empirical and scientific. The application of clinical science from a Western model in order to evaluate a subjective system such as Ayurveda may not be entirely appropriate.

However, there are points of similarity between the two systems. Probably the prime emphasis within the Ayurvedic system is on appropriate nutrition. Equally, Western medicine is increasingly concerned about the importance of a suitable diet. Ayurvedic practice often focuses upon the problem of an unbalanced diet in increasing the toxins in the body. It argues that when we do not eat in a healthy way, digestion is impaired, and waste matter is not passed out from the body efficiently. This leads to the accumulation of harmful chemicals in the body, which ultimately will lead to illness. Although some Ayurvedic treatments are designed to eliminate these toxins, the recommended approach is to have a balanced and natural diet in the first place. In this sense, Western and Ayurvedic approaches are largely in unison.

The Ayurvedic model of physiology becomes apparently more intuitive when it argues that the body is controlled by a central system of energy. This is said to pass energy around the body through a series of channels, and that one of the key purposes of Ayurvedic treatment is to ensure that these channels are functioning properly. This hypothesis is less-susceptible to Western-style empirical verification, and yet it appears to have a useful explanatory function within the Ayurvedic paradigm.

The attraction of Ayurveda for the counter-cultural movement of the 1960s concerned partly features of Ayurveda such as its naturalistic and holistic approach, but also because there was at the time a developing antipathy towards some features of Western medicine. Drugs companies were becoming increasingly powerful, and society was concerned about the side effects of some drugs. Doctors had considerable power in terms of supporting a particular treatment strategy, and such strategies sometimes involved treatment of an invasive nature. Some patients began to feel that they should be more involved in the determination of the treatment plan, and that such a plan should take into account wider factors than the specific illness under investigation.

As Ayurveda has become more and more well-known beyond the confines of India, it has become an increasingly commercialized phenomenon. However, in order to achieve this commercialization in the West those people managing Ayurveda as a product have had to comply with the norms and standards of Western commercial life. In order to give it credibility colleges and other educational institutions have been established devoted to teaching Ayurveda. These colleges offer courses and qualifications in Ayurveda, thus giving it a certain legitimacy in the eyes of the general public and of those who wish to receive treatment. Ayurvedic professionals can thus list their qualifications in much the same way as professionals in other fields. At the same time, however, the spiritual elements in Ayurveda have to some extent been lost. Much the same happened as yoga was popularized in the West. Hatha yoga became seen as a system of exercise rather than as part of a holistic spiritual practice.

Perhaps the most interesting phenomenon to arise from the commodification of Ayurveda in the West has been the importation of a Western model of Ayurveda back to India. Western tourists visiting southern India, in particular, can now stay at Ayurvedic spas and clinics, established on Western lines, and offering a Westernized form of Ayurveda. This phenomenon can be perceived, depending upon one's point of view, as an inevitable consequence of cultural globalization or as an unfortunate simplification and commercialization of a long-established and refined cultural tradition.

The increasingly close relationship between Ayurveda and the West has made a number of demands upon the traditional Ayurvedic model. The Western obsession with regulation and quality control has lead to demands for greater standardization of Ayurvedic products. Practitioners are becoming more and more aware that they need to conduct formal research on Ayurvedic remedies, and to publish their findings in academic journals, as is the practice within Western medicine. As at the moment there are some procedural problems in establishing the credibility of Ayurvedic medicines, there is an emphasis in Western-oriented centres on the use of massage and other 'external' treatments.

Traditionally, Ayurvedic practitioners were community doctors who received support from the people they treated. However, during the British colonial administration, there was little encouragement for Ayurveda, as Western medicine was gradually introduced. Today, however, teaching and training in Ayurveda in India is being modelled on the Western system with university courses, nationally recognized certification and postgraduate research up to doctoral level. As early as 1922 Benaras Hindu University realized that it would be important to have courses which incorporated elements of Ayurveda and Western medicine. Today it has a Faculty of Ayurveda within its Institute of Medical Sciences. It offers a Bachelor degree in Ayurveda, Medicine and Surgery (BAMS) and a range of postgraduate courses. It also has a medicinal herb garden, devoted to the cultivation of plants used in Ayurvedic treatment. In 1967 Gujarat Ayurved University was established. The institution concentrates entirely on the teaching of Ayurvedic philosophy and practice and also offers a BAMS degree and postgraduate research programmes in Ayurveda. Many other institutions of higher education in India are now offering such courses.

Ayurveda has thus now established a position for itself in both the Western-oriented health industry and as a serious system of medical treatment. There may still be some way to go before it is fully accepted within Western medical schools, but as with acupuncture, Western doctors are beginning to recognize its potential.

Further reading

Batie, H. F. (2003) *Healing Body, Mind and Spirit: A Guide to Energy-Based Healing*. St Paul, MN: Llewellyn Publications.

Heaven, R. and Charing, H. G. (2006) *Plant Spirit Shamanism*. Rochester, VT: Destiny Books.

Lad, V. (1993) *Ayurveda: The Science of Self-healing – A Practical Guide*. Twin Lakes, WI: Lotus Press.

Lad, V. and Frawley, D. (1986) *The Yoga of Herbs: An Ayurvedic Guide to Herbal Medicine*. Twin Lakes, WI: Lotus Press.

Pole, S. (2012) *Ayurvedic Medicine: The Principles of Traditional Practice*. London: Singing Dragon.

Zhao, X. (2006) *Ancient Healing for Modern Women*. New York: Walker.

11

Yoga, mysticism and spiritual consciousness

Summary

As part of the challenge to orthodoxy in society, the counter-culture sought new approaches to achieving enlightenment, a sense of meaning and what Maslow termed 'self-actualization'. The Hindu tradition provided different ways of achieving some kind of spiritual meaning in life, with hatha yoga, meditation, tantric techniques and a range of mystical insights. Some people experimented with astrology, alchemy, neo-paganism and divination, but arguably the primary perspective was one derived from Indian religion. This chapter explores the interest in spirituality within the counter-culture, and in particular the contribution of Hindu mysticism.

The eclecticism of the 1960s

The 1960s was a period in which young people began to appreciate that they could draw upon a wide range of different influences in terms of music, art, fashion and world views. During the nineteenth century and first half of the twentieth century, there had been extensive contacts between Europe and other parts of the world, but the relationship had been one largely based upon colonialism. European countries had been aware of other cultures, and of their music, art and religion, but had tended to view these cultural productions through the eyes of a European culture which had generally been viewed as superior. This eurocentric perspective applied standards and criteria to the artefacts of other cultures, which were based upon the standards normally used to judge Western European culture. Within this viewpoint, cultural products from the East, from Africa or South America, were often perceived as interesting, but not something to be taken too seriously. There were exceptions to this, for example, in the nineteenth century the scholarly work on Hindu scriptures, but this was largely the prevalent perspective.

By the time of the 1960s, however, a number of factors had combined to create a more open and accepting approach to world cultures. The increased access to higher education in the West provided young people with the intellectual insights to appreciate other cultures. Increased travel opportunities enabled young people to see these cultures at first hand. In addition, political changes such as the independence movements in colonial countries created a climate in which developing countries were more assertive about their own languages and cultures. This, combined with increasing migration, usually from former colonies to the country of former colonial power, added to the possibilities for cultural dispersion. Thus, even before the advent of the Internet, worldwide social changes in the 1960s were beginning to have an effect on the interchange of cultures and ideas.

The 1960s also saw an increasing acceptance of the value of indigenous cultures, where previously these had been either ignored or at best regarded as 'primitive' and representing an early stage in human intellectual development. There was a gradual realization that the cultures of, for example, indigenous Americans and indigenous Australians were far more sophisticated than had previously been assumed. In particular it was realized that they had a complex spiritual relationship with their environment, which enabled them to live in harmony with nature. The environmental movement in the West began to acknowledge that there was much they could learn from these ancient cultures. Moreover, it was also realized that the spirituality of indigenous peoples, although marked by an absence of such features as scriptural texts, was none-the-less significant in that it integrated the various elements of their life experience.

Both before and immediately after the Second World War, young people largely inherited and accepted the religious traditions of their parents and family. In the West these traditions were in the main represented by various Christian denominations. Moreover, there tended to be an acceptance of the veracity of these belief systems in an absolute sense. That is, the tenets of the different Christian denominations were, to a large degree, accepted and unchallenged. There was also little tendency for people to compare religions, according to various criteria, and perhaps to decide that they preferred one belief system to another.

The 1960s, however, saw a gradual transition from absolutism in terms of religious belief towards a more relativistic position. People, and perhaps young people in particular, now had the knowledge, and sometimes actual personal experience, to compare the different religions of the world. Not only could they now change their religion, but they could also construct their own personal spiritual position by combining elements from different major and minor faiths. In particular, this encouraged some people to look back at the spiritual history of Western Europe to paganism and shamanism, and to explore ways in which they could take elements from these systems to create new religions. The 1960s thus saw the development of many new religious movements, a significant number of which were derived from Hindu origins.

Underpinning the increasingly relativistic position adopted by young people at this time was the assumption that there are many different ways to acquire spiritual experience and to gain a direct understanding of the divine. In addition, the rather more radical position is that these different routes to God are of equal legitimacy. One can analyse this general transition in religious belief in terms of a number of different continua, including a gradual change from an emphasis on religious teaching to an emphasis upon religious experience. The absolutist position in terms of religion tended to emphasize the acquisition of religious teaching and dogma, whereas the 1960s saw a trend towards an emphasis upon religious experience.

This can be seen as explaining the increasing interest in Eastern religions during the decade. It can be argued, for example, that traditions such as Zen, Taoism and Hindu Tantra, while possessing scriptural texts, do place an emphasis upon the importance of practical spiritual experience. Those who hold this position would argue that scriptures do give us religious truths, but that we can never fully understand those truths unless we can convert them into practical experience. Hence the emphasis, in the religions mentioned earlier, on meditation and chanting, for example, is to create a living religious experience. The young people of the 1960s were thus generally dissatisfied with the learning of religious 'truths' and wanted above all, to understand religion directly, through their own empirical experience.

As with many periods in human development, the 1960s demonstrated some trends which seemed to be in opposition to each other. There was still an enormous impetus to improve the living conditions of people in a material sense, and in particular in terms of housing. Large cities still retained many of the small terrace houses typical of the nineteenth-century industrial expansion. By the early 1960s there was an impetus to demolish these and build accommodation up to modern standards. The solution of the period was to build tower blocks, often on the outskirts of big cities, to house displaced people from the city centres. The Red Road development in Glasgow, which commenced in the mid-1960s, and later gave its name to an award-winning film, was typical of the time. Such developments may for a relatively short time have met the physical needs of residents, but it gradually became evident that they were not meeting the psychological, social or indeed spiritual needs of people.

The internal life

The response of the counter-culture to this type of development was to place an emphasis upon the 'internal' life of human beings rather than the 'external'. It pointed out that for their happiness and sense of well-being, human beings not only needed material comfort but also required a sense of internal, spiritual harmony. Young people of the time thus sought philosophies and world views which emphasized the internal life and the search for personal development. This perhaps explains the attraction of Indian religious experience at the time in the sense that it focused less on adherence to scriptures and formal teachings and more on the personal spiritual search of the individual.

This personal journey upon which many young people embarked in the 1960s also had important social consequences. In the 1950s and earlier, people had tended to remain attached to the religious traditions of their family or social group. However, with the advent of the 1960s there was a much greater tendency for young people to seek a spiritual experience which was not part of their family tradition. This was a small but important step towards more religious and cultural integration in society. Music has been an area in which people have found stimulation from the Hindu tradition. Quite apart from the Beatles, some jazz musicians and composers have been notable for their interest in Hinduism. The saxophone player John Coltrane (1926–1967) was an example of a musician with very eclectic views on religion and spirituality.

John Coltrane was reared within the African-American Methodist Church tradition, but gradually developed a strong interest in Hinduism and Indian mysticism. He studied Indian scriptures such as the Bhagavad Gita and explored the works of philosophers such as Krishnamurti. He also meditated regularly, and indeed 'Meditations' was the title of one of his albums. In terms of his personal belief system, John Coltrane drew upon a very wide range of religious traditions. He appears to have held the view that there were many different ways in which one could have an experience of God. He was also deeply committed to what he saw as the spiritual nature of music (Cole, 2001). In his view he felt that music could have a very positive influence on the lives of people, and that there was a deep connection between music and religion. In a sense, he seems to have viewed his music as a way of improving the world and the lives of other human beings. John

Coltrane made a particular study of Indian music, and this is reflected in the names of some of his LPs such as 'Om'. One of his most famous LPs was 'A Love Supreme' which referred to his deep feelings for God (Whyton, 2013).

His interest in Hinduism was shared with his second wife, Alice Coltrane (1937–2007) who was also a jazz musician. In particular she made a study of Hindu religious songs termed 'bhajans' and explored these as the basis for some of her own music. The titles of some of her compositions, for example, 'Hare Krishna' and 'Sita Rama', reflect her strong interest in Hinduism. Alice Coltrane was influenced by the Hindu teacher, Swami Satchidananda, and especially by his notion that one of the prime functions of spirituality was to help individuals to reach the best of which they are capable. The idea of helping people reach their maximum potential was one which she and her husband sought to encourage through their music. John Coltrane died relatively young in 1967.

Another musician who has been greatly influenced by Indian music is the guitarist and composer John McLaughlin. He was born in 1942 in Doncaster, England and has worked in a number of genres including jazz, rock and classical Indian music, combining them in his own distinctive style. In the 1960s he played with Georgie Fame among other groups, and later collaborated with Miles Davis. McLaughlin's interest in Indian music lead him to play the veena, an instrument related to the sitar. Around 1970 he started to follow the teachings of the Bengali religious teacher Sri Chinmoy, and later adopted the name Mahavishnu John McLaughlin.

Universalism in the Hindu religion

Chinmoy Kumar Ghose, later known simply as Sri Chinmoy, was born in what is now Bangladesh, in 1931. He died in 2007. As a student and young man he lived and studied at the Sri Aurobindo Ashram, in Puducherry. In 1964 he moved to New York in order principally to teach his spiritual philosophy to Westerners.

Sri Chinmoy's religious philosophy is characterized by a directness and simplicity, founded upon a few straightforward propositions (Chinmoy, 2000, 2010). One of the key elements of his philosophy is that God can be perceived in many different ways, but that this does not alter the essential qualities or nature of God. An analogy might be that we can shine beams of light on to an object from different directions. This will illuminate the object in different ways and cast very different shadows, giving the object a varied appearance. However, this variety of appearance is superficial and does not alter the essential quality of the object. The latter remains the same.

Just as there is one God who may be viewed in very different ways by different people, and different religious belief systems, there is also one 'Truth'. God and Truth are synonymous. Truth may also be viewed in very different ways by different religions, but fundamentally according to Sri Chinmoy, there is only a single Truth, and only one truthful way of contemplating the world.

For Sri Chinmoy truth is synonymous with the realization of God. Of course, this begs the question rather, as to the nature of God. However, within this perspective, God is the same as the highest, most noble and most moral qualities within each human being. The sum total of these divine qualities is the 'self' or 'original self' which all mystics try to discover. Sri Chinmoy argued that in all religions, spiritual seekers try to identify with, and to comprehend, this highest truth. Each of the world's principal religions has developed ways of helping their adherents to find this highest truth and to merge with it. These strategies include meditation, prayer, contemplation, the study of scriptures, chanting and many other methods. They are all methods, however, which lead to the same goal, the merging and union with the divine which is within us all. In some religions this divine element is known as God, while in other religions such as Buddhism, this goal may be a spiritual state of mind. Nevertheless all religions are aiming at the same goal, and the true seeker, from whatever religious tradition is looking for the same sense of oneness with the divine.

In this sense, a feeling of unity with God is the same as having discovered ones true self. In this state one exists in a condition of harmony and peace with the world. The relationship between Man and God is a reciprocal one. On the one hand, the presence of God within human beings enables them to make contact with the highest qualities within themselves. It enables human beings to recognize the highest moral principles of which they are capable. On the other hand, without human beings to act as a vehicle, God would not be able to demonstrate such higher ethical qualities.

Sri Chinmoy argued that these higher, noble qualities are often the justification for people claiming that their religion is superior to other religions. Chinmoy argued that such claims are not indicative of a 'true' religion. In other words as all religions in his view lead to the same divine reality, it is not possible to claim that one religion is superior to another. It may be possible, however, for people to argue that a particular religion is more appropriate for them, in terms of their personality or the manner in which they relate to God. Sri Chinmoy pointed out that religions should try to develop a sense of empathy with each other rather than attempting to prove that they are in some way better. He argued that it was antithetical to the true nature of a religion to try to demonstrate that it was superior to another system of religion. Rather, each faith should try to see the value in other belief systems, as opposed to creating a sense of competition with them.

We can recognize the genuine nature of persons' spiritual search by the way in which they conduct themselves in their daily lives. The manner in which they relate to other people, and for example, the kindness which they show, is a reflection of their spirituality. According to Chinmoy, the external existence of a person is a reflection of his or her internal spiritual existence.

Sri Chinmoy also argued for the relevance of yoga to all religions. He viewed yoga as a strategy whereby human beings could experience the reality of God in everyday life. The process whereby people can realize the presence of God within them goes beyond the nature of a specific religion. In fact Chinmoy suggested that when people practised yoga, it was not necessary for them to abandon their own traditional religion. The crucial issue was for people to seek God in their personal life and to try to attain the highest spiritual consciousness of which they were capable.

It is not difficult to see how this type of approach to spirituality found favour with the young people of the 1960s counter-culture. Unlike the traditional religious experience of the West, there were no fixed rules about how to conduct their spiritual lives. They could choose their own way to a spiritual experience, combining religious forms from different religious traditions. They no longer needed to adhere to what some saw as the rather oppressive morality of traditional Christianity. They could construct their own value system for their journey through life. This affirmation of the legitimacy of individual freedom was a central aspect of the philosophy of the 1960s.

When one culture is transplanted into a different host culture, it is usually the case that the transplanted culture has to adapt to the new one if it is to flourish. To some extent this is what happened when yoga was first introduced to the West. There has always tended to be a focus upon hatha yoga and the practice of the asanas rather than upon yoga as a philosophy or as a technique to develop self-awareness. One of the first people to introduce yoga systematically to the West was a Latvian-born religious teacher, Indra Devi (1899–2002). During her early life she developed an interest in Indian thought and philosophy, and in the late 1930s travelled to India and became a disciple of the famous teacher Krishnamacharya. After many years of study and practice of yoga, she travelled to the United States and in 1948 she established a school of yoga in Hollywood. She concentrated on teaching hatha yoga as a means of developing physical fitness, flexibility of the body and mental tranquillity (Devi, 1965, 2002). Her teaching was accepted enthusiastically by many of the Hollywood film stars, who saw yoga as a means of enhancing their capacity to do their job. Greta Garbo, Gloria Swanson and Olivia de Havilland among others were students of Indra Devi. Marilyn Monroe (1926–1962) was also a devoted student of yoga. Indra Devi became accepted internationally as a leading teacher of yoga. Throughout her life she was deeply committed to the study of Hindu philosophy, and in the 1960s she became a student of Sathya Sai Baba. Throughout the 1940s and 1950s, however, yoga did not develop as a pastime or activity on a wide scale. It was not until the impact of Richard Hittleman (1927–1991) that yoga became popular on a really wide scale.

Hittleman came from a Jewish background in New York city, and in his early 20s studied with the teacher Ramana Maharshi. In 1957 he established a yoga school in Florida. Then in 1961 he took the step which brought an awareness of yoga into many households in the United States. He obtained a contract to create the first ever television programme which taught the principles of yoga. The programme was called 'Yoga for Health' and became extremely popular. He also wrote many books on yoga, which achieved large sales (Hittleman, 1983). His approach was not dissimilar to Indra Devi, in that he concentrated on the asanas, and then added later a discussion of the more philosophical aspects of yoga. His television programme started just as the counter-culture was first beginning to take place and have an impact, and this perhaps explains the almost unprecedented success Hittleman experienced in America. He became a leading figure in the developing field of alternative spiritualities; he was a friend and colleague of Alan Watts, and studied for a Masters degree in Oriental Mysticism at Columbia University. In his programmes and books, Richard Hittleman emphasized the straightforward nature of hatha yoga practice, and the way it could help people in their everyday lives. His popularity was also enhanced because he stressed that anyone could gain something from yoga practice, and that it was suitable for people of all ages and backgrounds. He also used his programmes and books to provide advice on healthy nutrition suitable for yoga practice, and was indeed giving the type of advice which today, 50 years later, has become very common.

When Hittleman taught about the philosophy of yoga, he adopted the perspective that within all of us is an element of the divine, of God, and that this is synonymous with what we call 'the Self'. Through the processes of meditation and yoga, he argued that we can identify with this 'Self'. During the 1950s and early 1960s there was a developing need among many Americans to find something in their lives which provided greater significance that simply the comforts of suburban living, and a materialistic set of values. This perhaps explains the remarkable success of Richard Hittleman's television programmes and of his books.

Ramana Maharshi had a considerable effect upon Hittleman in terms of helping him understand the underlying philosophy of yoga. He was born in Tamil Nadu in the south of India, and throughout his life he always asked his followers not to treat him as a special kind of person. Ramana Maharshi taught many aspects of Indian philosophy, but in terms of advising his followers on a technique to help their personal development, he recommended a method which he called 'self-enquiry'.

He argued that inside everyone is the concept of 'I', the person who we feel that we are. Thus, when we succeed at doing something, we tend to say to ourselves, 'I have succeeded at what I set out to do'. If we are in conversation with somebody, we tend to say, 'I think so and so, about this issue'. Therefore, every action which we undertake is related to the entity inside us, which we think of as the centre of ourselves; the 'I' which summarizes what we are. However, if we try to analyse the location of this 'I', it is very difficult to imagine where it might be. The more we think about the problem, the more it can occur to us, that the 'I' may not exist in the way which we previously thought. The more we think about it, we can have difficulty in working out how the 'I' does the things which we think it does. In addition, this way of looking at ourselves can be rather egoistic. The concept of the 'I' causes us to examine the world from a very egocentric viewpoint. We are always looking at the world in terms of ourselves, not of other people.

Ramana Maharshi recommends a process whereby through out our daily lives we constantly try to remind ourselves of what our 'I' is doing and thinking. When we do this regularly he argues that we will realize that the 'I' is not doing very much after all. It is really a kind of symbol to which we attach the things we have done. If we continue with this strategy, it is argued that the significance of the 'I' will gradually disappear. We will slowly lose the concept of the 'I', and in its place will be self-realization, the Self, or in fact, the divine within us. When this happens, and we are involved in a particular action, we will not think, 'I have been involved in doing that'. Rather, we will tend to think of an event simply taking place. This is a much less egotistical way of viewing the world.

Ramana Maharshi also pointed out that from this perspective many approaches to yoga and meditation relied upon the concept of 'I'. For example, one might think 'I have learned how to do a head stand', or 'I have learned how to sit in a lotus position'. Such thoughts are fundamentally ego-centred and relate to our concept of having achieved something. Such thoughts also set us in opposition to other people, as we are in competition with them, to see who can achieve the most asanas, or who can meditate for longest. It was much more productive to simply do the asanas, or simply to meditate, without thinking of the activities as something which had to be achieved.

Now this perspective can, if extended into everyday life, lead to a philosophy of living which is based much more on harmony rather than upon competition and conflict.

Other Hindu teachers advocated a similar position with regard to competition between people. Swami Rama (1925–1996) who was born in the Indian Himalayas spent a long period as a young man studying yoga and meditation. He became well-known during the 1960s for his apparent control over his autonomic nervous system, for example, allegedly having control over his heart beat. In 1971 he established the Himalayan Institute for Yoga Science and Philosophy, whose headquarter are in Pennsylvania. He spent much of his adult life teaching and writing in the United States (Rama, 1998, 1999).

Swami Rama pointed out that it was possible for people to live a normal life, mixing in the society of others, and still be a spiritual person. In other words, it is not necessary to be a renunciate or ascetic in order to develop spiritually. He argued that we can have material possessions, and lead a normal 'Western' life, without necessarily becoming attached to the objects we use or possess. Therefore, we might have a large, modern television in our apartment, and enjoy watching it in the evening, but we should not think that we 'possess' it in any way. We should not think of the television as 'belonging' to us. If we can adopt this frame of mind, then we will not be afraid of losing our material 'possessions'. We will just regard them as with us on a temporary basis, and perhaps improving our life for the time being. However, we will not feel possessive and acquisitive towards them. In any case, argued Swami Rama, thinking in terms of there being an 'I' within the human being can easily lead to thoughts of 'I have . . .', 'I possess . . .', and 'I want . . .'. In other words it is very easy to develop a materialistic perspective. Equally, after many years of yoga practice, some yogis develop the ability to perform difficult and unusual asanas, or to demonstrate other types of yogic powers. Swami Rama suggested that putting on any kind of show to demonstrate one's powers was antithetical to the true concept of yoga, as it was a form of egoism.

Swami Rama contrasted the approach of conventional world faiths with that of yoga. He argued that conventional, established religions sought to specify guidance for how people should conduct their lives. This might be in the form of moral injunctions, prescriptions for prayer, dietary requirements, rules for renunciation or the learning of scripture. However, he argued that such customs and requirements did not necessarily help an individual to find themselves. They were requirements for those who wanted to fit in with the accepted norms and values of the spiritual community of which they wished to be a part. Such customs, on the one hand, were more an indication of compliance rather than providing a route to self-illumination. Yoga, on the other hand, could be combined with any of the world's main religions. Yoga provided an entirely different approach, giving adherents a set of techniques and strategies which can be used to supplement conventional religious practice in order to help the individual towards self-realization.

It is not difficult to appreciate why this approach appealed more to young people in the 1960s compared with the traditional approach of major religions. Young people could select the particular combination of techniques which suited them, such as meditation, chanting or yoga asanas. What is more, compared with conventional religion, there was an enormous sense of informality. Spiritual practice could be conducted outdoors, and was not incorporated within a rigid theological hierarchy. Although yoga or Hindu mystical practices were often taught by a yogi or other teacher, the student was free to change teachers, or to adopt a different approach, with a minimum of formal notice. This informality combined with the freedom of young people to take a very individualistic approach to spirituality, gave the members of the counter-culture a very different potential for experiencing religion.

Further reading

Easwaran, E. (trans) (2007) *The Upanishads*. Tomales, CA: Nilgiri.
Feuerstein, G. (2001) *The Yoga Tradition: Its History, Literature, Philosophy and Practice*. Prescott, AZ: Hohm.
Greer, J. M. (2003) *The New Encyclopedia of the Occult*. St Paul, MN: Llewellyn.
Harvey, A. (ed.) (2001) *Teachings of the Hindu Mystics*. London: Shambhala.
Iyengar, B. K. S. (1979) *Light on Yoga*. New York: Schocken.
Underhill, E. (1955) *The Spiritual Life*. Harrisburg, PA: Morehouse.

PART THREE

The legacy in contemporary lifestyle

12

Overland to India – a modern pilgrimage

Summary

During the 1960s and early 1970s it was *de rigueur* for young people to follow the 'Hippie Trail' to India, travelling as cheaply as possible, stereotypically in an ancient camper van, painted in psychedelic colours. The typical route through Turkey, Iran, Afghanistan and Pakistan was not then generally hampered by the later wars and political conflicts, and it was possible to travel southwards to Goa or northwards to Kathmandu in a state of relative harmony with the local populations. Out of the experiences of these early travellers emerged the concept of budget travel for young people, and of the gap year. Some of these young travellers to India also went on to write about their experiences, and indeed to develop the travel guides which have become so popular with later generations of young people. This chapter examines the experience of the overland route to India and some aspects of its legacy.

Introduction – the route

There have doubtless been many factors since the time of Alexander the Great and earlier, which have encouraged people to travel from Europe towards the East. The desires for conquest, trade and the acquisition of wealth have probably figured fairly high on the list of motivational factors. However, it is not entirely clear that the seeking of wealth or other material benefits had much of an influence on the travellers of the 1960s. There is considerable evidence that those travelling overland to India were more influenced by ideas than by the gaining of material possessions. In fact, there was almost an element of inverted snobbery with regard to money, among the overland generation. Far from trying to travel in comfort having saved a great deal of money, there was a sense of competition about who could hitch-hike the farthest and spend no money, about who could find the cheapest and most insanitary of hotels, about who could sell the most blood to finance their onward travels and about who could survive the worst attack of dysentery without succumbing to medical help.

Most of the young people travelling overland to India in the 1960s and 1970s knew relatively little about their destination and even less about the countries they would pass through en route. It is worth remembering that during this period there were very few detailed travel guides of the type which are now readily available on the high street. The travellers of the 1960s had often to depend on stories and advice brought back to Europe by other young people, or picked up from contemporaries during the actual journey. However, they were motivated very often by books they had read about the 'mystic East' such as Hermann Hesse's 1922 novel 'Siddhartha', which had first become available in English in 1951 (Hesse, 2008). On the one hand, British accounts of India had to be considered in the context of the British rule of India. American authors, on the other hand, were able to look in a detached way at India, and the role of the British Raj. As a result of his journey around the world in 1895 and 1896, Mark Twain produced an interesting account of India in the book of his travels (Twain, 1989). Later, during the struggle for independence, the celebrated American journalists Webb Miller and Phillips Talbot, who both knew Gandhi personally, produced accounts of the events leading up to the creation of an independent India (Miller, 2011; Talbot, 2007). However, it was probably the visit of the Beatles to Rishikesh in February 1968, which was the ultimate trigger for the departure of many young people.

One of the main enabling factors for the overland journey from Europe to India in the 1960s and 1970s was the relative political stability of the countries to be encountered on the way. However, this travel phenomenon only lasted, in reality, for about a decade. In February 1979 the Iranian Revolution took place, making it more and more difficult for Westerners to traverse that country (Buchan, 2012). Then, later the same year in December, Russian troops invaded Afghanistan, effectively closing the country to overland travellers (Braithwaite, 2012). The decade of 1969 to 1979 had not been without difficulties for overlanders, with for example the 1971 Indo-Pakistan War which was linked to the fight for an independent Bangladesh. Nevertheless, given the political turbulence of more recent years, this period was remarkably peaceful for overland travellers, who were largely welcomed by the indigenous inhabitants of the area.

The first stage of the overland route took young people across Europe to Istanbul. The more intrepid and impecunious travelled as far as they could by hitch-hiking, while others employed their own transport ranging from saloon cars to camper vans. Some purchased seats on the various antiquated buses which went to and fro on the overland trail. The route typically took people across Belgium or France, Germany, Austria, Yugoslavia and Bulgaria to Istanbul. For those with a little more money there was the Direct-Orient Express, the descendent of the celebrated Orient Express of the inter-war years. It travelled from the Gare de l'Est in Paris, directly to Sirkeci Station in Istanbul, taking approximately 3 days. By the 1970s, however, the train had lost much of its former glory and consisted merely of several rather plain carriages which formed part of normal, more local trains. These carriages were shunted between trains at various stages of the journey. The route consisted of Lausanne, Milan, Venice, Belgrade, Sofia and finally Istanbul. The direct service finally ceased in 1977.

The route from London to India was of about 7,000 miles, and many young people at the time would embark with as little as 50 to 100 pounds to finance the trip. Whereas most British young people tended to travel overland from London to Delhi, some Americans flew to Istanbul and started their journey there, or even flew directly to India, returning Westwards to London by the overland route. It is worth remembering that compared with travel today, the overland generation of 50 years ago had to be a little more resourceful. The cash machine or ATM had not been invented, and people had to estimate the money they would need and take it all with them. If they lost their travellers cheques, or were robbed, they would need to find an agency to communicate with home in order to have replacement funds despatched. In the middle of Eastern Turkey or the Hindu Kush mountains, this could pose problems. There were of course no mobile phones, and access to telephones in many of the regions en route was impossible. It is also worth remembering that during the 1960s, very few ordinary families in Britain had a telephone landline in their house anyway, which made phoning home to the United Kingdom problematic. There were similarities in the United States, with up to a third of homes in some states not having a phone by 1970 (US Census Bureau, 2011). There were no credit cards, no computers and email, with the result that for the majority of young travellers the only effective communication was by letter or telegram, assuming they could find a post office.

The typical overland route continued Eastwards from Istanbul through Ankara, Sivas and Erzurum, crossing the Turkish–Iranian border just south of Mount Ararat. This area is extremely hot in summer, and inhospitably cold in winter, making travel a considerable challenge. The road passed through Tabriz, Tehran and Mashhad, entering Afghanistan in the direction of Herat.

The road looped south through Kandahar, and then north towards Kabul and Jalalabad. Afghanistan and Pakistan were linked by the road through the Khyber Pass, which was used by numerous 1950 vintage Chevrolet saloons converted to taxis (Docherty, 2007). The road passed into Pakistan through Peshawar, Rawalpindi and Lahore before entering India near Amritsar. Many young people had to leave their vehicles at the Pakistan–India border crossing because of the import duty into India. The typical route now continued across the north Indian plain via New Delhi, Agra and Kanpur, to Patna in the state of Bihar. Here the road turned north to cross the India–Nepal border at the small town of Raxaul. The town on the Nepalese side of the border is Birganj, and marks the beginning of the picturesque Tribhuvan Highway, which winds its way through the Himalayan foothills to Kathmandu, providing distant views of Everest on the way. The journey is about 100 miles from Birganj to Kathmandu, but the twists and turns of the road extend the journey time considerably.

Interacting with the local people

Compared with the situation today, young travellers of the time would have encountered relatively little animosity from the local people who lived along the 'hippie trail'. Young boys would sometimes throw stones at buses and cars as they wound their way along the valley floor of the Khyber Pass, but apparently more as a form of entertainment than through malice. In Peshawar it was no doubt a little daunting for Westerners in the market, to rub shoulders with tribesmen who carried ancient Lee-Enfield or Martini-Henry rifles balanced on their shoulders. Rifles seemed to be carried with the same sense of normality as one might carry a tennis racket in England. The rifles were nearly always copies of originals which have been obtained by various means. The separate parts were machined on small lathes often positioned on the floor outside people's houses.

In general however, young overlanders realized that there was little about which to be concerned. The proprietors of the tea houses, clothes and trinket shops in Afghanistan and Pakistan were welcoming of the young travellers who came from the West. They brought business certainly, but there were other reasons which accounted for their being generally accepted in a friendly way. Historically, the British people who had come to their countries were largely represented by a military hierarchy, who had sought to exercise dominion over the land and peoples of the area. These young travellers were different. They did not represent an affluent, military hierarchy who largely kept themselves aloof from local people – in fact, quite the contrary. Moreover, young Americans had no historical connection with being a colonial power in India.

It must have been evident to local people both on the overland route and in India and Nepal that young overland travellers represented a different culture and type of tourism to the affluent travellers of the colonial days. They generally had little money and stayed in very modest accommodation, often of the type which might be used by local people. Although some would still have had more disposable income than many local people, there was not the evident disparity of wealth which had existed in previous years. In India young people would often travel third class on the trains, and hence mix cheek by jowl with ordinary Indians. In the days of the Raj, the British in India with some exceptions tried above all to retain the 'British' way of life and to remain separate from Indian culture wherever possible. The result was often an exaggerated version of British culture. The overland generation, however, was by and large very interested in Indian culture and often tried to immerse themselves in the local way of life, wearing Indian-style clothes and eating very simple vegetarian food. They often sought accommodation in ashrams or for example, in Sikh gurdwaras, where there was often a culture of aiding travellers. This could have been viewed as exploitative by some people, but both ordinary Indians and Westerners gained from this close contact.

Young people were also able to learn about the role of the British in India and form judgements about the contribution which had been made to Indian society. The young people of the counter-culture had embarked on a journey to the East for a multiplicity of reasons. Some did not like the idea of a routine, career job and wanted to escape to a more independent, liberated life style. Others were no doubt alienated by the values of their parents, and more generally by the hierarchical, class-bound nature of society which still existed to some extent in the West. Interestingly, when they arrived in India, they found a society which was even more hierarchical than the one which they had left behind. It was also a society whose stratification was justified by some on religious grounds to the extent that the position of a person in the social hierarchy was judged to be a result of karma, or the way in which a person had acquitted themselves in previous existences. Some argued that this analysis merely compounded social differences since it appeared to justify the extreme wealth of a minority and the poverty of many Indians. They also found a society in which ordinary, lower-caste Indians deferred in the most subservient manner to higher-caste Hindus. Although as Westerners they were outside the caste system, their life style would sometimes incur a certain disdain on the part of higher caste, wealthy Indians, and this gave young people an appreciation of the position in society of ordinary Indians.

Once in India, they also found evidence all around them of the nature of the lives of the British in the days of the Raj (James, 1998). The usually overgrown British cemeteries on the outskirts of towns gave an insight into the precarious nature of life during the British Raj. The young age of many of the deceased bore witness to the hardships and dangers of life in the nineteenth and early twentieth centuries in India.

The British in India as a formative influence

What many of the overland generation did not perhaps realize was that the earliest travellers among them in the mid- to late 1960s were arriving in India only 20 years after independence on 15 August 1947. The manner in which they were received by the Indian population depended a great deal on the history of the relationship between the two countries and in particular on the experience of Indians during the period of British government. It is worth perhaps tracing some historical themes which had an effect on the attitudes of Indians to the young travellers of the 1960s and 1970s. The first formal connection between Britain and India could be said to be the Royal Charter of Elizabeth I, which established the East India Company in 1600 (Keay, 1993). The Company was literally a business enterprise devoted to trade with India and designed to maximize profit. It had to compete initially against other European interests, but with the Battle of Plassey, to the north of Calcutta in 1757, Britain consolidated its power. At Plassey, Robert Clive defeated a French army and the Indian troops of the Nawab of Bengal, thus gaining economic and military control of this important state. For 100 years until the Sepoy 'Rebellion' of 1857, the East India Company monopolized the very lucrative trade with India. During this period the raison d'être of the Company was trade and profit, supported to a certain extent by the use of military power in order to safeguard commercial interests and investment. Nevertheless, in order to facilitate trade, there needed to be close working relationships between the British and Indians. Company staff learned Indian languages, and where it was useful for trading purposes, immersed themselves in Hindu culture. At this time, very few unattached British women had come to India, and it was fairly common for members of the Company to form attachments with young Indian women. These were sometimes informal relationships, but in other cases couples married. There were however problems to be overcome. When the man's period of employment was over, he could not normally take his Indian wife back to Britain, and any children would not be employed by the East India Company when they grew up. The man was thus committing himself to remaining in India. To this day, it is possible for some people to trace back their ancestors to an Anglo-Indian marriage of this type.

The 1857 Indian 'Mutiny', or Sepoy Rebellion, lead however to a change of attitude on the part of the British (David, 2003). The most important political change was that from the following year India was ruled by the British Government. The Indian army was reinforced particularly with Sikh and Gurkha troops who had been loyal to Britain during the rebellion. The general approach of the British in India changed from that of a preoccupation with trade to an emphasis upon effective administration and government. As a result of this, many British officials kept somewhat aloof from the Indian population, in the supposed interests of objective and disinterested governance. There was also, in parallel, an attempt to appreciate some of the nuances of Hindu culture, as it was recognized that the roots of the 1857 rebellion lay in a certain arrogance and insensitivity towards Indian customs and culture. Victorian values prevailed during this period, and relationships between British men and Indian women were increasingly discouraged. This was also the period when unmarried British young women travelled out to India, specifically in search of a husband, constituting what was colloquially termed 'the fishing fleet'. After 1857, the British also realized that effective governance would depend on closer contact between India and Britain. In 1869 the Suez Canal opened, shortening dramatically the sea journey between London and Bombay (Karabell, 2003). In addition, one year later, the first submarine telegraph cable connected the two countries, enabling more secure communication.

The British Raj during Victorian times was a very hierarchical society, founded on relatively strict social strata. In this sense it mirrored in many ways, Indian society with its caste system. The system of castes, or varnas, consisting of Brahmins, Kshatriyas, Vaishyas and Shudras, tended to define to some extent, relationships between the British and Indians. Senior British army officers or members of the Indian Civil Service would tend to only mix socially with high caste Indians, and then only on formal occasions such as political events. This meant that senior British administrators might only tend to interact with ordinary Indians in their roles as servants. This may have given the British a somewhat distorted view of Indian society. There were exceptions however to the general assumptions about stratification in Indian society. Some members of the lowest Indian social stratum, the untouchables or 'schedules castes' as they are now termed rose to very senior positions in Indian society despite the discrimination against them. An example is K. R. Narayanan (1920–2005) who became President of India. In addition, some British army officers learned to speak Hindustani fluently in order to command Indian soldiers effectively. Inevitably, they acquired considerable understanding of Indian society.

Indians in general respected the way in which the British colonial rulers organized life in India. This was particularly true of the ordinary Indian agricultural workers in the villages. They often relied upon the British District Commissioner, in the Indian Civil Service, to resolve problems and disputes. Perhaps ironically, they often had more confidence in the representative of the colonial power than they did in the local rich Indian landowners, who they often saw as exploitative. They saw the District Commissioner as someone who would resolve problems in an impartial way, irrespective of the caste of the people involved. Ordinary Indians could thus have a positive experience of their dealings with the British army and the Raj in general.

When large-scale migration to Britain started in the 1960s, many Indians must have been surprised by what they saw. When they grew up to adulthood during the Raj, they would only have seen British people in positions of authority, whether in the army or civil service, or as managers of commercial enterprises. When Indians arrived in Britain in the 1960s they were astonished to see British men sweeping the roads, collecting refuse or doing labouring work on building sites. In India this was the type of work carried out exclusively by lower-caste people. Thus when Indians told their relatives back home about this phenomenon in letters, or during visits, they all must have concluded that Britain, like India, was very much a society structured along caste lines. When the young travellers of the counter-culture arrived in India in the late 1960s, in threadbare clothes and with very little money, ordinary Indians assumed that they were from ordinary, lower-caste families, in all probability escaping from exploitation by a rich ruling class – the kind of people who they had encountered ruling their country 20 to 30 years previously!

This analysis paved the way for a relatively close relationship between the young travellers and the ordinary Indian. All along the overland trail through Afghanistan, Pakistan, India and Nepal, young people found that in the tea houses, craft and clothes shops, local food markets and rest houses, locals were pleased to meet them not only for the trade but also to chat and find out what was happening in other countries. The travellers were interested in the culture and religion, and loved to interact with local people and to learn from them. This generally assured them a warm welcome. Importantly, young travellers were perceived as being of a similar social class to the local people. They did not drive expensive cars, and often travelled with the locals on public transport. Young people would therefore often be invited to local weddings, religious ceremonies, village events and generally to discuss the places they had travelled through.

Most young people in India made use of the railway system to travel around the sub-continent and found it an excellent way to meet Indians from a wide range of backgrounds, and hence to learn about Hinduism and Indian culture. The first railway line in India operated from Bombay to Thane in 1853, and some members of the East India Company began to realize its potential for trade. Manchester cotton entrepreneurs understood the potential benefits of transporting Indian cotton quickly and efficiently to the major ports of Bombay, Madras and Calcutta, for shipment to England. Equally, some elements of the army in India saw the potential for transporting troops. However, the real catalyst for railway expansion was the Mutiny of 1857. When the insurrection started, the British army found it very difficult to respond quickly to the main points of rebellion, because of the time taken to march an army in the heat of the summer. It was realized that an effective rail network would have transformed the situation and enabled order to be restored much more quickly, with many lives on both sides being saved. After the Mutiny, and the Indian administration passed to the British Crown, the rail network was expanded very quickly, and by 1870 it was possible to travel directly from Bombay to Calcutta. Among other advantages this linked the munitions factories at Calcutta with the rest of the country. Initially the administrators of the Raj wondered whether the Indians would use the railways a great deal. Although there would be some social divisions between first, second and third class, it was realized that in reality Indians of different castes would inevitably have to travel close together in the same carriages, and this might be unacceptable to them. In the result, this proved not to be a problem, and the railway system proved very popular. It helped to unite a country of different languages and cultures and made it possible for ordinary Indians to visit distant family members and to attend religious festivals which ordinarily would have been impractical. For young travellers in the 1960s, as indeed today, the railways enabled them to rub shoulders with Indians of all backgrounds. Indian railway carriages are innately very sociable places, and it was a very good way to learn about Indian customs and practices.

After the Mutiny, the administrators of the new Raj were very cautious about handing over the management of the railway system entirely to Indians, for fear of a new challenge to their authority. The development of relationships between British men and Indian women over the years of the East India Company had lead to a considerable community of Anglo-Indians who to some extent were socially isolated. They generally found it difficult to be accepted either by Indian or British society. However, because of their attachment to the British social system, they were often recruited to operate the railways, and this became an occupation with which the community was associated. The novel Bhowani Junction (Masters, 1960) explored the complex social pressures within this community. 'Bhowani' is a fictional town, although probably based upon Jhansi, in Uttar Pradesh, which today remains an important centre of rail travel.

One of the phenomena which struck the overlanders of the 1960s was the ease with which they could communicate in India. Through Turkey, Iran, and Afghanistan, English was not very widely spoken, but once the traveller reached Pakistan and India, the situation changed. India has over 20 languages which are principal or 'scheduled' languages in the Constitution of India. However, Hindi, the commonest language in the northern part of India, is the official language of the country and is used in government publications. It is written in the Devnagari script which is also used to write the scriptural language of Sanskrit. However, Hindi is spoken and understood very little in the southern part of India. English is in effect, the *lingua franca* of India, which explains why the travellers of the counter-culture could communicate relatively easily with ordinary Indians.

The reason for the popularity of English again lies historically in the aftermath of the 1857 rebellion. Once the administration of India passed to the British government through the Government of India Act of 1858, there was a general realization that the advances in technology prevalent in Europe should also be transferred to India. The expansion of steam ships between Britain and India shortened the journey time considerably, and transport in India was improved by the construction of canals. However, in order to implement new technological advances effectively there was an appreciation among the British that higher education opportunities for Indians needed to be improved. The universities of Bombay, Madras and Calcutta had been founded in 1857, but now underwent a rapid expansion. There were opportunities for Indians to be educated both in their mother tongue and in English in order to be able to work effectively with British engineers and technologists. Indians gradually became established in all areas of the functioning of the country. Not only did the understanding of English language begin to permeate the whole country, but it also greatly helped the travellers of the 1960s in understanding Hindu culture. One might also argue that this ability to interact internationally in English has in modern times helped Indian commercial and scientific progress, as evidenced for example by Bangalore becoming the centre of a thriving information technology and space research culture.

Young travellers in the 1960s would also have been surprised at the level of poverty in India, along with the evidence of strict social class divisions. After independence, there were consistent attempts by the Indian government to tackle discrimination against the Dalits or untouchables. The Untouchability (Offences) Act was passed in 1955, and measures were introduced involving positive action in order to assist untouchables in gaining better access to education and employment. Nevertheless, young people in the 1960s did not have to be in India long to see evidence of the way in which lower-caste people or untouchables were treated.

In both Britain and the United States they would have been aware of the differential treatment of people based upon social class. There was, for example, increasing discussion and awareness in the 1960s of the more limited opportunities of working class children in the education system, and the way in which this manifested itself in terms of later life chances. However, in India, young travellers were normally surprised at the more overt nature of the social class differences, in terms for example, of the everyday social interaction between different castes. There was very often clear social separation between people of higher and lower social status. In addition, although clear distinctions of wealth and standard of living existed in the West, these were much less evident than the quality of life distinctions in India. The scale and depth of the poverty evident in India made a lasting impression on young people. The manifestations of poverty included begging by large numbers of children, who lived permanently on the streets; the injuries and diseases which were everywhere evident, when in the West people would have been admitted to hospital and the number of homeless people apparently surviving by scavenging and recycling refuse which they could collect. Young people often spoke of the horror and helplessness when first confronted by such extremes of poverty, but of finally trying to exclude it from their minds through an inability to change the situation.

Young people coming to India in the 1960s sometimes had a rather unrealistic notion of Indian society. It was often perceived as a country in which people lived a relaxed, spiritual life in a largely idyllic, sub-tropical setting. In fact, when young people arrived, they were often overcome by the sheer sense of a struggle for survival in India rather than a pre-occupation with matters religious. It was true that say a men's hair-dresser working on the street would be surrounded by images of Hindu Gods, but if you wanted to find practitioners of yoga or meditation these usually had to be sought out in ashrams or specialist centres. The majority of people were pre-occupied with an economic struggle for survival.

Many of the young people who travelled to India were well-educated and had often been to university. Yet, disillusioned with a materialistic society, they had often rejected the idea of becoming established in a conventional career and had taken to travelling the world. There was no doubt a form of cognitive dissonance in some Westerners between their rejection of material opportunities and the continual struggle for survival of the people they met in India.

As the decade of the 1970s neared an end, and many of the opportunities for overland travel to India ended, this generation of young people had to find ways of adapting to their future lives. For many the return to a life of relative conformity in the West was not easy. However, the possibility of inexpensive travel of this type helped to create the concept of the 'gap year' for young people, which has since become so popular. The young people who went on this journey also brought back with them an understanding and tolerance of different cultures which in a perhaps diffuse way had an impact on Western attitudes to other cultures and countries.

Some young people, however, managed to combine their experience of the road to India with a future career. In July 1972 Tony and Maureen Wheeler, a young couple in their early 20s, set off to drive in their rather ancient vehicle to Asia. They sold their minivan in Afghanistan and then used a variety of means of transport until they finally reached Australia in December of 1972. The following year, a 94-page book was produced as a result of their travels, providing advice for young people wanting to make the overland route from Europe to Australia. The book 'Across Asia on the Cheap' was an immediate success and was followed by other travel books for young people. Thus was developed the 'Lonely Planet' brand.

The 'package tour' travel industry was only just developing in the 1960s, and the young people of the counter-culture opened up countries to cut-price travel which would not normally have been visited by travellers in any great numbers. In doing so, they paved the way for young people to explore less-travelled parts of the world on a shoestring. With regard to India, they took Western commercial enterprise with them and enabled both Westerners and Indians to export Indian cultural artefacts back to Europe. This saw the beginning of the commercialization of Indian religion and culture, and its integration into Western cultural life. It also laid the basis for a serious and scholarly study of Hinduism, and saw the expansion of the study of Hinduism within educational curricula in Britain at all levels from high schools to universities. Indian art influenced everything from clothes design to album covers, and affected all aspects of Western creative work.

Perhaps most significant of all, however, was that a generation of young people had the opportunity to travel to Eastern countries, not to seek conquest, riches or dominion over other peoples, but simply to learn and understand. They lived in Afghanistan when that country was at peace; they travelled around Iran, before the advent of an ideological conflict between it and the West and they saw traditional India before that country entered the era of space exploration. It is to be hoped that the impressions they brought back with them have contributed something to human peace and understanding.

Further reading

Brown, C. S. (1971) *Overland to India: A Practical Guide to Getting There Through Istanbul, Turkey, Iran, Afghanistan, and West Pakistan Cheaply, Happily, and Unhassled*. New York: Outerbridge & Dienstfrey.

May, G. G. (2008) *Overland to India*. Stockport: Rixon Groove.

Mehta, G. (1994) *Karma Cola: Marketing the Mystic East*. New York: Vintage.

Odzer, C. (1995) *Goa Freaks: My Hippie Years in India*. Northwood: Foxrock.

Tomory, D. (1998) *A Season in Heaven: True Tales from the Road to Kathmandu*. London: Lonely Planet.

Wells, B. (2008) *Snapshots of the Hippie Trail*. London: Lulu.

Worrall, J. (2012) *Travelling for Beginners: To Kathmandu in '72*. London: Amazon.

13

Meditation and a secular religion

Summary

In the 1960s students of Hindu culture were attracted to the practices of meditation and of the chanting of mantra. Originally this would have perhaps been under the guidance of a guru or of the leader of a Hindu religious organization. These practices would have been undertaken initially in a distinctly religious context. It is interesting to observe, however, that there has been a form of secularization of meditation, yoga and the use of mantra. Yoga is often taught solely as a form of physical exercise, and meditation as a means of maintaining a calm approach to life rather than exploring the spiritual element of these activities. This chapter analyses the gradual secularization of certain aspects of Hindu religious practice and their incorporation into mainstream life as techniques of physical and psychological well-being.

Introduction

One of the main underlying threads of the 1960s counter-culture was the idea of finding a world view which was completely different to that then existing in the West. To some extent rock music and the use of psychedelic drugs offered access to such an alternative world. However, the possibilities of Eastern culture, and in particular that of the Indian sub-continent, offered the greatest possibilities. Stories of the achievements of mystics and yogis abounded. Quite apart from the physical achievements of advanced hatha yoga practice, there were stories of yogis capable of swallowing acid, of levitation, of remaining buried for prolonged periods of time and of walking on hot coals. There were also stories of mystics in the Himalayas being able to traverse great distances extremely quickly and of being able to survive naked in extremely cold conditions. All such stories pointed to abilities and ideas, so different from normal experience in the West, as to suggest quite literally a totally different or 'counter culture'.

In the early 1960s, one of the strong appeals of the Indian sub-continent was the possibility of gaining access to such novel ideas, and the attention of young people inevitably turned to the relatively few examples of people who had tried before to do this. The United States had a particularly celebrated example in the traveller and student of Indian religions, Theos Bernard (1908–1947).

Bernard was born in California, but had grown up in Tombstone, Arizona. His parents both had a strong interest in Indian religion and this no doubt influenced him. At the age of 20 years he enrolled at the University of Arizona to study for a degree in law. During his undergraduate studies an Indian friend of his parents introduced him to the practice of hatha yoga, and he gradually developed considerable expertise. After he obtained his bachelor degree, he moved to New York, and enrolled at Columbia University on a MA course in Philosophy. Throughout his studies he maintained a strong interest in Eastern religions, and on completion of his MA he decided to embark on a visit to India and hopefully Tibet in order to further his understanding. He travelled to India in 1936, and after visiting different parts of the country, settled in Kalimpong in Bengal. This town in the foothills of the Himalayas had a considerable Tibetan Buddhist population. Bernard decided to embark on a serious study of Tibetan language as a precursor to his planned visit to Tibet. Later, after discussions with the British representatives in India and in Gangtok, he obtained the necessary authority to traverse Sikkim and eventually to enter Tibet.

Bernard's evident commitment to learning not only contemporary spoken Tibetan but also the classical written Tibetan language of the religious documents must have impressed the people he met in Lhasa. He was in Tibet for about four months, and during this time he made the acquaintance of leading members of the Lhasa government, and also key members of the Buddhist religious hierarchy. Bernard visited both Drepung and Ganden monasteries, and managed to negotiate permission from leading Tibetan monks, to export many examples of Tibetan manuscripts to the United States, including several hundred volumes of the main Tibetan Buddhist scriptures. Given the very small number of Westerners who had visited Tibet up to that point, reaching this agreement was a considerable achievement, and one which created the basis for the future of academic Tibetan studies in the

West. Indeed, upon his return to the United States, Bernard established the Tibetan Text Society in Santa Barbara, California, and he also started work on a guide to the grammar of the Tibetan language. From 1937 onwards he concentrated on writing books on a variety of subjects related to his travels and also to his studies of hatha yoga and meditation (Bernard, 2009, 2010). In 1942 he enrolled again at Columbia University, this time to undertake doctoral research. At the time there was no Department of Religious Studies at Columbia, and hence Bernard enrolled in the Department of Philosophy. Fortunately, a professor in that department, Herbert Schneider, had strong interests in comparative religion and indeed had been given the title 'Professor of Religion'. Professor Schneider took an interest in Bernard's research and applied to the University for permission to accept a doctoral thesis in the area of comparative religion. Permission was granted for the submission of the thesis within the philosophy department. This was the first time that doctoral research had been formally undertaken at Columbia in the area of comparative religion. Bernard submitted his PhD thesis in 1943 which was entitled 'Hatha Yoga: The Report of a Personal Experience'. Not only was the thesis accepted for the degree of PhD but also it was highly commended. The thesis was later published and became a widely read and influential book (Bernard, 2007).

Theos Bernard would not have known at the time, but his work on Hatha Yoga was the starting point for the development of the study of comparative religion at Columbia University. Through the impetus of this thesis, and the interest and enthusiasm of staff at the University, a Department of Religion was established in 1961, and later in 1966 a Professor of Sanskrit was appointed. Thus by the 1960s undergraduate and research students were able to follow in the footsteps of Theos Bernard and study Indian religions.

Bernard decided to travel again to India in 1947, with a view to collecting more manuscripts from monasteries in the Western Himalayas. However, this was the period during which India acquired independence, and there was considerable conflict between Hindu and Muslim communities. On his return journey from the monasteries he had visited, he was passing through the Kulu region in the state of Himachal Pradesh, when he was shot and killed. It seems likely that the motivation for the murder was either robbery or a case of mistaken identity. The further sadness for his family was that his body was never found. Although only 39 years when he was killed, he achieved an enormous amount in terms of spreading a knowledge of yoga, and of Indian and Tibetan culture in the West.

Fortunately, many of the artefacts, manuscripts and documents which he brought back to the United States as a result of his first expedition have not been lost. Some are kept in the Beinecke Rare Book and Manuscript Library at Yale University, while others are in the Theos Bernard Collection, at the East Asian and Bancroft Libraries at the University of California, Berkeley.

Throughout his travels and studies in India and Tibet, Theos Bernard tried to acquire an understanding of traditional yoga practice as exemplified by contemporary yogis. He made strenuous efforts to identify suitable teachers so that he could develop an appreciation of the traditions of hatha yoga on the Indian sub-continent. He was only too aware that even traditional yoga teachers differ somewhat in the emphasis they place on aspects of the practice, but Bernard tried to synthesize what he saw as the core of the teachings. In his writings he tried to set down what he saw as the key, traditional teachings of Indian and Tibetan gurus.

In particular, in yoga he stressed the relationship between the development of the body and the understanding of mental processes. For him, the physical aspects of the postures and the use of breathing exercises were simply a precursor to developing a control of the mind. Yoga was thus ultimately a spiritual process and not simply a matter of developing and exercising the body.

Time and again Bernard alluded to the need for regular and systematic practice in yoga. He described the training programmes which he had undertaken, and explained that a serious and determined approach was required if expertise was to be developed. He always stressed the importance of having the guidance and help of a good teacher.

Even though Hatha Yoga had developed within a Hindu religious context, Bernard did not appear to take the view that any one religion was superior to another. He saw yoga as potentially having an integrative function in religion, in that it was relevant to many different types of religious practice. He felt that one thing which many people had in common was an inability to control the way in which their mind functioned, and the way in which random thoughts often gained control over their mind. One of the best ways to gain control over the mind was to use breathing exercises, for example, those which involved regular breathing practice. Such practice would calm the mind and enable the individual to develop an analytic and reflective approach to their thoughts. The individual would then be less under the influence of thoughts which simply appeared in the mind and would be able to exercise greater mental concentration. Bernard also pointed out that when the mind was focusing upon pleasurable experiences of any kind, then this would not encourage progress in yoga.

Although Theos Bernard was instrumental in informing the West about contemporary yoga practice, it can be argued that he did not attempt to amend the practice in order to make it more accessible to people. It does not appear that for him yoga was in any way a commodity, even though he did deliver many lectures in order to draw attention to his travels and his findings.

Although yoga has in many ways gradually become more secularized, Theos Bernard sought to retain its fundamental spiritual dimension.

The spread of yoga in the West

Although Theos Bernard's achievements in terms of the academic and practical study of yoga were extremely impressive, he perhaps did not unfortunately live long enough to have a worldwide impact. Born ten years after Bernard, an Indian yoga practitioner named B. K. S. Iyengar was to have such an impact. He was born in the state of Karnataka in southern India in a relatively poor family. His father was employed as a schoolteacher, and the family had to rely upon growing a small amount of vegetables in order to subsist. In 1918 there was an influenza pandemic, which had a serious effect upon the health of Iyengar's mother. In its turn, her ill health affected her baby, and Iyengar was weak and unwell as a child. By 1934 when Iyengar was 16 years of age, he was still not physically strong, and the decision was taken to send him to Mysore where his brother-in-law, S. T. Krishnamacharya, was well-known as a teacher of yoga. The idea was that the discipline of hatha yoga might improve his health and physical conditioning. Although he did not always find Krishnamacharya to be a sympathetic teacher, Iyengar began to realize that yoga practice was beginning to have a positive impact on his health. Once he appreciated the potential benefits of yoga he became motivated to practice diligently. His extensive practice resulted in his gaining something of a local reputation as a yoga teacher.

During the 1930s and 1940s Iyengar continued with his studies of yoga, gradually extending his reputation in India. It was during this time that he began to develop some of the ideas that would eventually become the system known as Iyengar Yoga. He first of all realized that it was yoga that had helped him recover from his childhood illnesses, and that there was no reason why yoga could not help others recover from physical disabilities. He therefore began to see the potential of yoga, not just for a few people, but for anyone at all who was willing to make the effort to practise. As Iyengar developed his ideas about using yoga to assist people with medical difficulties, he began to place a lot of emphasis upon improving the suppleness and physical capacity of the body. He also insisted that his students position themselves correctly when practising the asanas. Sometimes students were not physically able to adopt the correct positions for asanas, either because of illness, age or inflexibility. Iyengar had noted that sometimes celebrated yogis of the past had employed physical supports to assist students in attaining the correct asana positions. Students might, for example, lean against naturally occurring objects such as trees or rocks to gain support. When it seemed appropriate Iyengar decided to adopt this philosophy in his own teaching and to use a combination of such objects as cushions or straps in order to help his students. This enabled them to attain the correct asana position, and as they gradually became more adept, to gradually relinquish the use of the support technique. Such aids enabled Iyengar's students to master postures with much less possibility of injury and to move on more rapidly to more complex asanas. This was important for Iyengar, because one of his key principles was that it was necessary to plan a clear sequence of asanas which would benefit the student. He also devised a series of asanas which he considered would be beneficial to help someone with a specific medical ailment. The use of physical aids also enabled students to maintain a particular asana for much longer than would normally have been possible. This enabled them to gain much greater benefits from the posture than would normally have been possible.

Iyengar also placed great emphasis upon the practice of pranayama or breathing exercises. While his students were performing asanas, he taught them the most beneficial systems of breathing. He was of the view that a correct approach to breathing helped to link the physical aspects of yoga with meditation practice. Iyengar encouraged his students to focus their meditation upon the asana which they were carrying out. In this way, the hatha yoga, the pranayama and the meditation became an integrated activity. The result was a feeling of calm and of sensitivity towards one's surroundings.

During the early 1950s Iyengar met the violinist Yehudi Menuhin, and the two men became close friends. Menuhin became a student of yoga and encouraged Iyengar to teach more in the West. Menuhin had a wide circle of contacts and recommended to them Iyengar's approach to yoga. Iyengar introduced his system of yoga to a range of people including the then Queen of Belgium and Nikita Krushchev. Iyengar always believed in the principle that yoga should and could be made available to everyone. He introduced adaptations to classical hatha yoga which made the discipline attractive and relevant to the West, and today Iyengar's teaching approach has become almost synonymous with hatha yoga. In 1966 he wrote the best-selling book 'Light on Yoga', which helped to turn Iyengar into a worldwide personality and increasingly popular author (Iyengar, 2001, 2006, 2013).

Meditation in the West

One of the features of the period of the 1960s, particularly in the United States, was that subjects such as meditation started to make an appearance within formal academic courses in universities. This was an interesting and significant development. During the medieval period in Europe the study of theology or divinity was restricted to a Christian perspective, and within such a paradigm there was the assumption that students were committed to the normative doctrinal principles prevalent within the Christian Church. This tradition continued into the twentieth century with the continued assumption that arguably the major role of departments of theology was to provide academic training for those who would ultimately assume holy orders within a Christian denomination. Part of the iconoclastic challenge of the 1960s, however, was that first religion or religions were a fitting subject of academic study, irrespective of the nature of the religion or of its cultural origins. Secondly, and perhaps even more radical, was the notion that aspects of religious traditions could be analysed and discussed within our higher education system, not exclusively as a religious idea, but as what might be described as a therapy or a humanistic psychology. In 1968 at the University of California, Berkeley, Eknath Easwaran, an Indian academic, delivered one of the early academic courses in meditation, within the US higher education system.

Easwaran was born in the state of Kerala in southern India in 1910. He always stressed the significant role played by his maternal grandmother in his religious development. It was from her that he acquired the appreciation of trying to live spiritually each day. He grew up during the period of the British rule in India, and also while Gandhi was leading the independence movement. Easwaran was deeply influenced by Gandhi and in particular by his philosophy of non-violence. As a young man he studied English Literature and also read widely on Christianity. At the University of Nagpur he obtained first-class honours degrees in literature and in law. He returned to the university as an academic and ultimately became the Head of the Department of English. During the development of his academic career he did not, however, lose sight of his spiritual interests and practice. Although deeply committed to his own Hindu tradition, and especially to the Bhagavad Gita, he became very interested in other religions. In particular he came to believe in the idea that all of the world's main religions could enable someone to attain profound spiritual insights.

In 1959 Easwaran was the recipient of a Fulbright scholarship to work at the University of California, Berkeley, and two years later he founded the Blue Mountain Centre of Meditation. By this time he had become well-known in California as a speaker on Hinduism. He also established a publishing company, the Nilgiri Press, in Berkeley, and wrote a number of books on meditation and related issues (Easwaran, 1978, 2010, 2011).

Easwaran is perhaps best-known for his approach to meditation which became known as 'Passage Meditation'. The central concept of this approach is the repetition, usually under the breath, of a selected extract from the writings within one of the world's major religions. The extract is usually selected because it has some special significance or meaning for the meditator. It may be chosen from scriptures, or perhaps from the writings of a religious teacher. According to Easwaran, the repetition of the passage, and implicitly the reflection upon the meaning, has a positive effect upon the way we view the world. The repetition of such a passage is not essentially the equivalent to repeating a mantram. A passage is longer and offers greater opportunity for reflection on the content. A mantram is a short phrase or syllable, the repetition of which is also advocated by Easwaran. The use of mantra is advantageous in calming the mind and helping to discipline it in terms of controlling the arising of negative thoughts. Easwaran was very positive about the use of mantra and felt that they contributed a great deal to the control of the mind. The use of a passage and of a mantram were the two main meditation techniques advocated by Easwaran. He felt that they were very helpful in enabling us to control the rising and falling of ideas in the mind and in encouraging mental concentration. Moreover, they also helped the mind to operate more slowly, with a calmness and tranquillity.

As a central element in meditation, Easwaran wanted to help us to avoid discriminating between those things which we thought we liked and those things which we did not like. His argument was that once we consider something desirable, we become unhappy if we cannot have it. It is much better he considered to be impartial towards material objects, and to avoid becoming attached to our desires.

Easwaran always emphasized that in order for someone to practise his form of meditation, they did not need to subscribe to any specific religious belief system. This system of meditation was open to all. Much more important were certain key principles of living one's life and of relating to other people. These include a lack of selfishness in our dealings with other people, and a consistent attempt to develop relationships of spiritual empathy with others.

Based upon his reflections on the world, and his practice of meditation, Easwaran made a number of important observations about the human condition. He noted, for example, that our minds are continually receiving new thoughts, and that in fact, many of them are negative in effect. He pointed out that we cannot always prevent thoughts arising in our minds, but that through meditation we need to practise just letting them fade away and leave us. Easwaran explained that many thoughts are responsible for the negative feelings of greed, desire, anger, irritation, pride, disdain and so on. Dwelling upon such thoughts over and over is a negative way of spending out time and ultimately has a negative effect upon. During meditation we should practise not responding to such thoughts and just letting them go.

He argued that very often it is not the behaviour of other people towards us which is significant, but our response to their behaviour. On the one hand, if someone is rude or condescending towards us, with effort, we can learn to ignore such behaviour, and continue calmly with our lives. On the other hand, if we think about that behaviour a great deal, it may make us feel angry and irritated, feelings which are not ultimately going to make us happy.

Easwaran saw meditation as a means of understanding life in a more positive and beneficial manner. Apart from helping us respond to others in a better way, it can also help us understand the phenomena of life and death in a more objective and balanced manner. He argued that life and death are not two separate periods of time, but are more like a continuum. From the point of our birth, events are set in train which gradually lead us to a point where our body ceases to exist and commences the process of dispersal and disintegration. This does not happen, however, just at the point of death, but is occurring throughout life as our body cells become older and less functional. For Easwaran, meditation can help us to see and understand the process of death and dying, rather than having an irrational fear of it.

Many Hindus do not use the term 'Hinduism' to describe their religion, but refer to it as 'sanatana dharma'. This term refers to the philosophy and moral principles which are at the heart of being human. Easwaran attempted to state the essential tenets of the sanatana dharma. He argued that in all human beings there exists a soul or a divine spirit which exists eternally. He went on to suggest that within all the main religions of the world there are systems of prayer, meditation and contemplation which enable all human beings to recognize and unite with this soul or atman. To achieve this should be the ultimate purpose for all human beings.

Easwaran pointed out that in the materialistic West, people often tended to concentrate on objects and on the world outside themselves. They looked for stimuli which were around them in order to find meaning in life. He advised them, however, to search within themselves in order to find happiness and spiritual fulfilment. One can see how well this message appealed to the young people of the 1960s counter-culture.

Meditation as a therapy

Prior to the mid-twentieth century, there tended to be an assumption in the West that the health of the body was generally not connected with the condition of the mind. In other words, our psychological state was not normally considered relevant to our physical state. However, a growing awareness of the practice of meditation, and of its psychological effects, began to suggest that not only were the mind and body connected, but also meditation could result in beneficial physical effects too.

In 1956 a Melbourne psychologist and psychiatrist named Ainslie
Meares (1910–1986) travelled to India and Nepal to study meditation
practices under different gurus. In Nepal he located a guru who taught him
a simple approach to meditation which he thought could be employed to
help relieve pain in those suffering from illness. Even though this was rather
a radical idea for the time in Western societies, Meares became more and
more convinced that meditation could in principle be used for therapeutic
purposes whether to help psychiatric patients or those suffering from
physical complaints.

Practices associated with meditation and contemplation have a long
history in the realm of religion, not solely within Eastern religions. The
Christian desert fathers, for example, employed such practices in Egypt in
the early centuries of the Christian era. Besides within Hinduism, meditation
has also had a central role in Buddhism. At the end of the Second World War,
during the American occupation of Japan, some American soldiers became
aware of the meditation practices of Zen Buddhism and took the ideas back
with them to the United States. It may well have been that they found the
peaceful, tranquil practice of meditation, a useful antidote to the terrible
stresses of warfare.

Through the 1950s and into the decade of the 1960s, a deeper
understanding of meditation began to appear in the West. It was appreciated
that it could be viewed either as part of a religious discipline or alternatively
as a secular activity linked to psychology or psychiatry. In the former case,
on the one hand, meditation tended to be viewed as a means of achieving
enlightenment, of having a direct experience of God or of some divine
principle and of achieving a different form of consciousness. It also tended
to be associated with a life of renunciation and discipline. On the other hand,
meditation in a secular context tended to be associated with the aim of
psychological growth, of acquiring an enhanced self-image and of gaining
more confidence, both personally and in connection to relationships with
other people. Through a process of secular meditation there was also the
feeling that one could develop more control of the mind, with a range of
associated advantages.

During the 1960s Meares started to use meditation as a means of
helping his patients whether suffering from psychological problems or from
illnesses such as cancer. In the latter case, the purpose was not to attempt
to cure the cancer, but to alleviate some of the symptoms and perhaps to
reduce the speed with which the disease spread. He wrote a best-selling
book entitled 'Relief without Drugs' (Meares, 1968).

Meares called his approach to meditation 'Stillness Meditation'. It involved
a fairly simple technique of trying not to clutter up the mind with random
thoughts. When thoughts arose they were gradually allowed to disappear from

the mind, resulting in a feeling of tranquillity. The purpose of this technique was to reduce stress levels and also the continual wrestling of thoughts in the mind, which often resulted in feelings of anxiety.

At the time Meares was in the avant-garde of the use of techniques such as meditation in a clinical context. Many of his professional peers were extremely sceptical about such trends in psychology and psychiatry, but there is now much more support for the use of meditation. This is thus an example of a technique embedded for thousands of years in religions which evolved in India, now becoming established in the West in both spiritual and secular contexts.

Further reading

Ashley-Farrand, T. (1999) *Healing Mantras: Using Sound Affirmations for Personal Power, Creativity and Healing.* London: Wellspring/Ballantine.
Ashley-Farrand, T. (2004) *Mantra Meditation.* Boulder, CO: Sounds True.
Devananda, S. V. (1999) *Meditation and Mantras.* Delhi: Motilal Banarsidass.
Goswami, S. D. (1991) *Prabhupada Meditations*, 2nd edn. New York: GN Press.
Hanegraaff, W. J. (1998) *New Age Religion and Western Culture: Esotericism in the Mirror of Secular Thought.* New York: State University of New York Press.
Kempton, S. (2010) *Meditation for the Love of It.* Boulder, CO: Sounds True.
Keshavadas, S. S. (2000) *Gayatri: The Highest Meditation.* Delhi: Motilal Banarsidass.
Williamson, L. (2010) *Transcendent in America: Hindu-Inspired Meditation Movements as New Religion.* New York: New York University Press.

14

The seeker and an alternative to the consumer society

Summary

The material re-construction which was necessary after the Second World War gave rise, through the 1950s, to a society pre-occupied with consumerism. This was rejected by the youth counter-culture of the 1960s, who sought a society based on different values including respect for the environment; avoidance of conflict; gender, religious and racial equality and genuine democratic participation in society. Hinduism, with its lack of a centrally imposed ideology, its tolerance of other views and its emphasis upon non-violence, provided an influential set of alternative values. In addition, its tradition of encouraging people to find their own spiritual identity supported the sense of individualism popular with young people. This concluding chapter explores the theme of the 'individual seeker' within the counter-culture, and the extent to which this can be related to the influence of Hinduism.

Introduction

On the face of it at least, there would appear to be clear philosophical differences between the societal systems of the West and that of India. In the West there is an apparent sense of individualism which is linked to an economic system of free-market liberalism. When Thomas Jefferson in 1776 sketched out a draft of the US Declaration of Independence, he may have been thinking of the spirit of individualism when he wrote that citizens have the right to 'life, liberty and the pursuit of happiness'. Some may argue of course that liberty and individualism are not necessarily associated. The liberty of the individual may depend not upon any qualities inherent in the individual, but upon the type of political system assured by the collectivity. Equally, the pursuit of happiness by the individual may well-conflict with the happiness of others. Nevertheless, in the Declaration of Independence there is an implicit emphasis upon the rights and equality of the individual.

In Indian society a rather different emphasis has evolved. Perhaps the central concept of the Hindu religion is dharma, and an understanding of this concept has traditionally informed the relationship between the individual and the collective society. The Hindu religion, or to use the term often preferred in India, 'sanatana dharma', rests upon the assumption that there is a spiritual and moral system which pervades life and the universe. If the universe and all aspects of human existence within it are to function properly, then human beings must accept their responsibility to support this moral system as best they can. This responsibility may involve such actions as behaving ethically in personal relationships, protecting the environment, carrying out the expected religious rituals, helping and respecting members of the family and working hard at one's traditional occupation. One might sum this up by saying that there is a responsibility to support the norms and values of the established collectivity. This responsibility is a duty which comes about when one is born into Hindu society. This duty is what is meant by dharma.

Therefore, the fundamental quality of Hindu society is normative and associated with the support of the collectivity. Nevertheless, there are strong elements within this essentially religious society which support ideas of individuality. Hinduism is not a religion with a central authority figure or a single set of authoritative scriptures. While people may generally tend to follow family traditions in terms of religion, there is considerable freedom for people to use their own judgement in selecting a religious teacher, choosing scriptural texts to read, making offerings to deities and selecting a location for a pilgrimage. One might thus describe Hindu society as individualistic within the context of a broad commitment to the collectivity.

Counter-cultural ethics

The counter-culture of the 1960s superficially gave the impression of a hedonistic individualism. Unconventional clothes, the use of drugs, a liberal approach to sex, rock music, festivals, a rejection of capitalist economic systems, squats and a philosophy of 'do your own thing', all conspired to give the impression of a hippie sub-culture which was predominantly concerned with the pursuit of pleasure and excitement. It can be argued, however, that this is a relatively superficial analysis. The principal goal of the counter-culture was, as its name implies, to provide an alternative to the prevailing culture which had developed since the Second World War. It was not, however, just a matter of an alternative. The fundamental idea was to challenge the prevalent society with a different set of values, and hence to change it. The wearing of colourful, non-standard clothes challenged the accepted norm of the suit and narrow tie. The use of drugs carried the additional excitement that it was illegal. For some, the rejection of the institution of marriage was not so much a dislike of fidelity and living as a couple rather than the act of challenging the institution of marriage and the conventions which accompanied it. Hence the counter-culture proposed alternatives to the existing society, not primarily in the pursuit of individual pleasure, but in order to try to move society in a different direction.

The young people of the counter-culture were interested in establishing social movements which would in their view help to create a fairer and more ethical society. The use of different types of habitation was a case in point. When young people took over empty inner-city housing and turned it into squats, it was only partly about living an alternative lifestyle. Symbolically, this was just as much concerned with demonstrating the waste of having usable housing standing empty when there were so many homeless, or poorly housed people. Another case in point was the growth of vegetarianism during the 1960s. It was gradually realized that it was much more efficient in terms of energy usage to eat vegetables rather than to eat animals which themselves lived off vegetable matter. This was quite apart from ethical questions about killing animals for food. Hence vegetarianism was not simply a hippy lifestyle choice, but a rational means of employing the planet's resources more effectively. Many of the fashions of the 1960s were not so much concerned with individual choices, but rather with a sense of responsibility towards society.

In fact, much had been learned in the 1960s from India, where a majority of the population were vegetarian, and where there was considerable respect for animals, particularly the cow. In India, the concept of vegetarianism was closely linked to the concept of ahimsa or non-violence towards other living organisms.

The 1960s was an era of protest against war and violence, epitomized in the hippy catchphrase of 'peace and love'. The principal target of anti-war protest was the conflict in Vietnam, and many members of the public may have assumed that 'draft dodgers' or others who did not enlist were simply avoiding their obligations as citizens, were afraid to fight, were showing solidarity with the enemy or were communists. Whatever the truth or otherwise in individual cases, the passage of time has provided space for different interpretations of the Vietnam War, and of the role of those who objected to it at the time. The reality of the war in Vietnam was generally evident throughout its duration, because of the capacity of journalists to send images directly back to the United States. It was thus difficult for ordinary American citizens to be unaware of the effects of the use of napalm, defoliants, carpet bombing and the many acts of gratuitous cruelty on both sides of the conflict. Gradually the American population began to view the war as unjust and unethical. Although the anti-war protesters were initially seen as opposing a legitimate American foreign policy to prevent the spread of communism, the protesters slowly began to win the moral debate and to establish the case that America was involved in an immoral war. Although some might have argued at the time that the anti-war protesters were exceeding their rights as individual citizens by challenging on a large scale the legitimately established policies of their government, today in retrospect, many would see the counter-cultural protesters as pointing to the cruelties and illiberal nature of an unjust war. They may at the time have appeared to be interested more in their own individual freedom, but in fact they were arguing for the intrinsic freedoms of whole societies to have the right to live in peace.

Statements of principle

One of the most significant critiques of the nature of American society in the 1960s was the so-called Port Huron Statement (Hayden, 2005). This was a policy statement issued on behalf of an organization called Students for a Democratic Society in June 1962. Formed initially in 1960 this organization aimed to transform the political process in the United States, using strategies such as direct social action, and participative decision making. The Port Huron Statement is a detailed policy document drafted largely by Tom Hayden who later became a leading figure in the counter-cultural movement (Hayden, 2008). The Statement was named after Port Huron, Michigan which was the location of the first major gathering of the Society. There is within the Statement, a detailed analysis of the perceived ills of American society, and by implication the alleged failings of other Western societies. Throughout the 1960s the Statement provided a set of political and social aspirations for the counter-cultural movement.

One of the major cornerstones of the Port Huron Statement was the continued 'Cold War' between the Eastern and Western blocs, and the inability of American administrations since the Second World War to ameliorate the situation. There was in the early 1960s a genuine fear in the West of the possibility of total annihilation through a nuclear conflict with the Soviet bloc, and young political activists placed a great deal of the blame for this upon the US administration. Young people in particular felt they had no real influence over the political decision-making process, because the political system was not genuinely democratic.

The Port Huron Statement was also very critical of the treatment of black people in the United States and the continued prevalence of racist attitudes. It criticized the influence of large corporations, while the average person felt disempowered and impotent in the face of major national and international events. In general the Statement suggested that Americans no longer possessed an enthusiasm and optimism about the role of their country in the world. It was felt that individual people were distanced from those who took the major decisions which affected the future of the country.

In terms of a strategy to rectify this, the Statement proposed that non-violent protest would be the most effective means of raising awareness of these issues. The proponents of the Statement were very keen on using the influence of universities, both students and academics, to voice arguments about their concerns. They felt that universities were in a very good position to raise issues for debate, either through conventional teaching or by acting as a conduit for new ideas during seminars and conferences. The Port Huron Statement, appearing as it did at the start of the 1960s, to some extent acted as a reference point for the counter-culture throughout the decade. The passing of the Gulf of Tonkin resolution in 1964 provided President Johnson with the legitimacy for extending the conflict in Vietnam, and the latter became the prime locus of protest for the counter-culture. Nevertheless, the key principles enunciated in the Port Huron Statement and also applied to the philosophy of the protests against the Vietnam War.

The students who protested against American involvement in Vietnam during the mid-1960s had a very different set of values to their parents. The latter had been reared to accept the authority of both people and organizations who held power and social status. In particular, they tended to acknowledge the legitimate authority of the major institutions of society, the government, police, armed forces, legal and financial organizations. Their children, however, adopted a critical, analytical stance towards the received wisdom of society, and were more sceptical about simplistic interpretation of concepts. Hence patriotism, for example, was not viewed as a blind compliance with government policy. For some it was perhaps viewed as a qualified loyalty to one's government, within fairly closely circumscribed ethical limits. For others, a concept such as patriotism was seen as irrelevant and meaningless to young people who saw themselves essentially as citizens of the world rather than of a particular country. The counter-culture generation therefore may have considered that they had a greater sense of empathy with Vietnamese peasant farmers than with their own parents.

One of the important features of the counter-cultural generation is that as individuals they did not keep their political and social views to themselves but shared them to create a strong sense of group solidarity.

Symbols of change

A range of symbols was used to reinforce this sense of solidarity. Young people grew their hair, listened to rock music and wore unconventional clothes. Some items of clothing such as 'bell-bottom' jeans, Indian kaftans and leather thong sandals were almost de rigeur, but much was a question of individual taste. As the capitalist system was scorned by the counter-culture, many young people bought their clothes from second-hand shops, preferring to recycle clothes rather than purchase new ones. Many wore beads, rings, bracelets and scarves imported from India. Young people attempted to live as inexpensively as possible. They hitch-hiked rather than paying for transport and tried wherever possible to 'crash' on someone's floor in preference to paying for even communal accommodation. Members of the counter-culture tried as far as possible to live outside the limits of conventional society and to challenge traditional ways of life. Many of them had experience of higher education and were often despised by members of traditional society for, as they saw it, wasting their opportunities for a successful life and career. In many ways, members of the counter-culture were seeking a new formulation for living, one which was in harmony with the general principles of the Port Huron Statement, but which was also sufficiently individualistic for them to feel they were 'doing their own thing'.

One of the attractions of India and Hinduism for young people in the 1960s was the notion that it was possible to find a spiritual teacher who would enable them to 'find themselves'. To some extent this was the aim of Allen Ginsberg and his friend Peter Orlovsky when they travelled around India in 1962–1963. In Calcutta, Ginsberg visited the Nimtallah ghat, where dead bodies were cremated. There was an inevitable contrast with the attitudes to death in the West, where there tends to be a fear of dead bodies and of their disposal. In India, however, it seemed a much more natural process. Even though one could watch the actual disintegration of the body, which in one sense was unpleasant to experience; nevertheless, it enabled one to be much more objective and balanced about death. One tended to accept the process as part of the natural ebb and flow of life. Moreover, by experiencing openly the facts, however harsh, of human existence, it encouraged a more direct connection between human beings and the divine.

When young people travelled to India in the 1960s they were often interested in developing an understanding of the spiritual life. They saw India as having a different view of religion, when compared to the West. Their contact with religion in their home country had often involved notions of adherence to strict moral norms, which they usually viewed as unnecessarily oppressive. They wanted the freedom to develop a more individualistic view of spirituality. They perceived religion in the West as being reflected in a powerful and rich hierarchy, which historically had been as much interested in the influence which it could exert, as in helping ordinary people develop their own sense of the spiritual. In India, on the contrary, they saw individuals or small groups establishing their own ashrams, and developing their own styles of worship, apparently independent of the large temple organizations. Although there was an element of truth in this distinction between the two cultures, it involved a generalization which ignored the conformity within Indian society. Westerners also did not probably appreciate the way in which individuals were involved in networks of official religious organizations in India. In addition, for the devout Hindu, the achievement of spiritual enlightenment involves a conformity to religious duties and expectations. Only by conforming in this present existence, and if necessary in many future lives, with religious duties, can the individual achieve a state of enlightenment, and moksha, or escape from a continual cycle of birth and death.

Western travellers were often interested in examining these different tensions and comparing Indian society with the West. However, they often tried to explore Hinduism, not from the point of view of the religious hierarchies of the larger, established temple complexes but from the perspective of ordinary, often poor, Hindus. There were several reasons for this. Westerners were often impecunious and had no money to stay in the large international hotels of New Delhi or Bombay. Moreover, their style of dress did not fit in well with the image of expensive hotels. Their appearance gave the impression that they existed outside the scope of polite society – that they were outsiders. They certainly did not fit the image of the Western business people who frequented the hotels and restaurants of Connaught Circus. The attitude of many Westerners was one of exploring India, rather than trying to change it. They mingled with the poor, without passing judgement on the poverty, stayed in inexpensive rooms, ate the cheapest of food and did not attempt to separate themselves from India's masses. Many working-class Indians must have wondered about what motivated these young Westerners to come to India and live in close proximity with them. They would be more familiar with wealthy Westerners, who tried to avoid contact with India's poverty. They may have assumed that there were problems in Europe and America which persuaded young people to migrate to India in such numbers.

As young people returned to the West, they each brought with them their unique understandings of what they had seen in India. Although their stories fired the imagination of members of the counter-culture in the 1960s, it was a separate development which resulted in a more systematic understanding of Hinduism, particularly in the United States. During the mid-1960s, President Lyndon Johnson was committed to a range of measures to reduce racism and discrimination in the United States. In 1965, as one aspect of this strategy he signed the Immigration and Nationality Services Act, known sometimes as the Hart-Cellar Act. Until this Act, there had been restrictions upon immigration into the United States, generally based upon criteria such as nationality and country of origin. This Act, however, transferred the emphasis to criteria such as education and professional qualifications, potential employability and connections with any family members already resident in the United States. This change of criteria opened up the possibility of immigration to many new categories of people, including religious teachers. The Hindu gurus and swamis who came to teach in the United States during the 1960s and 1970s did so under the terms of this new Act. It was thus possible for different Hindu sects and denominations to become established in America, which, in ensuing years, lead to the building of a number of temples and meditation centres.

Hinduism and individuality

As the formal teaching of Hinduism expanded in the United States and Europe, there was a wider appreciation of the individualism inherent in its philosophy. Hinduism argues that many people without a spiritual perspective on life suffer under an illusion that the physical world with all its materialistic objects and possessions is the only significant reality. This illusion or maya can cause people to become overly attached to material goods. They therefore develop feelings of desire or kama for material objects. They spend their time striving to acquire yet more and more wealth. To look at it another way, they become obsessively concerned with egotistic ideas, and the acquisition of material things for themselves. The consequence of this, according to Hindu philosophy, is that the individual is caught in an endless cycle of birth and re-birth, with all its accompanying suffering. They do not break out of this cycle of samsara, since their state of delusion prevents them accumulating good karma through carrying out moral actions.

Hinduism prescribes certain strategies in order to enable people to mitigate the effects of their past actions, and to develop a better karmic record. In this way they can ultimately escape from samsara and achieve salvation. Several different branches of yoga have their own distinct approach to eliminating the effects of karma and helping the soul to achieve moksha.

Bhakti yoga concentrates upon the principle of devotion. The individual worships the divine, often in the form of a physical manifestation. However, bhakti is not simply a question of practising a number of rituals, but of devotion to the moral principles associated with a particular deity. Raja yoga focuses upon the control of the mind as a means to attaining enlightenment. Various techniques are suggested including the well-known asanas of hatha yoga. Other approaches include the practice of a very simple lifestyle, the use of various approaches to breathing (pranayama) and different techniques of concentration and meditation. Jnana yoga is associated with acquiring knowledge and understanding of the true nature of the human being, and in particular appreciating the divine nature of the human soul (Vivekananda, 1982b). This understanding is often founded upon detailed study, and the mastery of the other schools of yoga. Karma yoga is the yoga of moral action. This approach to yoga encourages people to participate in the world, but to do so in a particular way. We are urged to act in the world, but not to be concerned about the results of our actions. In other words, we should not act merely to acquire benefits for ourselves. We should, in fact, act in a manner which seems to us as being morally appropriate and dedicate that action to God. Any actions we take are therefore in Hindu terms, purified, and will contribute to our achievement of moksha.

The nature of individualism in Hinduism is rooted in the concepts of Jnana yoga. If we perceive the human soul as divine, that the Atman and Brahman are one and the same, and that in fact the entire material universe is synonymous with the divine, then this transforms our view of society and social conventions. It suggests a form of relativism in which one convention is essentially no different from another. The individual can thus find her or his personal way to salvation. As an example, one might consider the Aghori sect in India, which subscribes to a non-dualistic philosophy. Members of the sect as well-known for meditating and practising yoga at cremation grounds, for example, and for carrying a human skull with them as part of their rituals. Their practice of living at the very limits of convention serves at least partly to emphasize this non-dualistic view of life. By sitting close to cremated bodies they apparently reduce their fear of death, and emphasize that life and death are not separate realities, one to be loved and the other feared. In fact, they are part of the same reality, the same divine scheme of the universe. When Aghoris challenge many of the accepted norms of living, they are trying to reinforce our understanding of the unity of the universe and to help us realize that diversity can also be unity.

As a greater understanding of Hinduism evolved in the West during the 1960s and 1970s, devotees began to appreciate that it was acceptable philosophically to experiment with one's own way to find the divine. This was a different concept to religions which were based upon adherence to pre-conceived notions of truth and validity. Members of the counter-culture found an empathy between their own desire for self-expression and the ideas of individualistic, self-discovery which were inherent in Hinduism.

Further reading

Bloom, A. and Breines, W. (2010) *Takin' It to the Streets: A Sixties Reader*, 3rd edn. New York: Oxford University Press.

Cain, C. (ed.) (1999) *Wild Child: Girlhoods in the Counterculture*. New York: Seal Press.

Frank, T. (1998) *The Conquest of Cool: Business Culture, Counterculture, and the Rise of Hip Consumerism*. Chicago: University of Chicago Press.

Hayden, T. (2005) *The Port Huron Statement: The Vision Call of the 1960s Revolution*. New York: PublicAffairs.

Kolsbun, K. (2008) *Peace: The Biography of a Symbol*. Washington, DC: National Geographic.

Lemke-Santangelo, G. (2009) *Daughters of Aquarius: Women of the Sixties Counterculture*. Lawrence, KS: University Press of Kansas.

Lytle, M. H. (2006) *America's Uncivil Wars: The Sixties Era from Elvis to the fall of Richard Nixon*. New York: Oxford University Press.

Mathews, R. (2009) *Jobs of Our Own: Building a Stakeholder Society: Alternatives to the Market and the State*. Irving, TX: Distributist Review Press.

McCleary, J. B. (2004) *Hippie Dictionary: A Cultural Encyclopedia of the 1960s and 1970s*. Berkeley, California: Ten Speed Press.

Miles, B. (2005) *Hippie*. New York: Sterling.

References

Allsop, M. (2000) *Western Sadhus and Sannyasins in India*. Prescott, AZ: Hohm Press.

Aurobindo, S. (1993) *The Integral Yoga: Sri Aurobindo's Teaching and Method of Practice*. Pondicherry, India: Sri Aurobindo Ashram Trust.

—. (2006) *The Life Divine*, 7th edn. Pondicherry, India: Sri Aurobindo Ashram Publication Department.

Bernard, T. (2007) *Hatha Yoga: The Report of a Personal Experience*. New York: Harmony.

—. (2009) *Penthouse of the Gods*. New York: Harmony.

—. (2010) *Heaven Lies Within Us*. New York: Harmony.

Bhaskarananda, S. (2002) *The Essentials of Hinduism: A Comprehensive Overview of the World's Oldest Religion*. Seattle, WA: Viveka.

Bilton, M. and Sim, K. (1993) *Four Hours in My Lai*. New York: Penguin.

Braithwaite, R. (2012) *Afgantsy: The Russians in Afghanistan 1979–1989*. London: Profile.

Buchan, J. (2012) *Days of God: The Revolution in Iran and Its Consequences*. London: John Murray.

Buell, L. (ed.) (2006) *The American Transcendentalists: Essential Writings*. New York: Modern Library.

Burroughs, W. S. (1990) *Naked Lunch*. New York: Grove Press.

Carson, R. (1965) *Silent Spring*. London: Penguin.

Carter, D. (2005) *Stonewall: The Riots That Sparked the Gay Revolution*. New York: St Martin's Griffin.

Chinmoy, S. (2000) *The Wisdom of Sri Chinmoy*. San Diego, CA: Blue Dove Foundation.

—. (2010) *The Jewels of Happiness: Inspiration and Wisdom to Guide Your Life-Journey*. London: Watkins.

Chomsky, N. (1967) 'The Responsibility of Intellectuals', *The New York Review of Books*, 23.2.67 [Online] available at www.chomsky.info/articles/19670223.htm.

Cole, B. (2001) *John Coltrane*. Cambridge, MA: Da Capo Press.

Comfort, A. (1976) *The Joy of Sex: A Gourmet Guide to Lovemaking*. London: Quartet Books.

Coperthwaite, W. S. (2007) *A Handmade Life: In Search of Simplicity*. White River Junction, VT: Chelsea Green.

Dalgleish, M. and Hart, L. (2007) *Indian Head Massage in Essence*. London: Hodder Arnold.

Daniélou, A. (1994) *Complete Kama Sutra*. Rochester, VT: Park Street Press.

—. (trans J.-L. Gabin) (2003) *Shiva and the Primordial Tradition: From the Tantras to the Science of Dreams*. Rochester, VT: Inner Traditions.

Dass, R. (1997) *Journey of Awakening: A Meditator's Guidebook*, 2nd edn. New York: Bantam.

—. (2000) *Still Here: Embracing Aging, Changing and Dying*. New York: Riverhead Books.

—. (2004) *Paths to God: Living the Bhagavad Gita*. New York: Three Rivers Press.

David, S. (2003) *The Indian Mutiny 1857*. London: Penguin.

De Beauvoir, S. (1989) *The Second Sex*. New York: Vintage.

Devi, I. (1965) *Renew Your Life Through Yoga*. London: Allen and Unwin.

—. (2002) *Yoga for You*. Layton, UT: Gibbs M. Smith.

Dobbs, M. (2009) *One Minute to Midnight: Kennedy, Krushchev and Castro on the Brink of Nuclear War*. New York: Vintage.

Docherty, P. (2007) *The Khyber Pass: A History of Empire and Invasion*. London: Faber & Faber.

Doniger, W. and Kakar, S. (2002) *Kamasutra*. Oxford: Oxford University Press.

Easwaran, E. (1978) *Passage Meditation*. Berkeley, CA: Nilgiri Press.

—. (2007) *The Upanishads*. Tomales, CA: The Blue Mountain Center of Meditation.

—. (2010) *God Makes the Rivers to Flow*. Berkeley, CA: Nilgiri Press.

—. (2011) *How to Meditate*. Berkeley, CA: Nilgiri Press.

Feeney, P. (2012) *From Ration Book to e-Book: The Life and Times of the Post-War Baby Boomers*. Stroud: The History Press.

Fischer, L. (1997) *The Life of Mahatma Gandhi*. London: Harper Collins.

Forsthoefel, T. A. and Humes, C. A. (eds) (2005) *Gurus in America*. Albany, NY: State University of New York Press.

Forte, R. (ed.) (2012) *Entheogens and the Future of Religion*. Rochester, VT: Park Street Press.

Friedan, B. (2010) *The Feminine Mystique*. London: Penguin.

Fuller, R. B. (2008) *Operating Manual for Spaceship Earth*. Baden: Lars Müller.

Gaddis, J. L. (2005) *The Cold War: A New History*. London: Penguin.

Gautier, F. (2008) *The Guru of Joy: Sri Sri Ravi Shankar and the Art of Living*. London: Hay House.

Ginsberg, A. (1996) *Indian Journals*. New York: Grove Press.

—. (2009) *Howl, Kaddish and Other Poems*. London: Penguin.

Goffman, K. and Joy, D. (2005) *Counterculture Through the Ages: From Abraham to Acid House*. New York: Villard.

Graves, R. (2000) *Goodbye to All That*. London: Penguin.

Greene, J. M. (2006) *Here Comes the Sun: The Spiritual and Musical Journey of George Harrison*. London: Bantam.

Greer, G. (2006) *The Female Eunuch*. London: Harper Perennial.

Hawley, J. (2001) *The Bhagavad Gita: A Walkthrough for Westerners*. Novato, CA: New World Library.

Hayden, T. (2005) *The Port Huron Statement: The Visionary Call of the 1960s Revolutionary*. New York: Thunder's Mouth Press.

—. (2008) *Writings for a Democratic Society: The Tom Hayden Reader*. San Francisco: City Lights.

Hesse, H. (2008) *Siddhartha*. London: Penguin.

Hijiya, J. A. (2000) 'The Gita of J. Robert Oppenheimer', *Proceedings of the American Philosophical Society*, 144:2, 123–167.

Hittleman, R. (1983) *Yoga for Health*. New York: Ballantine.

Huxley, A. (1954) *The Doors of Perception*. London: Chatto & Windus.

Isherwood, C. (1980) *My Guru and His Disciple*. New York: Farrar, Straus, Giroux.

Iyengar, B. K. S. (2001) *Light on Yoga: The Definitive Guide to Yoga Practice*. London: Thorsons.

—. (2006) *Iyengar Yoga for Beginners*. London: Dorling Kindersley.

—. (2013) *Yoga: The Path to Holistic Health*. London: Dorling Kindersley.

James, L. (1998) *Raj: The Making and Unmaking of British India*. London: Abacus.

Jones, W. P. (2013) *The March on Washington: Jobs, Freedom and the Forgotten History of Civil Rights*. New York: W.W. Norton.

Karabell, Z. (2003) *Parting the Desert: The Creation of the Suez Canal*. London: John Murray.

Keay, J. (1993) *The Honourable Company: A History of the English East India Company*. London: HarperCollins.

Kemery, B. (2006) *Yurts: Living in the Round*. Layton, UT: Gibbs Smith.

Kerouac, J. (2008) *The Dharma Bums*. New York: Viking.

—. (2012) *On the Road*. London: Penguin.

Kesey, K. (2005) *One Flew Over the Cuckoo's Nest*. London: Penguin.

Koestler, A. (2005) *Darkness at Noon*. London: Vintage.

Krishnamurti, J. (1995) *The Book of Life: Daily Meditations with Krishnamurti*. New York: Harper Collins.

—. (1999) *This Light in Oneself: True Meditation*. Boston, MA: Shambhala.

—. (2010) *Freedom from the Known*. London: Rider.

Lad, U. and Lad, V. (1997) *Ayurvedic Cooking for Self-Healing*, 2nd edn. Albuquerque, NM: The Ayurvedic Press.

Lad, V. (1999) *The Complete Book of Ayurvedic Home Remedies: A Comprehensive Guide to the Ancient Healing of India*. London: Piatkus.

Leary, T., Metzner, R. and Alpert, R. (1964) The Psychedelic Experience. New York: Kensington.

Long, J. D. (2009) *Jainism: An Introduction*. London: I.B. Tauris.

Lovelock, J. (1995) *Gaia: A New Look at Life on Earth*. Oxford: Oxford University Press.

Maslow, A. H. (1976) *Religions, Values and Peak-Experiences*. New York: Penguin.

—. (1999) *Toward a Psychology of Being*, 3rd edn. New York: John Wiley.

Masters, J. (1960) *Bhowani Junction*. London: Penguin.

Matthews, M. (2010) *Droppers: America's First Hippie Commune, Drop City*. Norman, OK: University of Oklahoma Press.

Meares, A. (1968) *Relief Without Drugs: How You Can Overcome Tension, Anxiety, and Pain*. London: Souvenir Press.

Miller, W. (2011) *I Found No Peace: A Journey Through the Age of Extremes*. London: deCoubertin.

Millett, K. (1970) *Sexual Politics*. New York: Doubleday.

Muller-Ortega, P. E. (1989) *The Triadic Heart of Siva – Kaula Tantricism of Abhinavagupta in the Non-Dual Shaivism of Kashmir*. Albany, NY: State University of New York.

Narayan, R. K. (2000) *The Mahabharata: A Shortened Modern Prose Version of the Indian Epic*. Chicago: Chicago University Press.

Nearing, H. and Nearing, S. (1973) *Living the Good Life: How to Live Sanely and Simply in a Troubled World*. New York: Schocken Books.

Olsen, R. (2012) *Handmade Houses – A Century of Earth-Friendly Home Design*. New York: Rizzoli.

Oonk, G. (ed.) (2007) *Global Indian Diasporas: Exploring Trajectories of Migration and Theory*. Amsterdam: Amsterdam University Press.

Osho (1998) *The Book of Secrets*. New York: St Martin's Griffin.

—. (2002) *Love, Freedom, Aloneness: The Koan of Relationships*. New York: St Martin's Press.

—. (2009) *Tantra: The Supreme Understanding*. London: Watkins.

—. (2011) *The Tantra Experience: Evolution Through Love*. New York: Osho Media International.

Pais, A. (2006) *J. Robert Oppenheimer: A Life*. Oxford: Oxford University Press.

Poros, M. V. (2010) *Modern Migrations: Gujarati Indian Networks in New York and London*. Stanford, CA: Stanford University Press.

Prabhavananda, S. and Isherwood, C. (trans) (1975) *Shankara's Crest-Jewel of Discrimination*. Hollywood, CA: Vedanta Society of Southern California.

Prabhupada, A. C. B. S. (1989) *Bhagavad Gita As It is*. Los Angeles, CA: ISKCON.

Radha, S. S. (2005) *Mantras: Words of Power*. Spokane, WA: Timeless Books.

Radhakrishnan, S. (1993) *The Bhagavadgita*. New Delhi: Harper Collins.

Rama, S. (1998) *Meditation and Its Practice*. Honesdale, PA: Himalayan Institute Press.

—. (1999) *Living with the Himalayan Masters*. Honesdale, PA: Himalayan Institute Press.

Rampuri, B. (2010) *Autobiography of a Sadhu: A Journey into Mystic India*. Rochester, VT: Destiny Books.

Reuben, D. (1969) *Everything You Always Wanted to Know About Sex But were Afraid to Ask*, 2nd edn. New York: David McKay.

Rice, E. (1990) *Captain Sir Richard Francis Burton: A Biography*. Cambridge, MA: Da Capo.

Richardson, M. (2006) *Surrealism and Cinema*. Oxford: Berg.

Ross, K. (2002) *May '68 and Its Afterlives*. Chicago: University of Chicago Press.

Roszak, T. (1995) *The Making of a Counter-Culture: Reflections on the Technocratic Society and Its Youthful Opposition*. Berkeley, CA: University of California Press.

Russell, P. (1976) *The TM Technique: An Introduction to Transcendental Meditation and the Teachings of Maharishi Mahesh Yogi*. London: Routledge & Kegan Paul.

Saraswati, P. C. (2006) *The Vedas*. Mumbai: Sudakshina.

Schendel, W. V. (2009) *A History of Bangladesh*. Cambridge: Cambridge University Press.

Sellier, G. (trans K. Ross) (2008) *Masculine Singular: French New Wave Cinema*. Durham: Duke University Press.

Sessa, B. (2012) *The Psychedelic Renaissance*. London: Muswell Hill Press.

Shindler, C. (2012) *National Service from Aldershot to Aden: Tales from the Conscripts, 1946–62*. London: Sphere.

Sieden, L. S. (1989) *Buckminster Fuller's Universe*. Cambridge, MA: Perseus.

Sivananda, S. S. (2005) *Sadhana: A Text Book of the Psychology and Practice of the Techniques to Spiritual Perfection*, 8th edn. Shivanandanagar, India: The Divine Life Society.

Southall, B., Vince, P. and Rouse, A. (2002) *Abbey Road: The Story of the World's Most Famous Recording Studios*. London: Omnibus Press.

Spess, D. L. (2000) *Soma: The Divine Hallucinogen*. Rochester, VT: Park Street Press.

Sutton, N. and Randerwala, H. (2013) *The Power of Dharma: The Universal Moral Principle*. Luton: Global Break.

Swami Vishnudevananda (1960) *The Complete Illustrated Book of Yoga*. New York: Julian Press.

Talbot, P. (2007) *An American Witness to India's Partition*. New Delhi: Sage.

Thoreau, H. D. (1962) *Walden and Other Writings*. New York: Bantam.

Twain, M. (1989) *Following the Equator: A Journey Around the World*. Mineola, NY: Dover.

US Census Bureau (2011) *Historical Census of Housing Tables*. Washington, DC: US Department of Commerce.

Van Lysebeth, A. (1995) *Tantra: The Cult of the Feminine*. Boston, MA: Red Wheel/Weiser.

Vatsyayana (trans R. Burton) (1962) *Kama Sutra of Vatsyayana*. New York: Medical Press of New York.

—. (1963) *The Kama Sutra*. London: George Allen & Unwin.

Vivekananda, S. (1982a) *Raja Yoga*. New York: Ramakrishna–Vivekananda Center.

—. (1982b) *Jnana-Yoga*. New York: Ramakrishna–Vivekananda Center.

Watkins, E. S. (1998) *On the Pill: A Social History of Oral Contraceptives 1950–1970*. Baltimore, MD: The John Hopkins University Press.

Watts, A. (1957) *The Way of Zen*. New York: Pantheon.

—. (1972) *In My Own Way: An Autobiography 1915–1965*. New York: Pantheon.

—. (1988) *Psychotherapy, East and West*. New York: Random House.

Whiteside, A. (2008) *HIV/AIDS: A Very Short Introduction*. Oxford: Oxford University Press.

Whyton, T. (2013) *Beyond 'A Love Supreme': John Coltrane and the Legacy of an Album*. Oxford: Oxford University Press.

Willbanks, J. H. (2007) *The Tet Offensive: A Concise History*. New York: Columbia University Press.

Williams, K. (1997) *The Prague Spring and Its Aftermath: Czechoslovak Politics 1968–1970*. Cambridge: Cambridge University Press.

Yogananda, P. (1998) *Autobiography of a Yogi*. Los Angeles, CA: Self-realization Fellowship.

Yogashram, V. G. (2012) *The Complete Life of Krishna: Based on the Earliest Oral Traditions and the Sacred Scriptures*. Rochester, VT: Inner Traditions.

Yorke, M. (2011) *Holy Men and Fools*. [Online] available at www.youtube.com/watch?v=grDKdmUcGig.

Glossary

Ahimsa a Sanskrit term which may be translated as 'non-violence'. In its more general sense it is a moral principle that we should not do harm to any living organism. This includes not only by physical acts but also by what we say.

Asanas the postures which are used in the hatha yoga tradition.

Ashram a Hindu religious community, usually centred around a guru and his or her teachings.

Ayurveda a traditional and ancient form of medicine associated with Hinduism. Some of its remedies are regarded as 'alternative', and at odds with modern scientific medicine.

Baby boomers the generation which was born in the period immediately after the Second World War.

Beat Movement an informal group of poets and writers during the 1950s in America, characterized by avant-garde and stream of consciousness styles of writing. They were influenced to different degrees by Eastern spiritualities. Jack Kerouac and Allen Ginsberg were notable members.

Bhagavad Gita a Hindu scripture, part of the Mahabharata epic. It covers the advice given by Krishna on how human beings should address the great ethical dilemmas which confront them in life.

CND an acronym for the Campaign for Nuclear Disarmament which was founded in 1957.

Counter-culture a sub-culture which develops within the predominant culture of a society, and which reflects considerably different values.

Dharma this is the general duty or responsibility of human beings to live their lives in harmony with the moral forces which govern the universe. In Hinduism it is sometimes interpreted as following the duties of the caste into which one is born.

French New Wave this was a French cinema movement of the early 1960s, which in terms of both theme and style, was a challenge to existing cinema. It was closely associated with the European counter-culture.

Gaia hypothesis a theory which conceives of the earth as a biological system which ideally is in a state of equilibrium in order to support life. If we permit certain elements of this equilibrium to become dysfunctional, then there may be a threat to some forms of life.

Ghats large steps which lead down to the Ganges, notably at Benaras. In some places the ghats are used by bathers who want to immerse themselves in the river, while at others the ghats are used for the cremation of the dead.

Haight-Ashbury a region of San Francisco where many hippies and other members of the American counter-culture lived during the 1960s.

ISKCON an acronym of the International Society for Krishna

Consciousness, which was founded by Swami Prabhupada in 1966.

Iyengar Yoga an approach to hatha yoga based upon the teachings of B. K. S. Iyengar.

Karma by living according to dharma, human beings accumulate the consequences of this, and gain 'good karma'. If we do not live in harmony with dharma, then we suffer the effects of this, and acquire 'bad karma'. Karma is thus the moral law of cause and effect. If we fulfil our dharma, we will lead a happy and harmonious existence, both in this life and subsequent lives.

Mala in Hinduism a string of meditation beads traditionally consisting of 108 beads. The mala is used as an aid in the recitation of mantra.

Marshall Plan an American post-Second World War strategy to help with the reconstruction of Europe.

Maya in general terms maya is the illusion that there is a distinction between human consciousness and the divine force which permeates the universe. Once we realize that the two are synonymous, then we can become enlightened, and escape from samsara, the continuous cycle of birth and death.

Moksha the state of spiritual enlightenment or liberation, which is the ultimate goal of the Hindu faith. The attainment of moksha indicates that one has escaped from the cycle of samsara. The various practices of yoga are traditionally considered to be the main method to attain moksha.

Port Huron Statement a radical critique of American society written in the early 1960s by Tom Hayden.

It concentrated on the need for peace in the world, and an end to racial conflict.

Puja this is a religious ceremony in which one pays homage to a deity. The act of puja may take a variety of forms, including prayers, rituals, the making of offerings or the chanting of mantra.

Sadhu a wandering Hindu ascetic.

Sattvic food this is food which is pure and untainted, and has been obtained through processes which cause no harm to other living things.

Shankara a Hindu philosopher born in the eighth-century CE, in what is now Kerala, and who acted as an advocate for Advaita Vedanta.

Soma a liquid which was drunk during ancient Vedic ceremonies, and which is believed to have had hallucinogenic properties. Its exact composition is unknown.

Stillness Meditation a system of meditation therapy developed by the Australian psychologist, Ainslie Meares.

Transcendental Meditation a form of meditation developed by Maharishi Mahesh Yogi. The technique uses mantras, spiritual syllables which are repeated.

'Wind of Change' expression derived from a speech by former British Prime Minister, Harold Macmillan, referring to independence movements in British colonies in the early 1960s.

Wolfenden Committee a committee which reviewed the law in Britain on homosexuality. The committee reported in 1957 and recommended a liberalization of legislation.

Woodstock well-known music festival held in the United States in August 1969.

Index

Abhedananda, Swami 34
Advaita vedanta 48
Aghori 37
ahimsa 86
Ahmedabad 11
AIDS 97
Allahabad 11
Alpert, Richard 39
American Civil War 21
Amritsar 88
Anquetil-Duperron, Abraham 14
Arjuna 50
asana 107
Ashoka 20
ashram 106
Auroville 110
avatar 54
Ayurveda 120

Baby-boomer 31
Baez, Joan 22
Bangladesh 13, 67
Bay of Pigs 4
beat generation 9, 15
Beatles, The 62
beatnik 9
Benaras Hindu University 99, 127
Bengal 158
Bernard, Theos 158–61
Bhagavad Gita 14, 49–52
Bhaktivedanta Manor 113
Blavatsky, Helena 14
brahman 46–8, 52
Buddhism 13, 20, 59
Buddhist Society 32
Burroughs, William 9
Burton, Sir Richard 98

Campaign for Nuclear
    Disarmament (CND) 83
Carson, Rachel 21
Cassady, Neal 9, 75
caste 60, 149
censorship 96
Chandra 70
chillum 76
Chinmoy, Sri 133
Chomsky, Noam 24
Civil Rights 7, 21, 83
Cochin 49
Coltrane, John 132
Columbia University 9, 158–9
Cuba 4

Dalai Lama 12
dalits 152
Dandi 89
de Beauvoir, Simone 24
Devi, Indra 135
Diggers 19
Dubček, Alexander 85
Dylan, Bob 22–3

East India Company 148
Easwaran, Eknath 163
Emerson, Ralph Waldo 118
equality
    gender 7
    race 7
existentialism 25

feminism 25
flower power 24, 118
Ford, Gerald 7
Frieden, Betty 26

Gaia hypothesis 119
Gandhi, Mahatma 19–20, 55,
    83, 89
Ganges 37, 63
Garcia, Carolyn 75
gay rights 7, 27–8
ghats 11
Ghose, Aurobindo 110
Ginsberg, Allen 8–13, 18
Goa 65
Graves, Robert 117
Greenwich Village 28
Greer, Germaine 27
Gujarat 87
guna 121
guru 32–3, 108
Guthrie, Arlo 23

Haight-Ashbury 18
Harrison, George 62, 113
Harvard University 10, 39
Havens, Richie 40
Hesse, Hermann 144
hippie 17–18
HIV virus 97
Hoffman, Abbie 24
holi 53
Huxley, Aldous 35, 73

impermanence 20
integral yoga 40, 110
International Society for
    Krishna Consciousness
    (ISKCON) 13, 76, 113
Isherwood, Christopher 35
Iyengar, B.K.S. 161–2

Jain religion 20, 86
Jallianwala Bagh 88
Jefferson, Thomas 169
Johnson, Lyndon 22

Kama Sutra 98
Kathmandu 65, 146
Kennedy, John F. 4, 22, 26, 102
Kent State University 23
Kerala 49
Kerouac, Jack 8, 75
Kesey, Ken 74

King, Martin Luther 22, 84
Krishna 13, 59
Krishnamurti, Jiddu 14, 109
Kumbh Mela 36, 77

Lawrence, D.H. 3, 94
Leary, Timothy 39, 71
Lennon, John 63
Lincoln Memorial 22
Lovelock, James 119
LSD 73

Macmillan, Harold 4
Mahabharata 50
Maharaj Ji 39
Maharishi Mahesh Yogi 57
Maharshi, Ramana 136
mala 38
Mandela, Nelson 90
mantra 12
Marshall Plan 7
McCartney, Paul 63
McDonald, Country Joe 23
McLelland, David 71
Miller, Henry 94
moksha 47
murti 54
My Lai massacre 23

Narayanan, K.R. 149
Nimtallah ghat 174
non-dualism 48

Oppenheimer, J. Robert 49
Orlovsky, Peter 11
Osho 36, 57

Parks, Rosa 21
Parliament of World Religions 14
Port Huron Statement 172–3
Prabhavananda, Swami 34
Prabhupada, Bhaktivedanta
    Swami 13, 76
psychedelic drugs 71

racial segregation 22
Ram Dass 39
Rama, Swami 138
Ramakrishna 14, 34

Robins Report 8
Roychoudury, Malay 12

sadhu 12, 37, 78–9
Sai Baba, Sathya 136
sanatana dharma 53, 170
sanskrit 12, 35, 49
Saraswati, Swami 58
Sarnath 11, 20
Sartre, Jean-Paul 24
Satchidananda, Swami 39–40
satyagraha 87
Shankar, Ravi 62
Shankara 47
Shiva 78
Sivananda, Swami 111
Snyder, Gary 10, 33
soma 69–70
Stonewall Inn 28
Swaminarayan 114

tantra 100
Tet offensive 91
Theosophical Society 14
Thoreau, Henry David 118
Tolstoy farm 19
Transcendental meditation 57, 61
Transcendentalism 119

True levellers 18
Trungpa, Chögyam 13

Upanishads 14, 33, 47–9
Uttarkashi 58

Vaishnavite Hinduism 13
Varanasi 11, 65
Vatsyayana 98
Vedanta 34
Vedas 46
Viet Cong 7, 84
Vietnam War 22, 84, 91
Vivekananda, Swami 14, 34

Walden 118
Watts, Alan 32–3
Whitman, Walt 119
Wilkins, Charles 14
Winstanley, Gerrard 19
Wolfe, Tom 74
Wolfenden, Lord 27
Woodstock festival 23, 39

yoga 135–9
Yogananda, Paramhansa 66

Zen 9–11